Zinn
and the
Art
of
Mountain Bike Maintenance

by Lennard Zinn,
senior technical writer of *VeloNews*

Illustrated by Todd Telander

VELOPRESS • BOULDER, COLORADO

VeloPress
1830 N. 55th. Street
Boulder CO 80301
USA

An imprint of Inside Communications

ISBN 1-884737-15-3

First Edition 1996
1 2 3 4 5 6 7 8 9 10

Manufactured in the United States of America

contents

a tip of the helmet to....

My heartfelt thanks go out to Todd Telander, whose illustrations made the
procedures more intelligible and beautiful; to my editors and in-house support
system, Charles Pelkey and Mark Saunders, for separating the wheat from the
chaff and adding more wheat when necessary; to Terry Rosen, for bugging
me to write this book for so many years; to Mike Sitrin of VeloPress, for doing
the same and promising to publish it when I did; to Felix Magowan, John
Wilcockson and David Walls of Inside Communications for their financial
support and encouragement; to John Muir and Robert Pirsig, for writing such
great books to encourage this effort; and to Joy Straka and Michael Lichter
for the cover photography.

Thanks also to Brett Lindstrom for his assistance with the glossary.
For technical assistance with the details, thanks to Shimano, Rock Shox,
Answer Products, Doug Bradbury, Wayne Stetina, Steve Hed, Ken Beach,
and to Scott, John, and Rusty at Louisville Cyclery (Louisville, CO).

I also want to thank my entire family for all of their support and inspiration:
Emily and Sarah, my daughters, for showing me that books can be written,
completed, and published at a prolific rate, Dad and Mom, for encouraging
me my whole life, Rex and Steve, for their suggestions, Kai, Ron, and Dad,
for being authors themselves and an inspiration to me, and Marlies, for taking
the kids when I needed it.

Thanks, Sarah, for proving Groucho Marx right.

dedication

To Sonny, my wife, without whose support
this book could not have been written;
or at least a few more decades
would have passed before it got done.

introduction

"**P**eace of mind isn't at all superficial, really. It's the whole thing. That which produces it is good maintenance; that which disturbs it is poor maintenance. What we call workability of the machine is just an objectification of this peace of mind. The ultimate test's always your own serenity. If you don't have this when you start and maintain it while you're working you're likely to build your personal problems right into the machine itself."

— ROBERT M. PIRSIG, from *Zen and the Art of Motorcycle Maintenance*

ABOUT THIS BOOK

This book is intended for those with an interest in maintaining their own mountain bikes. Most importantly, this book has been written for mountain-bike owners who do *not* think they're capable of maintaining their own bikes. In *Zen and the Art of Motorcycle Maintenance*, Robert Pirsig explores the dichotomy between the purely classical and purely romantic views of the world. Pirsig's exploration of this dichotomy can certainly be applied to mountain biking. Riding a mountain bike is generally a romantic experience of emotion, inspiration and intuition, even when solving the complex physics of how to negotiate a technical section of trail without putting your foot down. Mountain-bike mechanics, however, is a purely classical structure of underlying form dominated by reason and physical laws. The two fit eloquently together. Each is designed to function in a particular way, and one without the other would be missing out on half the fun.

the basic beast

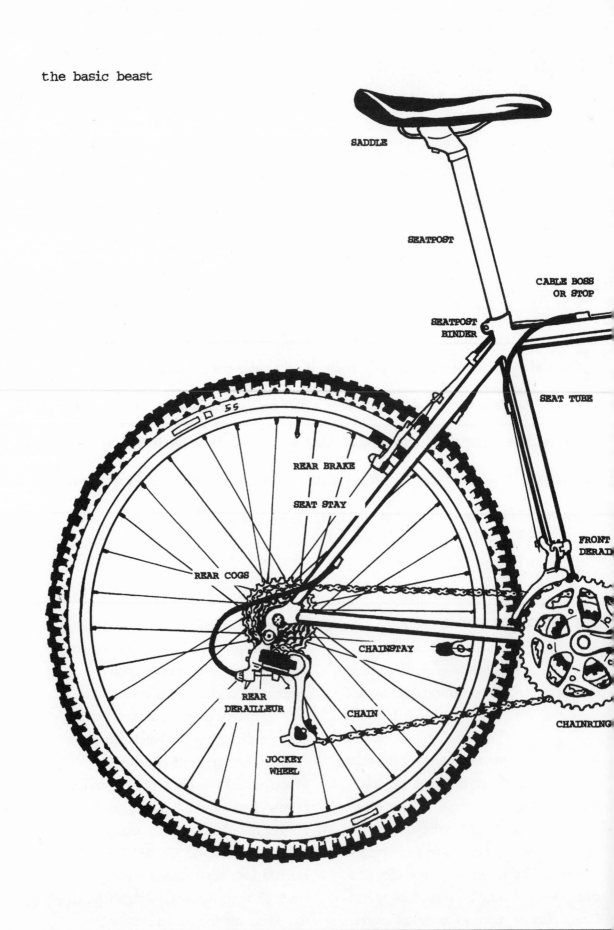

SADDLE

SEATPOST

CABLE BOSS
OR STOP

SEATPOST
BINDER

SEAT TUBE

REAR BRAKE

SEAT STAY

FRONT
DERAI

REAR COGS

CHAINSTAY

REAR
DERAILLEUR

CHAIN

CHAINRING

JOCKEY
WHEEL

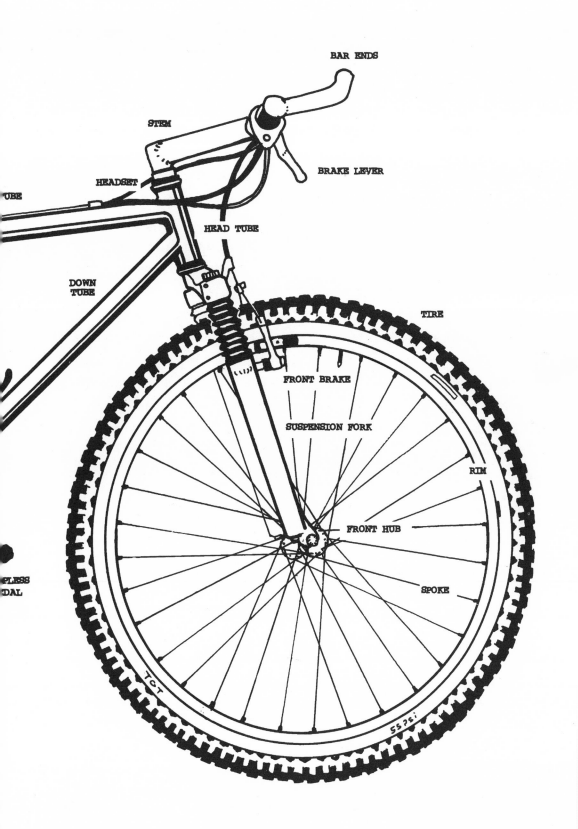

BAR ENDS

STEM

BRAKE LEVER

HEADSET

HEAD TUBE

DOWN
TUBE

TIRE

FRONT BRAKE

SUSPENSION FORK

RIM

FRONT HUB

SPOKE

intro

The step-by-step procedures in this book, coupled with the exploded diagrams are so simple to follow that even the pure romantic can discover a passion for spreading new grease on old parts. The romantic can also appreciate how success at bike mechanics requires that the procedures are done with a certain sense of love. If not, frustration will take over, and all the care you imagined putting into your mountain bike will be lost, along with the joy of riding.

Zinn and the Art of Mountain Bike Maintenance is organized in such a way that you can pick maintenance tasks appropriate for you. The repairs illustrated on these pages require no special skills to perform; anyone can do them. It takes only a willingness to learn.

Mountain bikes are notoriously hardy creatures. You can keep one running an awfully long time just by changing the tires and occasionally lubricating the chain. Chapter 2 is about the most minimal maintenance your bike requires. If that's the only chapter you end up using, you will have gotten your money's worth by avoiding some unpleasant experiences out on the trail.

This book was not originally intended for shop mechanics. For that reason, I have not included the lists of parts specifications such a mechanic might need. Nonetheless, when combined with a specifications manual, this book can be a useful, easy-to-follow reference for shop mechanics and serious home mechanics.

WHY DO IT YOURSELF?

There are a number of reasons why you would want to maintain your own mountain bike. Obviously, if done right, it is a lot cheaper to do it yourself than to pay someone else to do it. This is certainly an important factor for those riders who live to ride and have no visible means of support. Self-mechanicing is a necessity for that crew.

As your income goes up and the time available to maintain your bike goes down, this becomes less-and-less true. If you're a well-paid professional with limited free time, it probably does not make as much *economic* sense to maintain your own bike. However, you may find that you enjoy working on your bike for reasons other than just saving money. Unless you have a mechanic whom you trust and to whom you bring your bike regularly, you are not likely to find anyone else who cares as much about your bicycle's smooth operation and cleanliness as you do. Furthermore, if you love to ride and have only a limited time to do it, you probably can't afford to *not* be able to fix mechanical breakdowns that occur on the trail.

It is a given. Breakdowns *will* happen, even if you have the world's best mechanic working on your bike. It really takes away from my enjoyment of a ride if I have something on my bike that I do not understand well enough to know whether it is likely to last the ride, and how to fix it if it does not.

There is an aspect of bicycle mechanics that can be extremely enjoyable in-and-of itself, almost independent of riding the bike. Bicycles are the manifestation of elegant simplicity. Bicycle parts, particularly high-end components, are meant to work well and last a long time. With the proper attention, they can shine both in appearance and in performance for years to come. There is real satisfaction in dismantling a filthy part that is not functioning well, cleaning it up, lubricating it with fresh grease, and reassembling it so that it works like new again. Knowing that I made those parts work so smoothly, and that I can do it again when they get dirty or worn, is rewarding. I am eager to ride hard to see how they hold up, rather than being reluctant to ride for fear of breaking something.

There is also something very liberating about going on a long ride and knowing that you can fix just about anything that might go wrong with your bike out on the trail. Armed with this knowledge and the tools to put it into action, you will have more confidence to explore new areas and go farther than you might otherwise.

In 1995, I took a day to ride the entire 110-mile White Rim Trail loop in Utah's Canyonlands. It is as desolate as you can imagine out there, and I was completely alone with the sky, the sun and the rocks for long stretches. I had a good mileage base in my legs, so that I knew I was physically capable of doing the ride during the limited daylight hours of late October. I had checked, replaced, or adjusted practically every part of my bike in the days before the ride. I had also tried out the bike on long rides close to town. Finally, I added to my saddle bag tool kit a few tools that I do not ordinarily carry.

I knew that there was very little chance of anything going wrong with my bike, and with the tools I had, I could fix almost anything short of a broken frame on the trail. Armed with all of this knowledge and experience, I *really* enjoyed the ride! I stopped and gawked at almost every breathtaking vista, vertical box canyon, or colorful balanced rock or arch. I even took a few scenic detours. I knew that I had a good cushion of safety, so I could totally immerse myself in the pleasure of the ride. I had no nagging fear of something going wrong to dilute the experience.

If you have a degree of confidence in your abilities as a bike mechanic, you might even be willing to share your love of the sport with other, less-experienced, riders. You'll enjoy bringing new people along, particularly if you know that you can fix their bikes.

HOW TO USE THIS BOOK

Skim through the entire book. Skip the detailed steps, but look at the exploded diagrams and get the general flavor of the book and what's

rigid

inside. When it's time to perform a particular task, you'll know where to find it, and you will have a general idea of how to approach it.

Todd Telander, the book's illustrator, and I have done our best to make these pages as understandable as possible. Exploded diagrams are purposefully used instead of photographs to show more clearly how each part goes together. The first time you go through a procedure, you may find it easier to have a friend read the instructions out loud as you perform the steps.

Obviously, some maintenance tasks are more complicated than others. I am convinced that anyone with an opposable thumb can perform virtually any repair on a bike. Still, it pays to

spend some time getting familiar with the really simple tasks, such as fixing a flat, before throwing yourself into complex jobs, such as building a wheel.

Tasks and tools required are divided into three levels indicating their complexity or your proficiency. Level 1 tasks need Level 1 tools and require of you only an eagerness to learn. Level 2 and Level 3 also have corresponding tool sets and are progressively more difficult. All repairs mentioned in this book are classified as Level 1, unless otherwise indicated, and the tools are shown in Chapter 1.

Each chapter starts with a list of required tools in the margin. If a section involves a higher level of work, there will

fully suspended

intro

be an icon designating the level and tools necessary to perform the tasks in that section. At the end of several chapters, there is a troubleshooting section. This is the place to go to identify the source of a certain noise or particular malfunction in the bike. There is also a comprehensive troubleshooting guide in the appendix.

THE MOUNTAIN BIKE

This is the creature to whom this book is devoted.

All of its parts are illustrated and labeled on pages eight and nine. Take a minute to familiarize yourself with these now and then refer back to this diagram whenever necessary.

The mountain bike comes in a variety of forms, from models with rigid frames and forks to models with high-zoot front and rear suspension systems. A mountain bike generally comes with 26-inch knobby tires. Tire variations are abundant and include everything from studded snow tires to smooth street tires and everything in between.

I believe that by clearly spelling out the steps necessary to properly maintain and repair a bicycle, even those who see themselves as having no mechanical skills will be able to tackle problems as they arise. With a little bit of practice and a willingness to learn, your bike will suddenly transform itself from a mysterious black box, too complicated to

the beast exploded

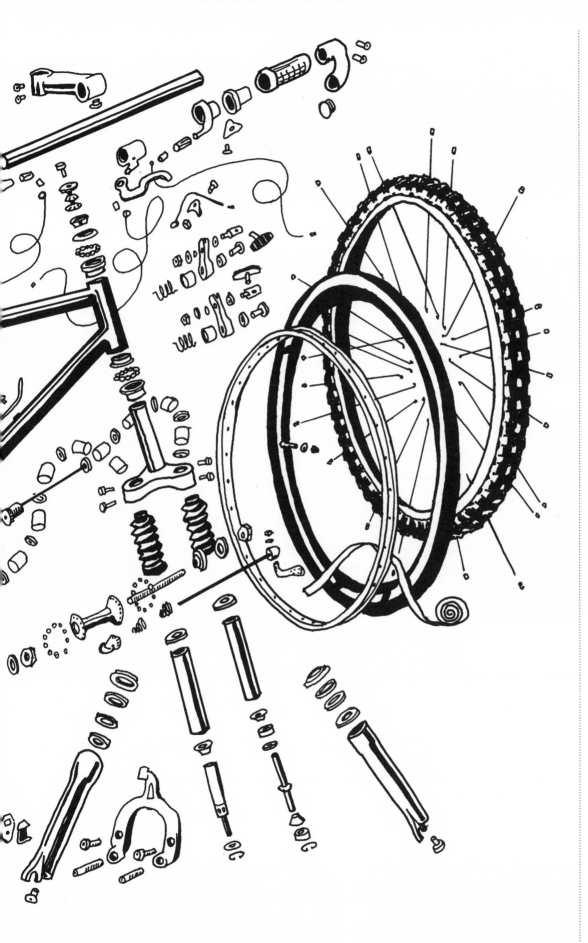

hybrid

tamper with, to a simple, very understandable machine that is a delight to work on. Just allow yourself the opportunity and the dignity to follow along, rather than deciding in advance that you will *never* be able to do this. All you have to do is follow the instructions and trust yourself.

So, set aside your self image as some one who is "not mechanically oriented" (and any other factors that may stand in the way of you making your mountain bike ride like a dream), and let's start playing with your bike!

tools

> "The right tool for the right job"
>
> — MR. NATURAL

You can't do much work on a bike without tools. Still, it's not always clear exactly which tools to buy. This chapter will clarify what tools you should consider owning, based on your level of mechanical experience and interest.

As I mentioned in the introduction, the maintenance and repair procedures in this book are classified by their degree of difficulty. All repairs mentioned are classified as Level 1, unless otherwise indicated. The tools for Levels 1, 2 and 3 are pictured and described on the following pages. In addition, a list of the tools needed in each chapter are shown in the margin at the beginning of each chapter.

For the uninitiated, there is no need to rush out and buy a large number of bike-specific tools. With only a few exceptions, the "Level 1 Tool Kit" consists of standard metric tools. In a more compact and lightweight form, this is the same collection of tools I recommend carrying with you on long rides. The "Level 2 Tool Kit" contains several bike-specific tools, allowing you to do more complex work on the bike. "Level 3" tools are extensive (and expensive), and ensure that your riding buddies will show up not only to ask your sage advice, but to borrow your tools as well. If you are one to loan tools, you might consider marking your collection, so as to help recover those items that might otherwise take a long time finding their way back to your workshop.

LEVEL 1 TOOL KIT

Level 1 repairs are the simplest and do not require a workshop, although it is nice to have a good space to work. You will need the following tools:

- **Tire pump** with a gauge and a valve head to match your tubes (either Presta or Schrader).

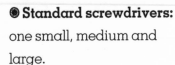

- **Standard screwdrivers:** one small, medium and large.
- **Phillips-head screwdrivers:** one small and one medium.
- Set of three **plastic tire levers**.
- At least two **spare tubes** of the same size and valve type as those on your bike.
- Container of regular **baby powder**. It works well for coating tubes and the inner casings of tires.
- **Patch kit.** Choose one that comes with sandpaper instead of a metal scratcher.
- One **6-inch adjustable wrench** (a.k.a., "Crescent wrench").
- **Pliers:** regular and needle-nose.
- Set of **metric Allen wrenches** that includes 2.5mm, 3mm, 4mm, 5mm, 6mm, and 8mm sizes. Folding sets are available and work nicely to keep your

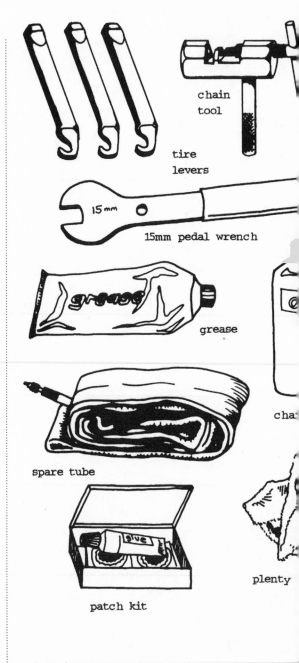

chain tool

tire levers

15mm pedal wrench

grease

spare tube

patch kit

plenty

wrenches organized. I also recommend buying extras of the 4mm, 5mm, and 6mm sizes.

- Set of **metric open-end wrenches** that includes 7mm, 8mm, 9mm, 10mm, 13mm, 14mm, 15mm and 17mm sizes.
- **15mm pedal wrench**. These are thinner and longer than a standard 15mm wrench.
- **Chain tool** for breaking and

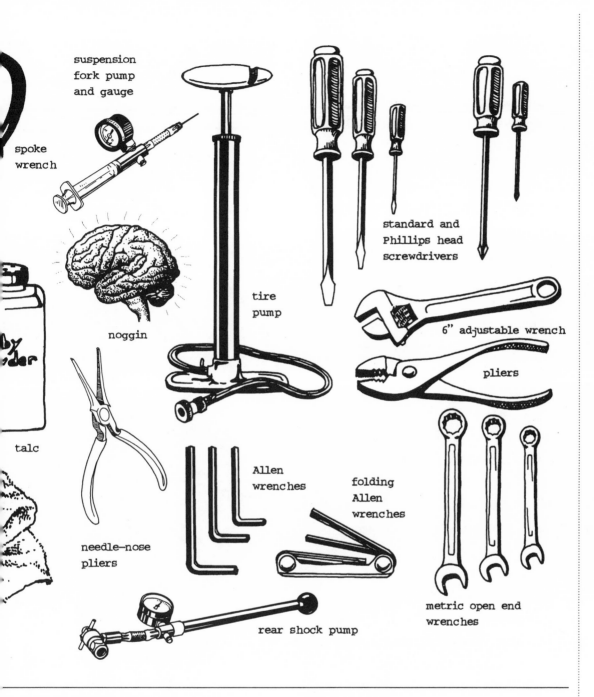

suspension fork pump and gauge

spoke wrench

noggin

talc

tire pump

standard and Phillips head screwdrivers

6" adjustable wrench

pliers

needle-nose pliers

Allen wrenches

folding Allen wrenches

metric open end wrenches

rear shock pump

reassembling chains.

- **Spoke wrench** to match the size of nipples used on your wheels.
- **Tube or jar of grease**. I recommend using grease designed specifically for bicycles; however, standard lithium grease is okay.
- Squirt bottle or can of **chain lubricant.** Please choose one without harmful propellants.

- A lot of **rags**!

OTHER:

- Suspension forks and rear shocks using air/oil suspension usually come with a small air pump equipped with the appropriate head and gauge. If you have such a system, the pumps need to be part of your basic tool set.

LEVEL 2 TOOL KIT

 Level 2 repairs are a bit more complex, and I recommend that you use a well organized work space with a shop bench. Keeping your workspace well organized is probably the best way to make maintenance and repair easy and quick. You will need the entire Level 1 Tool Kit plus:

✪ **Portable bike stand**. Be sure that the stand is sturdy enough to remain stable when you're really cranking on the wrenches.

✪ **Shop apron** (this is to keep your nice duds nice).

✪ **Hacksaw** with a fine-toothed blade.

✪ Set of **razor blades** or a sharp shop knife.

✪ **Files:** one round and one flat.

✪ **Cable cutter** for cutting brake and shifter cables without fraying the ends.

✪ **Cable-housing cutter** for cutting coaxial-indexed cable housing. If you purchase a Shimano housing cutter, you won't need to buy the cable cutter, since it works well on both.

✪ Set of **metric socket wrenches** that includes 7mm, 8mm, 9mm, 10mm, 13mm, 14mm and 15mm sizes.

✪ **Crank puller** for removing crank arms.

✪ **Medium ball-peen hammer.**

✪ Two **headset wrenches**. Be sure to check the size of your headset before buying these. This purchase is unnecessary if you have a threadless headset and plan only to work on your own bike.

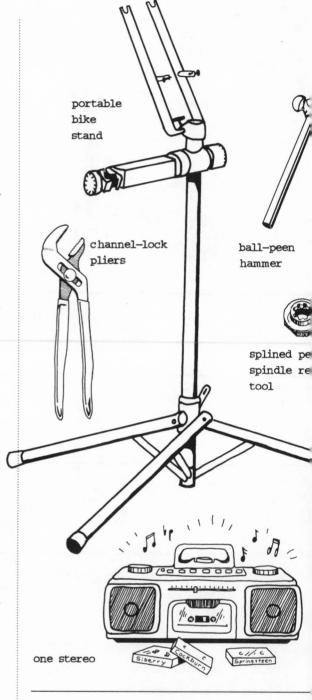

portable bike stand

channel-lock pliers

ball-peen hammer

splined pe spindle re tool

one stereo

✪ **Medium bench vise**.

✪ **Cassette cog lockring tool** for removing cogs from the rear hub.

✪ **Chain whip** for holding cogs while loosening the cassette lockring.

✪ **Bottom bracket tools**. For Shimano cartridge bottom brackets, you'll need

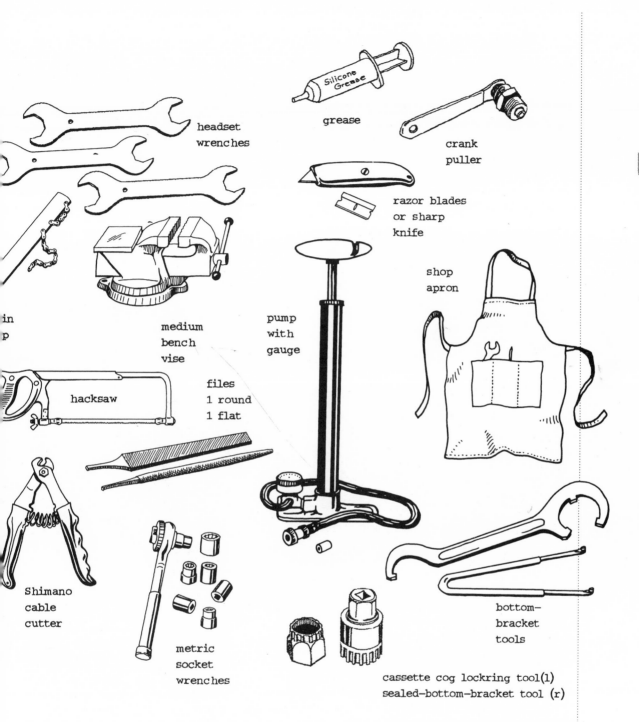

headset
wrenches

grease

crank
puller

razor blades
or sharp
knife

shop
apron

in
p

medium
bench
vise

pump
with
gauge

hacksaw

files
1 round
1 flat

Shimano
cable
cutter

metric
socket
wrenches

bottom-
bracket
tools

cassette cog lockring tool(l)
sealed-bottom-bracket tool (r)

the tool specifically made for their
bottom bracket; otherwise, you'll need
a lockring spanner and a pin spanner
to fit your bottom bracket.

⟡ **Channel-lock Pliers.**
⟡ **Splined pedal spindle removal tool.**
⟡ Tube of **silicone-based grease** if you

have GripShift and other non-lithium
grease for suspension forks.
⟡ One **stereo** with good tunes. This
is especially important if you plan
on spending a lot of time working
on your bike.

LEVEL 3 TOOL KIT

 If you are an accomplished Level 3 mechanic, you are now completely independent of your local bike shop's service department. This even includes building up brand-new frames. By now, you have a well-organized separate space intended just for working on your bike. Some elements of the Level 3 kit are obviously heavier-duty replacements for parts of the Level 2 kit.

✺ **Parts washing tank.** Please use an environmentally-safe degreaser.

✺ **Fixed bike stand**. Be sure it comes with a clamp designed to fit any size frame tube.

✺ **Large bench-mounted vise** to free stuck parts.

✺ **Headset press** used to install headset bearing cups. The press should fit all three cup sizes. Chris King headsets need a press that does not contact the pressed-in bearing. King sells inserts for regular headset presses to install his headsets.

✺ **Fork crown race punch** (a.k.a., slide hammer) for installing the fork crown headset race. (Thin Shimano or Chris King crown races require a second support tool to protect the crown race during installation.)

✺ **Headset cup remover**.

✺ **Star-nut installation tool** for threadless headsets.

✺ An **additional chain whip**. A second whip is handy for disassembling freewheels or old-style cassettes.

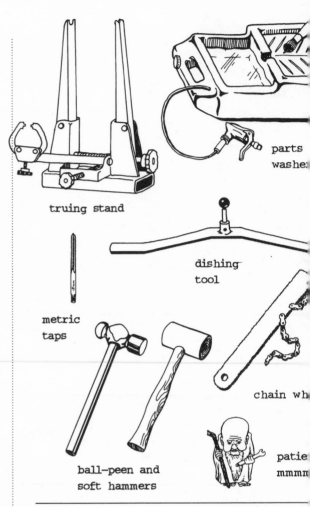

truing stand

parts washer

dishing tool

metric taps

ball—peen and soft hammers

chain whip

patience mmmm

✺ **Freewheel removers.** You should get removers for Shimano, Sachs and Suntour freewheels.

✺ **Large ball-peen hammer.**

✺ **Soft hammer.** Choose a rubber, plastic or wooden mallet to prevent damage to parts.

✺ **Torque wrench.** Torque wrenches are great for checking proper bolt tightness. There are many manufacturers who recommend using one when installing their components. I'll be honest, I don't use them all that often. Still, if you want to be thorough, it may be a good idea to pick one up at an automotive supply store.

✺ Set of **metric taps** that includes 5mm x

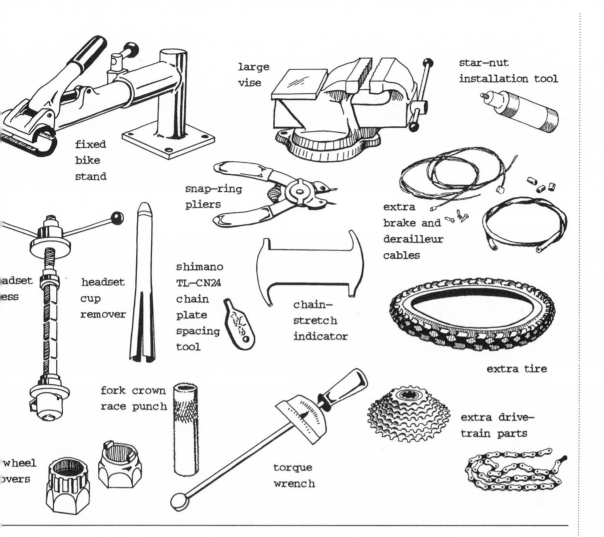

fixed bike stand

large vise

star-nut installation tool

snap-ring pliers

extra brake and derailleur cables

headset press

headset cup remover

shimano TL-CN24 chain plate spacing tool

chain-stretch indicator

extra tire

fork crown race punch

torque wrench

extra drive-train parts

wheel covers

0.8, 6mm x 1 and 10mm x 1. These work for threading bottle bosses, cantilever bosses, binder bolts, derailleur hangers, etc.

- Pair of **snap ring pliers** for removing snap rings from suspension forks, derailleurs and other parts.
- **Chain stretch gauge.** This handy little plastic item helps you quickly determine if a chain needs replacing.
- **Shimano TL-CN24 chain plate spacing tool,**
- **Truing stand** for truing and building wheels.
- **Dishing tool** for checking if that set of wheels you just built is properly centered.

- One healthy dose of **patience**, and an equal willingness to work and re-work jobs until they have been properly finished.

Other: This will save you from having to make a lot of last-minute runs to the bike shop for commonly used spare parts. Any well-equipped shop really requires several sizes of ball bearings, spare cables, cable housing, and a life-time supply of those little cable-end caps. You should also have a good supply of spare tires, tubes, chains and cogsets. If you expect to be working on suspension forks, be sure to have the proper lubricants and a few spare elastomers on hand.

NOW, IF YOU REALLY WANT A WELL-STOCKED SHOP:

The following tools are not even part of the Level 3 kit, and are not often needed for bike repairs. That said, they sure do come in handy when you need them.

- **English-threaded bottom bracket tap set.** This cuts threads on both sides of the bottom bracket while keeping the threads in proper alignment.
- **Head tube reamer/facer.** This tool keeps both ends of head tube perfectly parallel.
- **Bottom bracket shell facer.** Like a bottom bracket tap, this tool cuts the face of the bottom bracket shell, so they are parallel to each other.
- **Electric drill** with drill bit set for customizing.
- **Dropout alignment tools** (a.k.a., tip adjusters).
- **Derailleur hanger alignment tool** to straighten the derailleur after you shift into the spokes.
- **Cog wear indicator gauge** to determine if cogs are worn out.
- A full collection of **spoke wrenches**, and don't forget those new Spline Drive nipples.
- **Hydraulic oil** for overhauling hydraulic suspension systems.

SETTING UP YOUR HOME SHOP

I recommend keeping this area clean and very well organized. Make it comfortable to work in and easy to find the tools you need. Hanging tools on

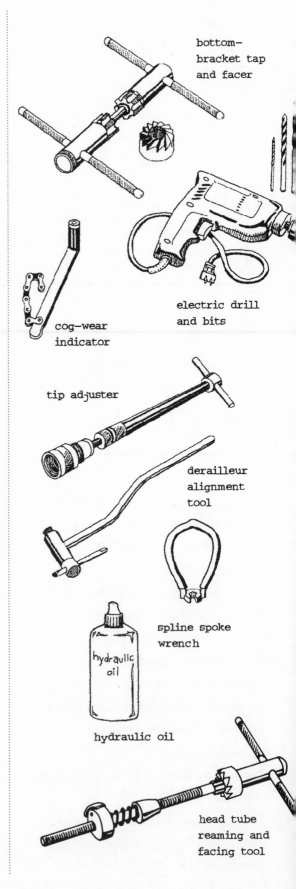

bottom-bracket tap and facer

electric drill and bits

cog-wear indicator

tip adjuster

derailleur alignment tool

spline spoke wrench

hydraulic oil

head tube reaming and facing tool

peg-board or slat-board or placing them in bins or trays are all effective ways to maintain an organized work area. Being able to find the tools you need will increase the enjoyment of working on a bike immensely. It is harder to do a job with love if you're frustrated about not being able to find the cable cutter. Placing small parts in one of those bench-top organizers with several rows of little drawers is another good way to keep chaos from taking over.

TOOLS TO CARRY WITH YOU WHILE RIDING

FOR MOST RIDING:

Keep all of this stuff in a bag under your seat or somehow attached to your bike. Some people may prefer a fanny pack. The operative words here are *light* and *serviceable*. Many of these tools are combined into some of the popular "multi-tools." Make sure you try all tools at home before depending on them on the trail.

❋ **Spare tube.** This is a no-brainer. Make sure the valve matches the ones on your bike.

❋ **Tire pump/CO$_2$ cartridge.** The bigger the better. Mini-pumps are okay, but they're slow. Make sure the pump is set up for your type of valves.

❋ At least two **plastic tire levers**, preferably three.

❋ **Patch kit.** You'll need something after you've used your spare tube.

❋ **Chain tool.** Get a light one that works.

❋ **Spare chain links** from your chain. If

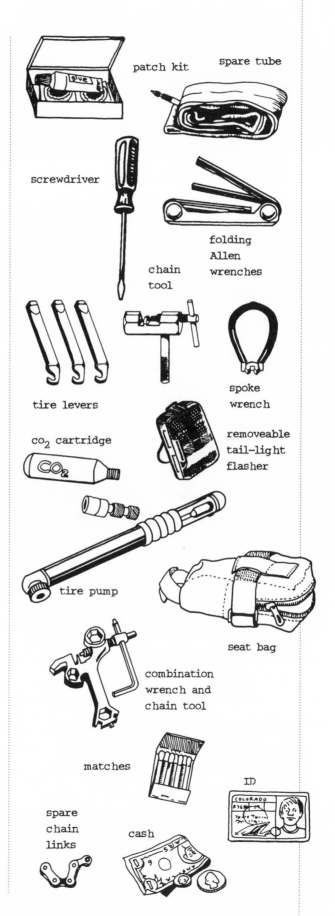

patch kit

spare tube

screwdriver

folding Allen wrenches

chain tool

tire levers

spoke wrench

CO$_2$ cartridge

removeable tail-light flasher

tire pump

seat bag

combination wrench and chain tool

matches

ID

spare chain links

cash

25

you're using a Shimano chain bring at least two "subpin" rivets.

❋ **Small screwdriver** for adjusting derailleurs and other parts.

❋ Compact set of **Allen wrenches** that includes 2.5mm, 3mm, 4mm, 5mm and 6mm sizes. (Some of you might need to bring along an 8mm too.)

❋ 8mm and 10 mm **open-end wrenches**.

❋ Properly sized **spoke wrench**.

❋ **Matches**, because you never know when you can be stranded overnight.

❋ **Identification**.

❋ **Cash** for obvious reasons and to repair side–wall damage

FOR LONG OR MULTI-DAY TRIPS:

This is, of course, in addition to proper amounts of food, water, and extra clothes.

❋ **Spare spokes**. *Innovations in Cycling* sells a really cool folding spoke made from Kevlar. It's worth getting one or two for emergency repairs on a long ride.

❋ Small plastic bottle of **chain lube**.

❋ Small tube of **grease**.

❋ **Compact 15mm pedal wrench**. Be sure to get one with a headset wrench on the other end.

❋ **Money**, or its plastic equivalent, which can get you out of lots of scrapes.

❋ A lightweight aluminized folding **emergency blanket**.

❋ **Rain gear**.

Note: Read Chapter 3 on emergency repairs before embarking on a lengthy trip.

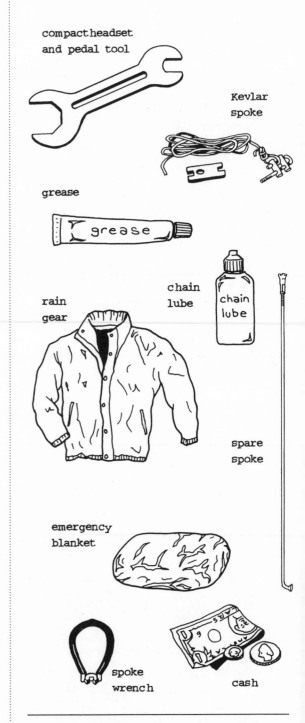

compact headset and pedal tool

Kevlar spoke

grease

rain gear

chain lube

spare spoke

emergency blanket

spoke wrench

cash

If you are planning a bike centered vacation, be sure to bring along a "Level 1" tool kit, some headset wrenches and incidentals like duct tape and sandpaper.

basic stuff

pre-ride inspection, wheel removal and general cleaning

*"**E**verything should be made as simple*

as possible, but not simpler"

— ALBERT EINSTEIN

This chapter covers three very basic, but important, maintenance procedures. It is a good idea to get in the habit of checking your bike *before* heading out on a ride.

Performing this inspection regularly could help you avoid delays due to parts failure. I won't even mention the injury risks you face by riding a poorly maintained bike. There are folks who just don't want to tamper with anything on their bikes. However, learning how to properly remove and reinstall a wheel is essential if you want to effectively deal with minor annoyances like flat tires or jammed chains. If you do

absolutely nothing else to your bike, keeping your chain clean will enhance the enjoyment of riding.

PRE-RIDE INSPECTION

❶ Check to be sure that the quick-release levers or axle nuts (the ones that secure the hub axle to the dropouts) are tight.

❷ Check the brake pads for excessive wear.

❸ Grab and twist the brake pads and brake arms to make sure the bolts are tight.

❹ Squeeze the brake levers. This should bring the pads flat against the rims (or slightly toed-in) without hitting the tires. Make certain that you cannot squeeze the levers all of the way to the handlebars. If you can, see Chapter 7 on brake adjustment.

5 Spin the wheels. Check for wobbles. Make sure that the rims do not rub on the brake pads.

6 Check the tire pressure. On most mountain bike tires, the proper pressure is between 40 and 60 pounds per square inch (psi). Look to see that there are no foreign objects sticking in the tire. If there are, you may have to replace the tube or patch it.

7 Check the tires for excessive wear or cracking.

8 Be certain that the handlebar and stem are tight and that the stem is lined up with the front tire.

9 Check that the gears shift smoothly. Make sure that the chain does not over-shift the smallest or biggest rear cog or the smallest or biggest front chainring.

wheel removal

---

releasing the brake

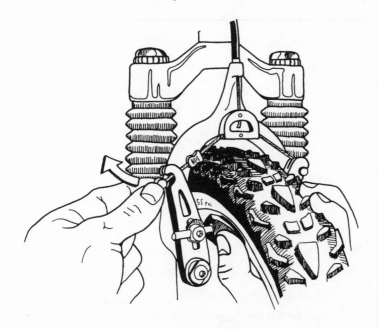

10 Check the chain for rust, dirt, stiff links or noticeable signs of wear. It should be clean and lubricated before you leave for a ride. The chain should be replaced on a mountain bike about every 500 miles of off-road or 1000 miles of on-road riding.

11 Apply the front brake and push the bike forward and back. The headset should be tight and not make "clunking" noises or allow the fork any fore-aft play.

12 If all this checks out, go ride your bike! If not, check the table of contents, go to the appropriate chapter and fix the problems before you go out and ride.

REMOVING THE FRONT WHEEL

You can't transport your mountain bike easily if you can't remove the front wheel. This is generally required for most roof racks, and for jamming a mountain bike inside your car. Wheel removal involves the quick-release skewer on most bikes and axle nuts on the low-end models. Remember that the wheel will not come out easily until the brake has been released.

RELEASING THE BRAKE

Most brakes have some sort of system to allow opening of the calipers so that the tire can pass between the pads. Most cantilever and U-brakes are released simply by holding the pads against the rim with one hand while pulling the enlarged head of the straddle cable out

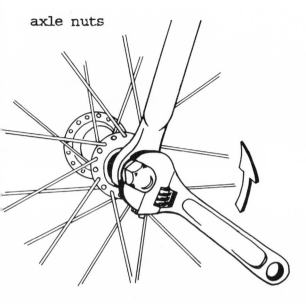

axle nuts

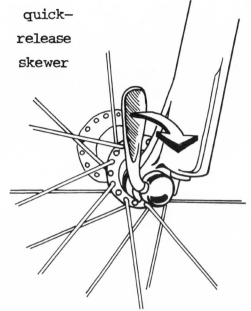

quick-release skewer

wheel
removal

of a notch in the top of the brake arm. Removing the straddle cable releases tension on the two brake arms, and they spring away from the rim.

Roller-cam brakes are released by pulling the cam down and out from between the two rollers while holding the pads against the rim. Many linkage brakes are released like cantilevers. Hydraulic rim brakes rely on methods specific to each model. Most rely on detaching the bridge connecting the piston cylinders together, so that they can be swung away. Most disc brakes allow the disc to fall away without releasing the pads. The Dia Compe disc brake requires opening a latch under the caliper securing it to the fork. The entire caliper can then be swung up and forward, allowing the wheel to come out.

DETACHING A WHEEL WITH AXLE NUTS

❶ Unscrew the nuts on the axle ends (usually with a 15 mm wrench) until they allow the wheel to fall out.

❷ Most mountain bikes have some type of wheel-retention system consisting of nubs or bent tabs on the fork ends (also known as "dropouts"), or an axle washer with a bent tooth hooked into a hole in the fork end. These systems prevent the wheel from falling out if the axle nuts loosen. Loosen the nuts enough to clear the retention tabs on the fork ends.

❸ Pull the wheel out.

DETACHING A WHEEL WITH A QUICK-RELEASE SKEWER

You don't even need a tool for this one.

❶ Pull the lever out to open it.

❷ After opening the quick-release lever, unscrew the nut on the opposite end of the quick-release skewer's shaft until it clears the fork's wheel retention tabs.

❸ Pull the wheel off.

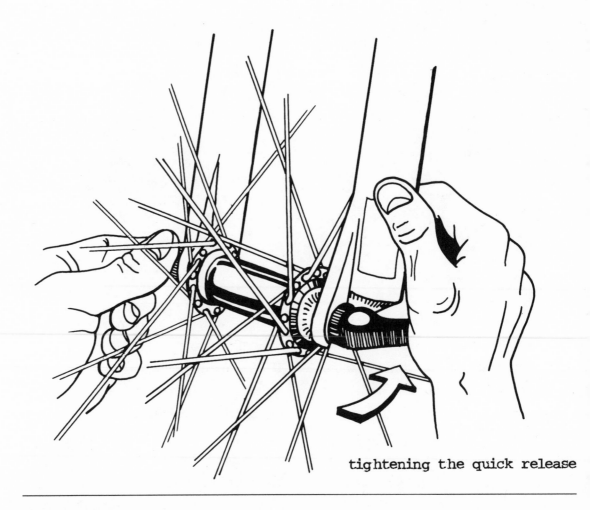

tightening the quick release

wheel
removal

INSTALLING
THE FRONT WHEEL

1 Leaving the brake open, push the wheel back in so that the axle sits fully into the dropouts. Lower the bike onto the wheel so that the bike's weight pushes the dropouts down onto the hub axle.

2 Tighten the axle nuts or quick-release skewer to secure it.

3 Check that the axle is tightened into the fork by trying to pull the wheel out.

TIGHTENING
THE QUICK-RELEASE SKEWER

The quick-release skewer is not a glori-fied wing nut and should not be treated as such.

1 Hold the quick release-lever in an open position, so that it is in a straight line with the axle.

2 Tighten the opposite end nut until it snugs up against the face of the dropout.

3 Flip the lever to the "closed" position and push it down until it is at a 90-degree angle to the axle. It should take a good amount of hand pressure to close the quick-release lever properly, leaving an imprint on your palm for a few seconds.

4 If the quick-release lever does not

removal and installation
of rear wheel

close tightly, open the lever again, tighten the end nut 1/4 turn and close it. If the lever cannot be pushed down flat, then the nut is too tight. Open the quick-release lever again, unscrew the end nut 1/4 turn or so, and try closing the lever again.

❺ Repeat this procedure until the quick-release lever is fully closed and snug.

When you are done, it is important to have the lever centered inside the tabs of the fork dropout, and pointing straight up or toward the back of the bike so that it cannot hook on obstacles and be accidentally opened.

CLOSING THE BRAKES

❶ With a cantilever or U-brake, hold the brake pads against the rim with one hand, while you hook the enlarged end of the straddle cable back into the end of the brake arm with your other hand. Generally, the steps required to close the brakes are the reverse of what you did to release them.

❷ Check the brakes by squeezing the levers. If everything is reconnected properly, you're done. Go ride your bike.

REMOVING THE REAR WHEEL

Removing the rear wheel is just like

removing the front, with the added complication of the chain and cogs.

❶ Shift the bike into the highest gear. This is the outermost and smallest rear cog. Do this by lifting the rear wheel off of the ground, turning the cranks and shifting.

❷ To release the wheel from the rear dropouts and the brakes, follow the same procedure as with the front wheel. When you push the wheel out, you will need to move the chain out of the way. This is usually a matter of grabbing the rear derailleur, twisting it back so the jockey wheels (pulley wheels) move out of the way, while pushing forward on the axle nuts or quick release with your thumbs, and letting the wheel fall as you hold the bike up. If the bottom half of the chain catches the wheel as it falls, lift the wheel and jiggle it upward to free it.

INSTALLING THE REAR WHEEL

❶ Check to make sure that the rear derailleur is shifted to its outermost position (highest gear).

❷ Slip the wheel up between the seatstays and maneuver the upper section of chain onto the smallest rear cog.

❸ Set the bike down on the rear wheel.

❹ As you let the bike drop down, pull the rear derailleur back with your right hand and pull the axle ends back into the dropouts with your index fingers. Your thumbs push forward on the

rear dropouts, which should now fall nicely down over the axle ends. Tighten the axle and rear brake the same way as you did on the front wheel. You're done. Go ride your bike.

CLEANING THE BICYCLE

Most cleaning can be done with soap, water and a brush. Soap and water are easier on you and the earth than stronger solvents, which are generally only needed for the drivetrain, if at all. In a pinch you can use a high-pressure pay car wash to clean your bike, but cleaning a bike this way is a bit like using a blowtorch to warm a baby bottle. It's a little too much, and it can be tough on your bike.

A bike stand is highly recommended when scrubbing the bike. In the absence of a bike stand, the bike can be hung from a garage ceiling with rope, or it can be stood upside down on the saddle and handlebars, or on the front of the fork and the bars.

❶ Remove the wheels.

❷ If the bike has a chain hanger (a little nub attached to the inner side of the right seatstay, a few centimeters above the dropout), hook the chain over it. If not, pull the chain back over a dowel stick or old rear hub secured into the dropouts.

❸ Fill a bucket with hot water and dish soap. Using a stiff nylon-bristle scrub brush, scrub the entire bike and wheels. Leave the chain, cogs, chainrings and derailleurs for last.

wheel removal

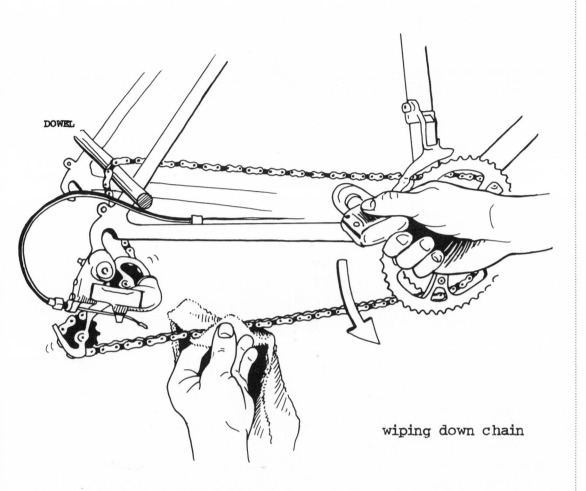

DOWEL

wiping down chain

---

❹ Rinse the bike with water, either by hosing it off or with a wet rag.

Avoid getting water in the bearings of the bottom bracket, headset, pedals or hubs. Also avoid getting water into the lip seals of suspension forks, as well as any pivots or shock seals on rear-suspension systems. Most frames and rigid forks have vent holes in the tubes to allow expanding hot gases to escape during welding. The holes are often open to the outside on the seatstays, fork legs, chainstays, and seatstay and chainstay bridges. Avoid getting water in these holes. This is especially true when using high-pressure car washes.

Taping over the vent holes, even when riding, is a good idea.

CLEANING DRIVETRAIN

The drivetrain consists of an oil-covered chain running over gears and derailleurs. It is all exposed to the elements, so it picks up lots of dirt. Since the drivetrain is what transfers your energy into the bike's forward motion, it should move freely. Frequent cleaning and lubrication keep it rolling well, and extend the life of your bike.

The drivetrain can often be cleaned sufficiently by using a rag and wiping down the chain, derailleur jockey

general
cleaning

33

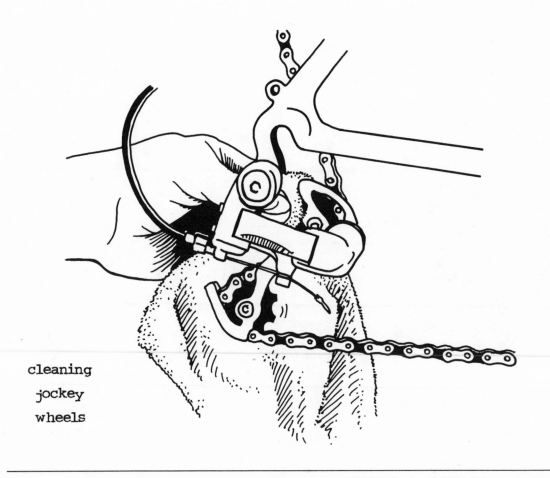

cleaning
jockey
wheels

wheels and chainrings.

❶ To wipe the chain, turn the cranks while holding a rag in your hand and grabbing the chain.

❷ Holding a rag, squeeze the teeth of the jockey wheels in between your index finger and thumb, as you turn the cranks. This will remove almost any buildup on the jockey wheels.

❸ Slip a rag in between cogs of the freewheel and work it back and forth to clean each cog.

❹ Wipe down the derailleurs and the front chainrings with the rag.

Your chain will last much longer if you perform this sort of quick cleaning regularly, followed by dripping chain lube on the chain and another light wipe down. You will also be able to skip those heavy duty solvent cleanings that are necessary when a chain gets really grungy.

You can also remove packed-up mud from derailleurs and cogs with the soapy water and scrub brush. The soap will not dissolve the dirty lubricant that is all over the drivetrain; rather the brush will smear it all over the bike if you're not careful. Use a different brush than the one you use for cleaning the frame. Follow it with a cloth wipe down.

SOLVENT CLEANING

If you determine that using a solvent is necessary, pick an environmentally

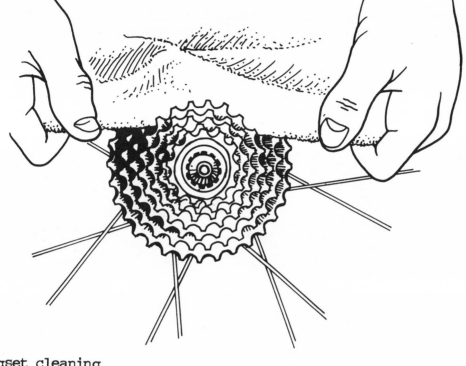

cogset cleaning

friendly one. Using one of the many citrus solvents on the market will minimize the danger of breathing the stuff or getting it onto and into your skin, and it will reduce a major disposal problem. Since all solvents suck the oils out of your skin, I recommend using rubber gloves, even with "green" solvents. A self-contained chain cleaner with internal brushes and a solvent bath is a convenient way to clean a chain (see page 36 for illustration). A nylon brush or an old toothbrush dipped in solvent is good for cleaning cogs, pulleys and chainrings, and can be used on the chain as well. Another way to clean the chain is to remove it and put it in a solvent bath.

❶ Follow the directions in Chapter 4 for removing the chain.

❷ Put the chain in an old water bottle about 1/4 full of solvent.

❸ Shake the bottle vigorously to clean the chain. Do this close to the ground, in case the water bottle leaks.

❹ Hang the chain up to dry.

❺ Install the chain on the bike, following the directions in Chapter 4.

❻ Drip chain lubricant into each of the chain's links and rollers.

❼ Lightly wipe down the chain with a rag.

You can re-use much of the solvent by allowing it to settle in a clear container over a period of days or weeks.

general
cleaning

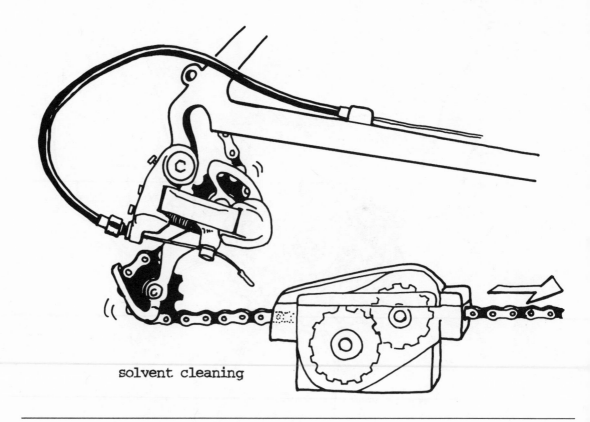

solvent cleaning

Decant and save the clear stuff and dispose of the sludge.

A clean bike invites you to jump on it, and it will feel faster. Corrosion problems are minimized, and you can see problems as they arise. A clean bike is a happy bike.

emergency repairs

how to get home when something big breaks or you get lost or hurt.

"**A**lways carry a flagon of whiskey in case

of a snake bite, and furthermore,

always carry a small snake"

— W. C. FIELDS

This chapter is included so you do not face disaster if you have a mechanical problem on the trail. If you ride your bike out in the boonies, sooner or later you will encounter a mechanical problem that has the potential to turn into an emergency. The best way to avoid such an emergency is to plan ahead and be prepared before it happens. Proper planning involves steps as simple as taking a few tools, spare tubes and a little knowledge.

If you have something break on the trail, there are procedures in this chapter to deal with most "emergencies,"

whether you have all of the tools that you need or not. You always have the option of walking, but this chapter is designed to get you home pedaling.

Finally, you may find yourself with a perfectly functioning bicycle and still be in dire straits because you're either lost, bonking or injured on the trail. Carefully read the final portion of this chapter for pointers on how to avoid getting lost or injured and what to do if the worst does happen.

If this chapter does nothing other than alert you to all of the dangers facing you out in the back country, then hopefully you'll prepare for them and this chapter will have accomplished its purpose.

RECOMMENDED TOOLS

The take-along tool kit for your seat bag is described in Chapter 1. If you're going to be a long way from civilization, take along the extra tools recommended for longer trips.

FLAT TIRES

If you have a spare or a patch kit:

Simple flat tires are easy to deal with. The first flat you get on a ride is most easily fixed by installing your spare tube (Chapter 6). Make sure you remove all thorns from the tire and feel around the inside of the tire for any other sharp objects. Check the rim to see that your flat wasn't caused by a protruding spoke or nipple or a worn rim strip.

After you run out of spare tubes, additional flats must be patched (also covered in Chapter 6).

No more spare tubes or patches

Now comes the frustrating part: You have run out of spare tubes, and have used up all of your patches (or your CO_2 cartridge is empty and you don't have a pump) and still you have a flat tire. The solution is obvious. You are going to have to ride home without air in your tire. Riding a flat for a long way will trash your tire and will probably damage your rim. Still, there are ways to minimize that damage. Try filling the space in the tire with grass, leaves or similar materials. Pack it in tightly and then remount the tire on the rim. This

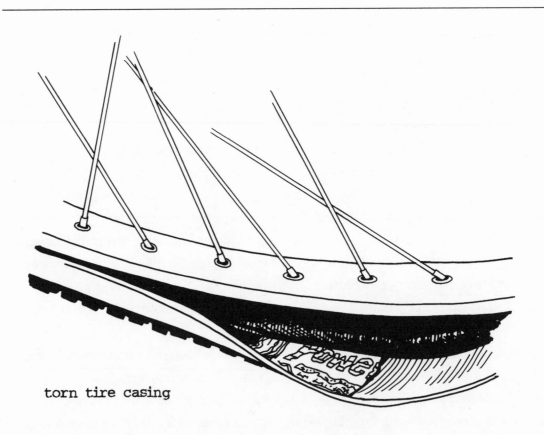

torn tire casing

should make the ride a little less dangerous, by minimizing the flat tire's tendency to roll out from under the bike during a turn.

Torn sidewall

If your tire's sidewall is torn, the tube will stick out. Just patching or replacing the tube isn't going to solve the problem. Without reinforcement, your tube will blow out again very soon. First, you have to look for something to reinforce the side wall. Dollar bills work surprisingly well as tire boots. The paper is pretty tough and should hold for the rest of the ride if you are careful. (I told you that cash will get you out of bad situations. Just don't try putting a credit card in there.) Business cards are a bit small but work better than nothing. You might even try an energy bar wrapper. You get the idea.

❶ Lay the cash or whatever inside the tire at the rip, or wrap it around the tube at that spot. Pack in as many layers as you can between the tire and tube to support the tube and prevent it from bulging out through the hole in the side wall.

❷ Put a little air in the tube to hold the makeshift reinforcement in place.

❸ Mount the tire bead on the rim. You may need to let a little air out of the tube to do so.

❹ After making sure that the tire is seated and the boot is still in place, inflate the tube to about 40 psi, if you are good at estimating without a gauge. Much less than 40 psi will allow the boot

to move around and may also lead to a pinch flat if you're riding on rocky terrain. This is not a perfect solution, so you will need to check the boot periodically to make certain that the tube is not bulging out again.

CHAIN JAMMED BETWEEN THE CHAINRING AND THE CHAINSTAY

If your chain gets jammed between the chainrings and the chainstay, it may be hard to get out if the clearance is tight. You may find that you tug and tug on the chain, and it won't come out, yet it somehow got in there. Well, chainrings flex, and if you apply some mechanical advantage, the chain will come free quite easily. Just insert a screwdriver or similar thin lever between the chainring and the chainstay, and pry the space open while pulling the chain out. You will probably be amazed at how easy this is, especially in light of how much hard tugging would not free the chain.

If you *still* cannot free the chain, disassemble the chain with a chain tool (Chapter 4), pull it out, and put it back together once it is back in the right place.

BROKEN CHAIN

Chains break quite often when mountain-bike riding, usually while shifting the front derailleur under load. The side force of the derailleur on the chain coupled with the high tension can pop a chain plate off the end of a rivet. As the chain rips apart, it can cause

broken
chain

39

collateral damage as well. The open chain plate can snag the front derailleur cage, bending it or tearing it off, or it can jam into the rear dropout.

When a chain breaks, the end link is certainly shot, and some others in the area may be as well.

❶ Remove the damaged links with the chain tool. (You or your riding partner *did* remember to bring a chain tool, right?) Again, the procedures for removing the damaged links and reinstalling the chain are covered in Chapter 4.

❷ If you have brought along extra chain links, replace the same number you remove. If not, you'll need to use the chain in its shortened state; it will still work.

❸ Join the ends and connect the chain (procedure for connecting a chain is in Chapter 4). Some lightweight chain tools and multi tools are more difficult to use than a shop chain tool. Some flex so badly that it is hard to keep the push rod lined up with the rivet. Others pinch the plates so tightly that the chain link binds up. It's a good idea to find these things out *before* you perform repairs on the trail. Try the tool out at home or at your local bike shop, this way you know what you're getting into before you reach the trailhead.

BENT WHEEL

If the rim is banging against the brake pads, or worse yet the frame or fork, pedaling becomes very difficult. It can

freeing jammed chain

chains

happen due to either a loose or broken spoke, or due to a badly bent or even broken rim.

LOOSE SPOKES

If you have a loose spoke or two, the rim will wobble all over the place.

❶ Find the loose spoke (or spokes) by feeling all of them. The really loose ones, which would cause a wobble of large magnitude, will be obvious. If you find a broken spoke, skip to the next section ("**Broken spokes**"). If you have no loose or broken spokes, skip to "**Bent rim**".

❷ Get out the spoke wrench that you carry for such an eventuality. If you don't have one, skip to "**No spoke wrench**" below.

❸ Mark the loose spokes by tying blades

of grass or the like around them.

❹ Tighten the loose spokes and true the wheel, following the procedures outlined in Chapter 6.

BROKEN SPOKES

If you broke a spoke, the wheel will wobble wildly.

❶ Locate the broken spoke.

❷ Remove the remainder of the spoke, both the piece going through the hub, and the piece threaded into the nipple. If the broken spoke is on the freewheel side of the rear wheel, you may not be able to remove it from the hub, since it will be behind the cogs. If so, skip to step 6 after wrapping it around neighboring spokes to prevent it from slapping around.

fixing broken chain

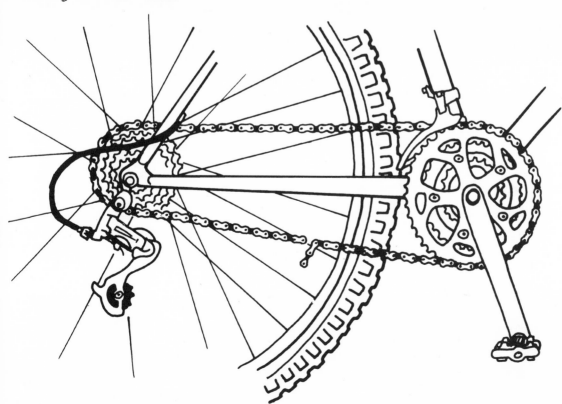

III

emergency

chains

loose spoke

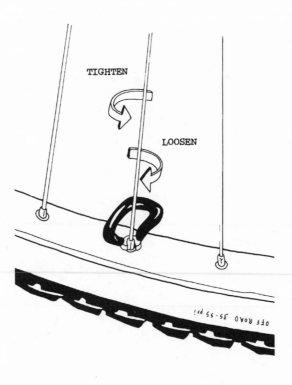

TIGHTEN

LOOSEN

OFF ROAD 35-55 psi

brake lever adjusting
barrel

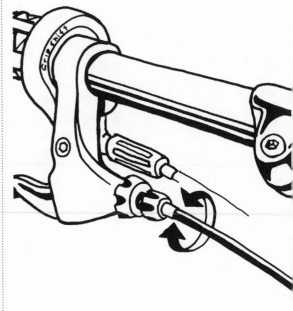

❸ Get out your spoke wrench. If you have no spoke wrench, skip to "**No spoke wrench**" below.

❹ If you brought a spare spoke of the right length or the Kevlar replacement spoke mentioned in Chapter 1, you're in business. If not, skip to step 6. Put the new spoke through the hub hole, weave it through the other spokes the same way the old one was, and thread it into the spoke nipple that is still sticking out of the rim. Mark it with a pen or a blade of grass tied around it. With the Kevlar spoke, thread the Kevlar through the hub hole, attach the ends to the enclosed stub of spoke, adjust the ends to length, tie them off,

and tighten the spoke nipple.

❺ Tighten the nipple on the new spoke with a spoke wrench, checking the rim clearance with the brake pad as you go. Stop when the rim is straight and finish your ride.

❻ If you can't replace the spoke and you do have a spoke wrench, bring the wheel into rideable trueness by loosening the spoke on either side of the broken one. These two spokes come from the opposite side of the hub and will let the rim move toward the side with the broken spoke as they are loosened. A spoke nipple loosens clockwise when viewed from its top. Ride home, as this wheel will rapidly get worse.

❼ Once at home, replace the spoke,

emergency

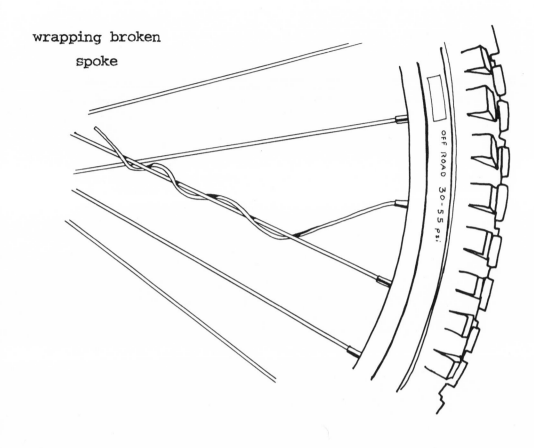

wrapping broken
spoke

OFF ROAD 30-55 psi

following the procedure in Chapter 6, or take it to a bike shop for repair.

NO SPOKE WRENCH

If the rim is banging the brake pads, but the tire is not hitting the chainstays or fork legs, just open the brake so that you can get home.

❶ Loosen the brake cable tension by screwing in the barrel adjuster on the brake lever. Remember that braking on that wheel is now compromised, so be careful.

❷ If that is not enough, and you have a wrench to loosen the brake cable (usually 5mm Allen), do so, and then clamp it back down (see Chapter 7).

❸ If this still does not cut it, or you have hydraulic brakes, you can remove both brake sides from the cantilever posts and pedal home slowly. You will usually need a 5mm Allen wrench for this. Do not attempt to ride a bike with open cantilever brake arms. The brake arms will flap around as you ride and may get caught in the spokes, which could crack your seatstay in a heartbeat.

If you want to straighten the wheel without using a spoke wrench, follow the procedures for dealing with a bent rim. Recognize that if you bend the rim by smacking it on the ground to correct for a loose or broken spoke, you will permanently deform the rim. Try to get

no spoke
wrench

43

fixing bent rim

home without resorting to this, since you will have to replace the rim.

BENT RIM

If your rim is only mildly out of true, and you brought your spoke wrench, you can fix it. The procedure for truing a wheel is explained in Chapter 6.

If the wheel is really whacked out, spoke truing won't do much. To get it to clear the brakes so that you can pedal home, follow the steps under **No spoke wrench**.

If the wheel is bent to the point that it won't turn, even when the brake is removed, you can beat it straight as long as the rim is not broken.

❶ Find the area that is bent outward the most and mark it.

❷ Leaving the tire on and inflated, hold the wheel by its sides with the bent part at the top facing away from you.

❸ Smack the bent section of the rim against the flat ground.

❹ Put the wheel back in the frame or fork, and see if anything has changed.

❺ Repeat the process until the wheel is rideable. You may be surprised how straight you can get a wheel this way.

DAMAGED FRONT DERAILLEUR

If the front derailleur is mildly bent, straighten it with your hands or leave it until you get home.

If it's just twisted on the seat tube, reposition it so the cage is just above, and parallel to, the chainrings, then tighten the derailleur in place with a

bent rim

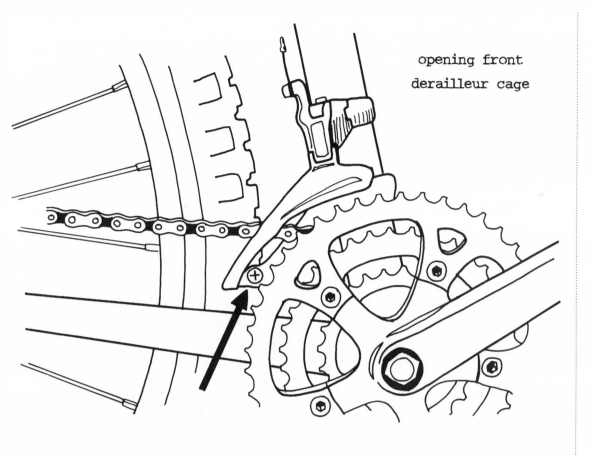

opening front
derailleur cage

emergency

5mm Allen wrench. If the derailleur is broken or so bent that you can't ride, you will need to remove it or route the chain around it.

With only a screwdriver:

❶ Get the chain out of the derailleur cage. To do this, open the derailleur cage by removing the screw at its tail.

❷ Bypass the derailleur by putting the chain on a chainring that does not interfere with it (either shift the derailleur to the inside and put the chain on the big chainring, or vice versa).

With Allen wrenches and a screwdriver (or a chain tool):

❶ Remove the derailleur from the seat tube, usually with a 5mm Allen wrench.

❷ Remove the screw at the tail of the derailleur cage with a screwdriver

❸ Pry open the cage, and separate it

from the chain. You could also disassemble the chain (Chapter 4), pull it out of the derailleur, and reconnect it.

❹ Manually put the chain on whichever chainring is most appropriate for the ride home. If in doubt, put it on the middle one.

❺ Tie the cable up so it won't catch in your wheel.

❻ Stuff the derailleur in your pocket and ride home.

DAMAGED REAR DERAILLEUR

If the derailleur just gets bent a bit, you can probably straighten it enough to get home. If the rear derailleur gets really bent or broken or one of the jockey wheels falls off, then you will not be able to continue with the chain routed through it. You will need to route

damaged rear
derailleur

the chain around the derailleur, effectively turning your bike into a single-speed for the duration of your ride.

❶ Open the chain with a chain tool (Chapter 4) and pull it out of the derailleur.

❷ Pick a gear combination in which you think you can make it home most effectively, and set the front derailleur over the chainring you have picked.

❸ Wrap the chain over the chainring and the rear cog you have chosen, bypassing the rear derailleur entirely.

❹ Remove any overlapping chain, making the chain as short as you can and still be able to connect the

ends together.

❺ Connect the chain with the chain tool as described in Chapter 4.

❻ Ride home.

BROKEN FRONT DERAILLEUR CABLE

Your chain will be on the inner chainring, and you will still be able to use all of your rear cogs. You have three options, depending on which chainring you want for your return ride:

Option 1. Leave it on the inner ring and ride home.

Option 2. Tighten the inner derailleur stop screw until the derailleur sits over the middle chainring. Leave the chain

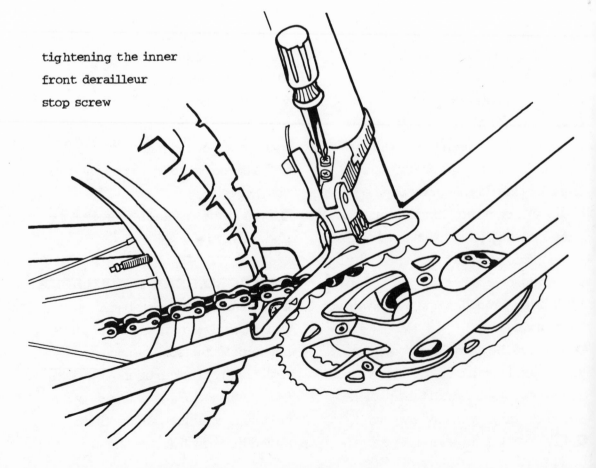

tightening the inner
front derailleur
stop screw

on the middle ring and ride home.

Option 3. Bypass the front derailleur by removing the chain from the derailleur and putting it on the big chainring. You can do this either by opening the derailleur cage with a screwdriver or by disconnecting and reconnecting the chain with a chain tool (Chapter 4).

Note: You have probably noticed by now that a chain tool is one of the handiest items you can take along. Like the credit card guys say: "Don't leave home without it."

BROKEN REAR DERAILLEUR CABLE

Your chain will be on the smallest rear cog, and you will still be able to use all three front chainrings. You have two options:

Option 1. Leave it on the small cog and ride home.

Option 2. Tighten the high-end adjustment screw on the rear derailleur (usually the upper one of the two screws) until it lines up over a larger cog. Move the chain to that cog and ride home. If you do not have a screwdriver, you can push inward on the rear derailleur while turning the crank with the rear wheel off of the ground to shift to a larger cog. Jam a stick in between the derailleur cage plates to prevent it from moving back

emergency

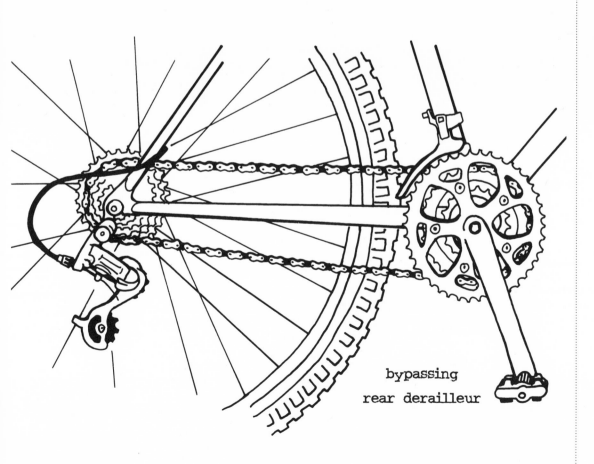

damaged
rear
derailleur
cable

bypassing
rear derailleur

down to the small cog. (See illustration on page 49.)

BROKEN BRAKE CABLE

Walk home, or ride slowly and carefully home if the trail is not dangerous.

FLAT SUSPENSION FORK

Not much you can do here. If you have a leaking air-oil fork, you will just have to ride back with it bottoming out the whole way. Go slowly and keep your weight back.

BROKEN SEAT RAILS OR SEATPOST CLAMP

If you can't tape or tie the saddle back on, try wrapping your gloves or some clothing over the top of the seatpost to pad it. Otherwise, remove the seatpost and ride home without a saddle.

BROKEN SEAT POST SHAFT

Splint it internally with a stick and ride very carefully. Failing that, remove the seatpost and ride home standing up.

BROKEN HANDLEBAR

It's probably best to walk home. You could splint it by jamming a stick inside and ride home very carefully, but the stick could easily break, leaving you with no way to control the bike.

flat suspension fork

———

broken seat rails

———

broken seat post

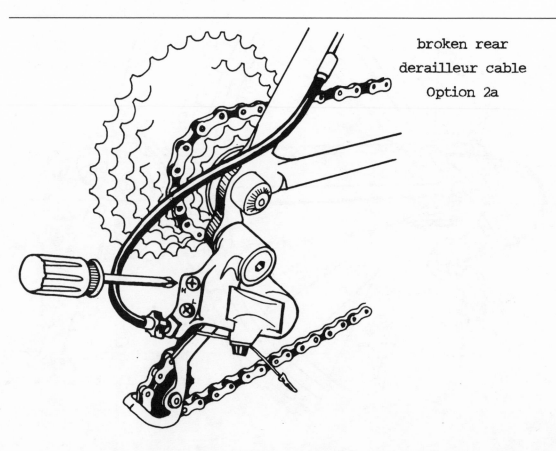

broken rear
derailleur cable
Option 2a

TRAIL SAFETY: AVOIDING GETTING LOST OR HURT, AND DEALING WITH IT IF YOU DO

Mountain biking in the back country can be dangerous. A rash of recent deaths and injuries underscores the need to prepare properly and to take personal responsibility for your own and others' safety when riding in deserted country. Two deaths near Moab, Utah, in the summer of 1995 highlight the risks inherent in the sport we love.

The two died in Moab while riding the Porcupine Rim trail, a favorite of visiting mountain bikers. The account of these two riders pinpoints a number of details that cost them their lives. The pair got lost on the descent off Porcupine Rim, missed the turn into Jackass Canyon, and then headed instead into Negro Bill Canyon — which divides the Porcupine trail from Moab's most famous ride, the Slickrock Trail. It may come as a surprise that people could die and go undiscovered for 17 days so close to a main highway into town (which was right below them) and two heavily traveled trails. But apparently they hadn't told anyone of their plans to ride this trail, so no one in town noticed when they did not return.

Their parents, not hearing from them for a few days, called the sheriff, and a search was mounted.

Once the two had lost their way, instead of riding back the way they had come, they had abandoned their bikes

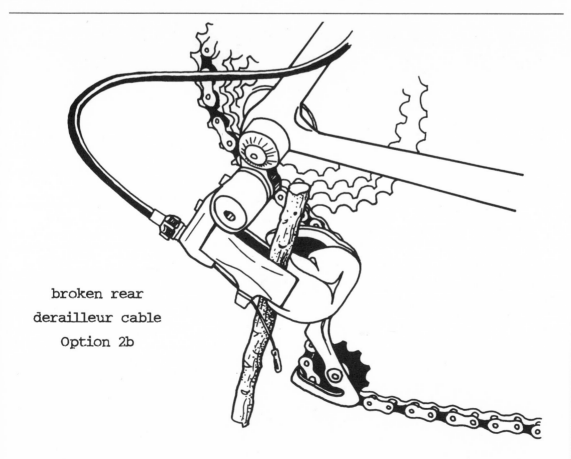

broken rear
derailleur cable
Option 2b

trail safety

and tried to walk down to the road. That road and the Colorado River are very close as the crow flies and are visible at a number of points ... but, due to the numerous cliffs, are quite difficult to reach. They climbed, fell or slid down to a ledge from which they apparently were unable to climb either up or down, and there they perished from exposure.

They died on a ledge, in such a way that they were very difficult to spot from the air. They had placed no items to indicate their positions to airborne spotters. Had searchers found their bikes, they could have concentrated the search on a small area. Regrettably, their bikes and helmets were picked up by a pair of passing riders who did not leave word with the authorities.

Eventually, a helicopter searcher saw the bodies on the ledge, and a Forest Service ranger rappelled 160 feet down to them. He was able to then walk out unaided, indicating that perhaps the riders were so injured, exhausted, delirious or hypothermic that they had been unable to take the same route out.

Cliffs, steep hills and an array of other natural features can also pose a risk. In the fall of 1995, another Moab rider barely managed to jump off his bike before it went hurtling over the edge of a cliff and dropped some 400 feet. Anyone who has ridden much in Moab can tell you that there are countless other places exposed enough to present a similar threat.

Even in seemingly safe areas, the risks can be high. Pro rider Paul Willerton came close to meeting his end on a relatively standard, cliffless, but isolated, trail near Winter Park, Colorado. Willerton crashed over his bars, and broke his leg. Unable to walk, he had to pull himself to safety using only his arms.

We all tend to think that nothing like this will ever happen to us. But things like this *can* happen, far too easily. This shouldn't discourage you from riding in the back country. It *should* encourage you to think and utilize the following 12 basic back-country survival skills — they could make the difference between life and death.

❶ *Always* take plenty of water. You can survive a long time without food, but not without water.

❷ Tell someone where you are going and when you expect to return. If you know of someone who is missing, call the police or sheriff.

❸ If you find personal effects on the ground, assume it could indicate that someone is lost or in trouble. Report the find and mark the location.

❹ If you get lost, backtrack. Even if going back is longer, it is better than getting stranded.

❺ Don't go down something you can't get back up.

❻ Bring matches, extra clothing and food, and perhaps a flashlight and an aluminized emergency blanket, in case you have to spend the night out or need to signal searchers.

7 If the area is new to you, go with someone who is familiar with it, or take a map and compass, and know how to use them.

8 Wear a helmet. It's hard to ride home with a cracked skull.

9 Bring basic first aid and bike tools, and know how to use them well enough to keep yourself and your bike going.

Walk your bike when it's appropriate.

10 Falling off a cliff is a poor alternative to taking a few extra seconds or displaying less bravado. Try riding difficult sections to improve your bike handling, but if the exposure is great or a mistake leaves you injured a long way from help, find another place to practice those moves.

Don't ride beyond your limits if you are

11 a long way out. Take a break. Get out of the hot sun. Avoid dehydration and bonk by drinking and eating enough.

Teach your friends all these things.

Keep in mind that your decisions not

12 only affect you, but they could also affect your riding partners and countless others. Realize that endangering yourself can also endanger the person trying to rescue you. Search and rescue parties are usually made up of helpful people, who will gladly come and save you, but no one appreciates being put in harm's way unnecessarily.

In summary, make appropriate decisions when cycling the back country. Learn survival skills, and prepare well. Recognize that just because you have a $4000 bike

and are riding on popular trails, you are not immune to danger. When ignorance makes us oblivious to danger, it sadly becomes the danger itself.

chains

> "**A** chain is only as strong as its weakest link"
>
> — ANONYMOUS

> "**A** sausage is only as good as its last link"
>
> — BLUTO

A bike chain is a simple series of links connected by rivets. Rollers surround each rivet between the link plates and engage the teeth of the cogs and chainrings. It is an extremely efficient method of transmitting mechanical energy from your pedals to your rear wheel. In terms of weight, cost and efficiency, the bicycle chain has no equal ... and believe me, people have tried to improve on it.

To keep your bike running smoothly, you do have to pay at least some attention to your chain. It needs to be kept clean and well lubricated in order to utilize your energy most efficiently, shift smoothly, and maximize chain life.

Chains need to be replaced frequently, since they stretch, which shortens the working life of other, more expensive, drivetrain components.

LUBRICATION

When lubricating the chain, use a lubricant intended for bicycle chains. If you want to get fancy about it, you can assess the type of conditions in which you ride and choose a lubricant intended for those conditions. Some lubricants are dry and pick up less dirt in dry conditions, some are sticky and therefore less prone to washing off in wet conditions.

❶ Drip a small amount of lubricant across each roller, periodically moving the chain to give easy access to the links

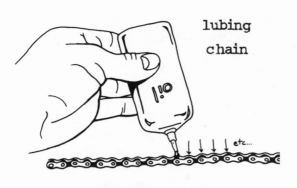

lubing chain

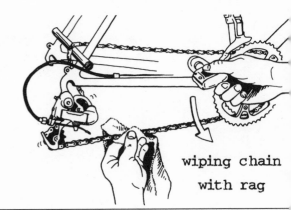

wiping chain with rag

you are working on. If you are in a hurry, you can turn the crank slowly while dripping lubricant onto the chain as it goes by. This is far better than not lubricating the chain, but it will cause you to apply too much lubricant. That, in turn, will cause the chain to pick up dirt faster, and you'll then wear out your chain sooner.

❷ Wipe the chain off lightly with a rag.

CLEANING

Cleaning the chain can be accomplished in a number of ways.

Frequent wiping and lubrication

The simplest way to maintain a chain is to wipe it down frequently and then lubricate it. If this is done prior to every ride, you will never need to clean your chain with a solvent. The lubricant softens the old sludge buildup, which is driven out of the chain when you ride. The problem is that the lubricant also picks up new dirt and grime. If new dirt and grime is wiped off and the chain is re-lubricated frequently, the chain will stay clean and supple. Chain cleaning can be performed with the bike standing on the ground

or in a bike stand.

❶ With a rag in your hand, grasp the lower length of the chain (between the bottom of the chainring and the rear derailleur lower jockey wheel).

❷ Turn the crank backward a number of revolutions, pulling the chain through the rag. Periodically rotate the rag to present a cleaner section of it to the chain.

❸ Lubricate the chain as above.

CHAIN-CLEANING UNITS

Several companies make chain-cleaning units that scrub the chain with solvent while it is still on the bike. These types of chain cleaners are generally made of clear plastic and have two or three rotating brushes that scrub the chain as it moves through the solvent bath. These units offer the advantage of letting you clean your chain without removing it from the bike. Regularly removing your chain is a pain and it shortens chain life. Most chain cleaners come with a non-toxic, citrus-based solvent. For your safety and other environmental reasons, I strongly recommend that you purchase

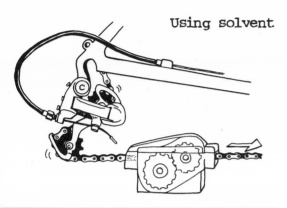

Using solvent

non-toxic citrus solvents for your chain cleaner, even if the unit already comes with a petroleum-based solvent.

Citrus chain solvents often contain some lubricants as well, so they won't dry the chain out. A really strong solvent will displace the oil from inside the rollers, and will later evaporate, leaving a dry, squeaking chain, that is hard to rehabilitate.

Procedure

❶ Remove the top and pour in solvent up to the fill line.

❷ Place the chain cleaning unit up against the bottom of the chain, and reinstall the top so that the chain runs through it.

❸ Turn the crank.

❹ Lubricate as above.

REMOVAL AND CLEANING

You can also clean the chain by removing it from the bicycle and cleaning it in a solvent. I recommend against it, because repeated disassembly weakens the chain. On a road bike, this is not much of an issue, but mountain-bike chains are more prone to breakage because of the

conditions in which they are used.

Chains generally break when shifting the front derailleur while pedaling hard. This can pry a link plate open so that the head of a rivet pops out of it, tearing the chain apart. Chain disassembly and reassembly expands the size of the rivet hole where you put it together, allowing the rivet to pop out more easily. Shimano supplies special "subpins" for reassembly of their chains that are meant to prevent this.

If you do disassemble the chain (see below for instructions), you can clean it well, even without a solvent tank. Just drop your chain into an old jar or water bottle half filled with solvent. Using an old water bottle or jar allows you to clean the chain without touching or breathing the solvent — something to be avoided even with citrus solvents.

Procedure

❶ Remove the chain from the bike (see "Chain removal" below).

❷ Drop it in a water bottle or jar.

❸ Pour in enough solvent to cover the chain.

❹ Shake the bottle vigorously (low to the ground, in case the top pops off).

❺ Hang the chain to air dry.

❻ Reassemble it on the bike (see "Chain installation" below).

❼ Lubricate it as above.

Allow the solvent in the bottle to settle for a few days so you can decant the clear stuff and use it again. I'll say it throughout the book — it is important to use a citrus-based solvent. It is not only

checking chain stretch

safer for the environment, it is gentler on your skin and less harmful to breathe. Wear rubber gloves when working with *any* solvent, and use a respirator meant for volatile organic compounds if you are not using a citrus-based solvent. There is no sense in fixing your bike so it goes faster if you end up becoming a slower, sickly bike rider.

CHAIN REPLACEMENT

As the rollers, pins and plates wear out, your chain will begin to stretch. That, in turn, will hasten the wear and tear on the other parts of your drivetrain. A stretched chain will concentrate the load on each individual gear tooth, rather than distributing it over all of the teeth that the chain contacts. This will result in the gear teeth becoming hook-shaped and the tooth valleys becoming wider. If such wear has already occurred, a new chain will not solve the problem. A new chain will not mesh with deformed teeth, and it is likely to skip whenever you pedal hard. So, before all of that extra wear and tear takes

place, get in the habit of replacing your chain on a regular basis.

How long it takes for the chain to stretch will vary, depending on chain type, maintenance, riding conditions, and strength and weight of the rider. Figure on replacing your chain every 500 to 1000 miles, especially if ridden in dirty conditions by a large rider. Lighter riders riding mostly on paved roads can extend replacement time to 2000 miles.

CHECKING FOR CHAIN STRETCH

The simplest method is to employ a chain-stretch indicator, such as the model made by Rohloff.

Another way is to measure it with a ruler. Chains are measured on an inch standard, and there should be exactly an integral number of links in one foot.

❶ Set one end of the ruler on a rivet edge, and measure to the rivet edge at the other end of the ruler.

❷ The distance between these rivets should be 12" exactly. If it is 12-1/16" or greater, replace the chain.

IV

chains

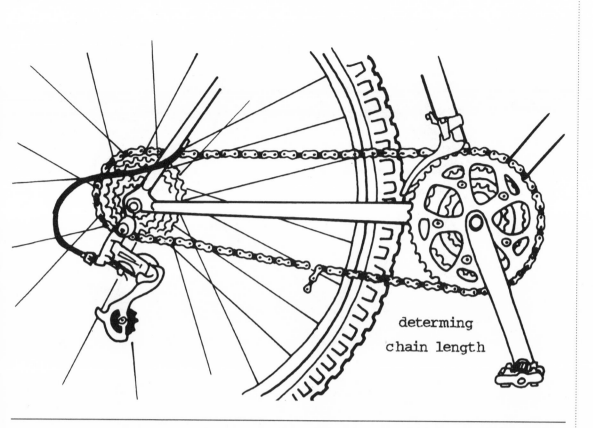

determing
chain length

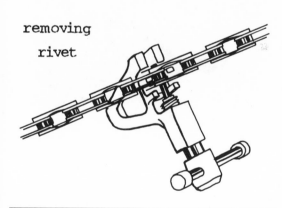

removing
rivet

removal and
installation

a new "subpin" for it, be careful to leave a millimeter or so of rivet protruding inward from the chain plate to hook the chain back together when reassembling.

CHAIN INSTALLATION

1. Determine the chain length:

If you are putting on a new chain, determine how many links you'll need in one of two ways.

Method 1. Assuming your old chain was the correct length, compare the two and use the same number of links.

Method 2. If you have a standard long-cage mountain bike rear derailleur on your bike, wrap the chain around the big chain ring and the biggest cog without going through either derailleur. Bring the two ends together until the ends overlap. Leave one full link of

CHAIN REMOVAL

The following procedure applies to all standard derailleur chains except those made by Taya, which snaps open when you flex the master link by hand.

❶ Place any link over the back teeth on a chain tool.

❷ Tighten the chain-tool handle clockwise to push the link rivet out. Unless you have a Shimano chain and

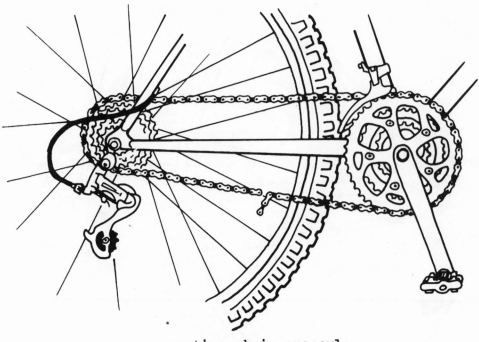

routing chain properly

overlap, and remove the rest.

2. Route the chain properly:

❶ Shift the derailleurs so that the chain will rest on the smallest cog in the rear and on the smallest chainring up front.

❷ Starting with the rear derailleur pulley that is farthest from the derailleur body (this will be the bottom pulley once the chain is taut), guide the chain up through the rear derailleur, going around the two jockey pulleys.

❸ Guide the chain over the smallest rear cog.

❹ Guide the chain through the front derailleur cage.

❺ Wrap the chain around the smallest front chainring.

❻ Bring the chain ends together so they meet.

3. Connect the chain:

Connecting a chain is much easier if the link rivet that was partially removed

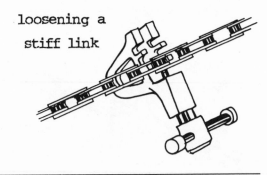

loosening a stiff link

when the chain was taken apart is facing toward you. Positioning the link rivet this way allows you to use the chain tool in a much more comfortable manner (driving the rivet toward the bike, instead of back at you).

CONNECTING
A STANDARD CHAIN:

❶ Push the ends together, snapping the end link over the little stub of pin you left sticking out to the inside between the opposite end plates.

❷ Push the rivet through with the chain

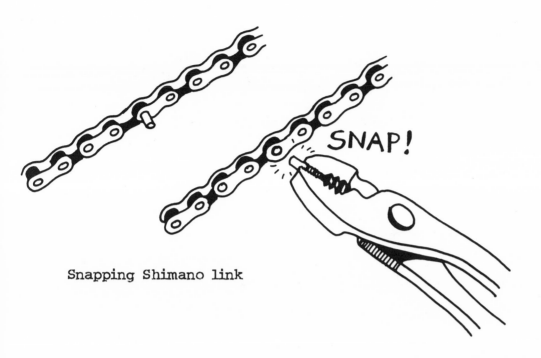

Snapping Shimano link

replacing
rivet

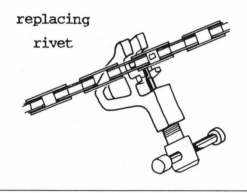

tool until the same amount protrudes on either end.

❸ Free the stiff link, either by flexing it back and forth with your fingers, or, better, by using the chain tool's second set of teeth as below.

❹ Put the link over the set of teeth on the tool closest to the rivet pusher.

❺ Push the pin a fraction of a turn to spread the plates apart.

CONNECTING A SHIMANO CHAIN:

❶ Make sure you have a Shimano

"subpin," which looks like a black rivet with a point on one end. It is twice as long as a standard rivet and has a breakage groove at the middle of its length. It comes with a new Shimano chain. If you are re-installing an old Shimano chain, get a new subpin at a bike shop. If you don't have a subpin and are going to connect it anyway, follow the procedure for **Connecting a standard chain**, but be aware that the chain is now more likely to break than if it was assembled with the proper subpin.

❷ Remove any extra links, pushing the appropriate rivet completely out.

❸ Line up the chain ends.

❹ Push the subpin in with your fingers, pointed end first. It will go in about halfway.

❺ With the chain tool, push the subpin through until there is only as much left protruding at the tail end as the other

connecting
Shimano
chains

59

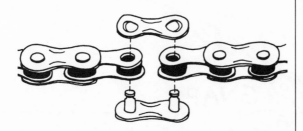

Taya chain master link

rivets in the chain.

5 Break off the leading half of the subpin with a pair of pliers.

5 The chain should move freely. If not, flex it back and forth with your thumbs at this rivet.

CONNECTING A TAYA CHAIN

1 Connect the two ends of the chain together with the master link that has two rivets sticking out of it.

2 Snap the outer master link plate over the rivets and into their grooves. To facilitate hooking each keyhole-shaped hole over its corresponding rivet, bow the plate with the protruding rivets so that the ends of the rivets are closer together.

connecting Taya chain

TROUBLESHOOTING CHAIN PROBLEMS

CHAIN SUCK

Sometimes the chain may not release from the bottom of the chainring as it travels to the bottom of the rear derailleur. It will come around and get "sucked" up by the inner or middle chainring until it hits the chainstay. This is called "chain suck." Sometimes, the chain becomes wedged between the chainstay and the chainring

A number of things can cause chain suck. To eliminate it, try the simplest methods first.

Reducing chain suck

1 Clean and lube the chain and see if it improves.

2 Check for tight links by watching the chain move through the derailleur jockey wheels as you slowly turn the crank backwards. Loosen tight links by flexing them side to side with your thumbs.

3 If chain suck persists, check that there are no bent or torn teeth on the chainring. Try straightening any broken or torn teeth you find with pliers.

4 If your chain still sucks, try another chain with wider spacing between link plates (if it is too narrow, it can pinch the chain ring). You can use a caliper to compare link spacing of various chains. Shimano has a link-spacing tool (TL-CN24) that checks link separation on their chainrings.

IV

chains

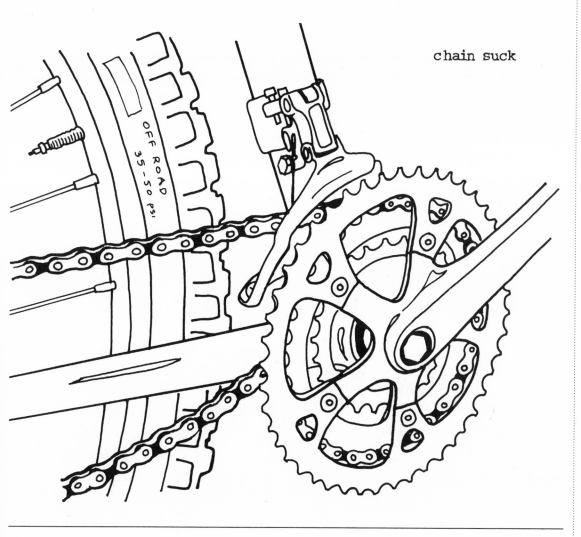

chain suck

TROUBLE—
SHOOTING

❺ If the problem still persists, a new chainring or an "anti-chain suck" device that attaches under the chainstays may help. Ask at your bike shop about what is available.

SQUEAKING CHAIN

❶ Wipe down and lubricate the chain.

❷ If the squeak does not go away after a single ride with fresh lubricant, replace the chain. (If the initial remedy does not work, the chain is too dry inside and probably rusted as well. They seldom heal from this condition. Life is too short and bike riding is too joyful to put up with the sound of a squeaking chain.)

SKIPPING CHAIN

There can be a number of causes for a skipping chain.

Filth

❶ Wipe off the chain, the cogs, the chainrings, and the rear derailleur jockey wheels.

❷ Lubricate the chain and try riding it again.

Stiff links

❶ Turn the crank backward slowly to see if a stiff chain link exists; a stiff link is unable to bend properly as it goes

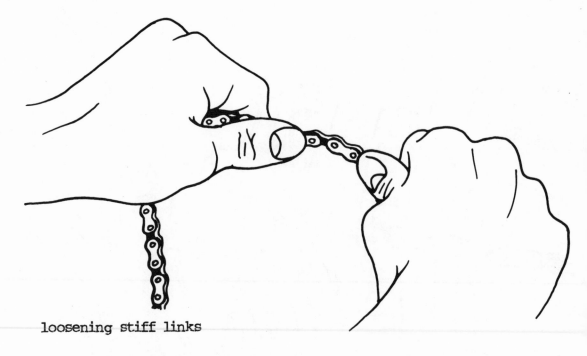

loosening stiff links

through the rear derailleur jockey wheels.

❷ Loosen stiff links by flexing them side to side between the index finger and thumb of both hands.

❸ Wipe down and lubricate the chain.

Stretched chain

If the chain is stretched, it will skip because it does not mesh well with the cogs. A new chain will fix the problem, if it has not gone on too long.

❶ Check for chain stretch as described above under "chain replacement."

❷ If the chain is stretched, replace it.

❸ If replacing the chain does not help or makes matters worse, see **Worn cogs** below.

Worn cogs

If you just replaced the chain, and it is now skipping, at least one of the cogs is worn out. If this is the case, it will probably skip on the cogs you use most

frequently and not on others.

❶ Check each cog visually for wear. If its teeth are hook-shaped, like breaking waves, the cog is shot and should be replaced. Rohloff makes a tool for checking cog wear.

❷ Replace the offending cogs or the entire cassette or freewheel. See cog installation in Chapter 6.

❸ Replace the chain as well, if you have not just done so. An old chain will wear out your new cogs rapidly.

Loose rear derailleur jockey wheel(s)

A loose jockey wheel on the rear derailleur can cause the chain to skip by letting it move too far laterally.

❶ Check that the bolts holding the jockey wheel to the cage are tight and use the appropriately sized (usually 3mm) Allen wrench.

❷ Tighten the jockey-wheel bolts if necessary, holding the Allen wrench close to the bend so that you don't have enough leverage to over-tighten them.

Maladjusted rear derailleur

If the rear derailleur is poorly adjusted or bent, it can cause the chain to skip, by lining the chain up between gears.

❶ Check that the rear derailleur shifts equally well in both directions and that the chain can be pedaled backward without catching.

❷ Adjust the rear derailleur by following the procedure described under the rear derailleur section in Chapter 5.

Bent rear derailleur
or derailleur hanger

If the derailleur or derailleur hanger is bent, adjustments won't work. You will probably know when it happened, either when you shifted your derailleur into your spokes, when you crashed onto the derailleur, or when you pedaled a stick or a tumbleweed through the derailleur.

❶ Unless you have a derailleur hanger alignment tool and know how to use it (Chapter 14), take the bike to a shop and have them check and correct the dropout hanger alignment. Some bikes, especially those made out of aluminum, have a replaceable (bolt on) right rear dropout and derailleur hanger, which you can purchase and bolt-on yourself.

❷ If a straight derailleur hanger does not correct the misalignment, your rear derailleur is bent. This is generally cause for replacement of the entire derailleur. See Chapter 5.) With some derailleurs, you can just replace the jockey wheel cage, which is usually what is bent. If you know what you are doing and are careful, you can sometimes bend a bent derailleur cage back with your hands. It seldom works well, but it's worth a try if your only other alternative is to replace the entire rear derailleur. Just make sure you don't bend the derailleur hanger in the process.

the transmission

derailleurs, shifters, and cables

V

"**M**ost Americans want to be somewhere else, but when they get there, they want to go home"

— HENRY FORD

3mm, 4mm, 5mm and 6mm Allen wrenches
flat-blade and Phillips screwdrivers (small and medium)
cable cutter
indexed housing cutter (Shimano)
pliers
grease
chain lubricant
hair spray (optional)

There is nothing like having your derailleurs working smoothly, predictably and quietly under all conditions. Knowing that you can shift whenever you need to inspires confidence when riding on difficult single-track sections. It really is a lot more pleasant to ride through beautiful terrain without the grinding and clunking noises of an out-of-whack derailleur.

Improperly adjusted rear derailleurs are a pretty common problem, which is surprising because derailleur adjustments have to be one of the easiest problems to correct. A few simple adjustments to the limit screws and the cable tension and you're on your way.

Once you see how easy it is, you will probably keep yours in adjustment all of the time.

THE REAR DERAILLEUR

The rear derailleur bolts to a hanger on the rear dropout. It moves the chain from one rear cog to another, and also takes up chain slack when the bike bounces or the front derailleur is shifted. Two jockey wheels (pulley wheels) hold the chain tight and help guide the chain as the derailleur shifts. Depending on the model, a rear derailleur has one or two springs that pull the jockey wheels tightly against the chain, creating a desirable amount of chain tension.

Increasing the tension on the rear derailleur cable moves the derailleur inward toward the larger cogs. When the

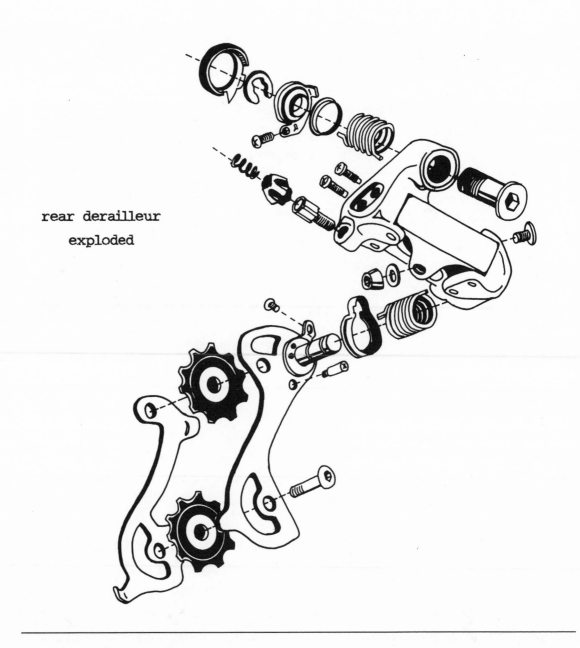

rear derailleur
exploded

cable tension is released, a spring between the derailleur's two parallelogram plates pulls the chain back toward the smallest cogs. The two limit screws on the rear derailleur prevent the derailleur from moving the chain too far to the inside (into the spokes) or to the outside (into the dropout). In addition to limit screws, most rear derailleurs have a cable-tensioning barrel adjuster located at the back of the derailleur, where the cable and cable housing enter it. This can be used to fine tune the shifting adjustment.

Rear derailleur installation

❶ Apply a small amount of grease to the derailleur's mounting bolt and then thread the bolt into the large hole on the right rear dropout.

❷ Pull the derailleur back so that the

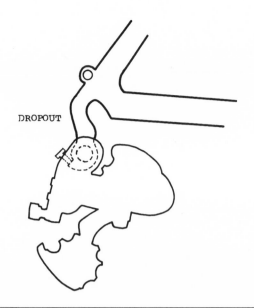

DROPOUT

limit screws

adjusting screw or tab on the derailleur
ends up behind the tab on the dropout.

❸ Tighten the mounting bolt until
the derailleur fits snugly against
the hanger.

❹ Route the chain through the jockey
wheels and connect it. (See Chapter 4,
Connecting a standard chain.)

❺ Install the cables and housings (see
Cable replacement below).

❻ Pull the cable tight with a pair of
pliers, and tighten the cable-fixing bolt.

❼ Follow the adjustment procedure
described below.

Adjustment of rear derailleur and right-hand shifter

Perform all of the following derailleur
adjustments with the bike in a bike
stand or hung from the ceiling. That
way you can turn the crank and shift
gears, while you put the derailleur
through its paces. Lubricate or replace
the chain (Chapter 4) so that the whole
drivetrain runs smoothly.

I. Limit screw adjustments

The first, and most important, rear
derailleur adjustment is the limit screws.
Properly set, these screws should make
certain that you will not ruin your frame,
wheel or derailleur by shifting into the
spokes or by jamming the chain between
the dropout and the smallest cog. It is
never pleasant to see your expensive
equipment turned into shredded metal.
All it takes is a small screwdriver to turn
these limit screws. Remember, it's *lefty
loosy, righty tighty* for these screws.

HIGH-GEAR-LIMIT SCREW ADJUSTMENT

This screw limits the outward movement
of the rear derailleur. You tighten or
loosen this screw until the derailleur
shifts the chain to the smallest cog
quickly but does not overshift.

How do you determine which limit screw
works on the high gear? Often, it will be
labeled with an "H," and it is usually the
upper of the two screws. If you're not
certain, try both screws. Whichever one

V

the transmission

high-gear-
limit screw
adjustments

moves the derailleur when the cable tension is released (and the chain is on the outside cog) is the one you're looking for. On most derailleurs, you can also see which screw to adjust by looking in between the derailleur's parallelogram side plates. You will see one tab on the back end of each plate. Each is designed to hit one of the limit screws at each end of the movement. Shift into your highest gear, and notice which screw is touching one of the tabs; that is the high-gear-limit screw.

low-gear-limit screw adjustment

❶ Shift the chain to the large front chain ring.

❷ While slowly turning the crank, shift the rear derailleur to the smallest rear cog (highest gear).

❸ If there is a bit of hesitation in the chain while you shift, loosen the cable a little to see if it is stopping the derailleur from moving out far enough. Do this by turning the barrel adjuster clockwise, or by loosening the cable-fixing bolt.

❹ If the chain still won't drop smoothly and without hesitation to the smallest cog, loosen the high-gear-limit screw 1/4 turn at a time, continuously repeating the shift, until the chain repeatedly drops quickly and easily.

❺ If the derailleur throws the chain into the dropout, or it tries to go past the smallest cog, tighten the high-gear-limit screw 1/4 turn and re-do the shift. Repeat until the derailleur shifts the chain quickly and easily into the highest gear without throwing the

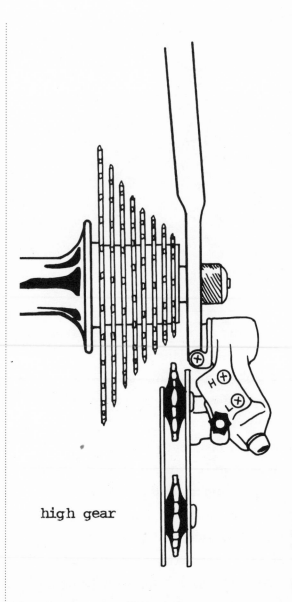

high gear

chain into the dropout.

LOW-GEAR-LIMIT SCREW ADJUSTMENT
This screw stops the inward movement of the rear derailleur, preventing it from going into the spokes. This screw is usually labeled "L," and it is usually the bottom screw. You can check which one it is by shifting to the largest cog, maintaining pressure on the shifter, and turning the screw to see if it changes the position of the derailleur.

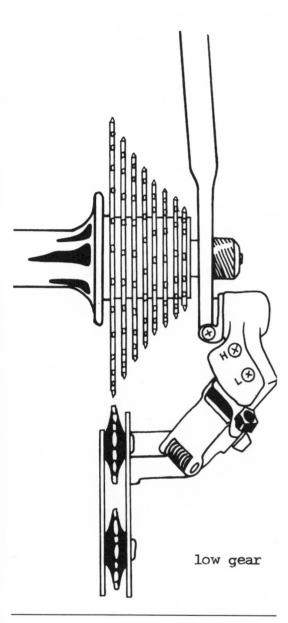

low gear

❶ Shift the chain to the inner chainring on the front. Shift the rear derailleur to the lowest gear (largest cog). Do it gently, in case the limit screw does not stop the derailleur from going into the spokes.

❷ If the derailleur touches the spokes or shifts the chain over the largest cog, tighten the low-gear-limit screw until it does not.

❸ If the derailleur cannot bring the chain onto the largest cog, loosen the screw 1/4 turn. Repeat this step until the chain

shifts easily up to the cog, but does not tap the spokes.

II. Cable-tension adjustment
INDEXED REAR SHIFTERS

With an indexed shifting system (one that "clicks" into each gear), it is the cable tension that determines whether the derailleur moves to the proper gear with each click.

❶ With the chain on the large chain-ring in the front, shift the rear derailleur to the smallest cog. Keep clicking the shifter until you are sure it will not let any more cable out.

❷ Shift back one click; this should move the chain smoothly to the second cog.

❸ If the chain does not climb to the second cog, or if it does so slowly, increase the tension in the cable by turning one of the cable barrel adjusters (either on the derailleur or on the shifter) counterclockwise. If you run out of barrel adjustment range, re-tighten both adjusters, loosen the cable-fixing bolt and pull some of the slack out of the cable. Tighten the fixing bolt and repeat the adjustment. (see page 70)

❹ If the chain overshifts the second cog or comes close to overshifting, decrease the cable tension by turning the barrel adjuster clockwise.

❺ Keep adjusting the cable tension in small increments while shifting back and forth between the two smallest cogs until the chain moves easily in both directions.

❻ Shift to the middle chainring in the front and onto one of the middle rear

cable–tension
adjustment
———
indexed rear
shifters

cogs. Shift the rear derailleur back and forth a few cogs, again checking for precise and quick movement of the chain from cog to cog. Fine tune the shifting by making small adjustments to the cable-tensioning barrel adjuster.

7 Shift to the inner ring in the front and to the largest cog in the rear. Shift up and down one click in the rear, again checking for symmetry and precision of chain movement in either direction between the two largest cogs. Fine tune the barrel adjuster until you get it just right.

8 Go back through the gears. With the chain in the middle chainring in front, the rear derailleur should shift smoothly back-and-forth between any pair of cogs. With the chain on the big chainring, the rear derailleur should shift easily on all but perhaps the largest one or two cogs in the rear. With the chain on the inner chainring, the rear derailleur should shift easily on all but perhaps the two smallest cogs.

non-indexed shifters

NON-INDEXED (FRICTION) SHIFTERS

If you do not have indexed shifting, adjustment is complete after you remove the slack in the cable. With proper cable tension, when the chain is on the smallest cog, the derailleur should move as soon as the shift lever does. If there is free play in the lever, tighten the cable by turning the cable barrel adjuster on the derailleur or shifter counterclockwise. If your rear derailleur has no barrel adjusters, loosen the cable clamp bolt, pull some slack out of the cable with pliers, and re-tighten the clamp bolt.

FINAL DETAILS OF REAR DERAILLEUR ADJUSTMENT

You can get a bit more precision by adjusting the small screw that changes the derailleur's position against the derailleur hanger tab on the right rear dropout. With the chain on a middle cog, adjust the screw so that the upper jockey wheel is very close to the cogs. You'll know that you've moved it in too closely when it starts making noise.

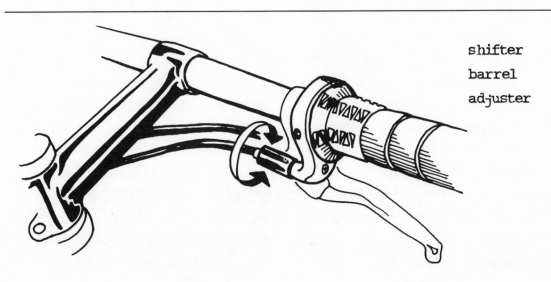

shifter barrel adjuster

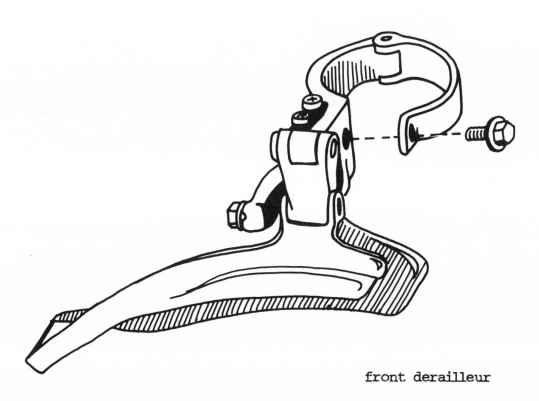

front derailleur

THE FRONT DERAILLEUR

The front derailleur moves the chain over the chainrings. The working parts consist of a steel cage, a linkage and an arm attached to the shifter cable. The front derailleur is attached to the frame, usually by a clamp surrounding the seat tube. Some Shimano models attach to the face of the bottom bracket. Shimano's top-of-the-line XTR front derailleur mounts both to the face of the bottom bracket and to a braze-on boss on the seat tube.

Front derailleur installation
Band type

❶ Clamp the front derailleur around the seat tube.

❷ Adjust the height and rotation.

❸ Tighten the clamp bolt.

Bottom-bracket-mounting type
front derailleur

 ❶ Remove the bottom bracket. (See Chapter 8.)

❷ Slip the derailleur bracket over the right-hand bottom bracket cup, and start the cup into the bottom bracket shell a few threads.

❸ With less expensive models, place the C-shaped stabilizer around the seat tube to fix the rotational adjustment. With the XTR bottom-bracket-mounted derailleur, loosely screw the mounting bolt into the special braze-on designed for it.

❹ Tighten the right-hand bottom bracket cup against the bottom bracket face.

❺ With the XTR bottom-bracket-

proper cage alignment

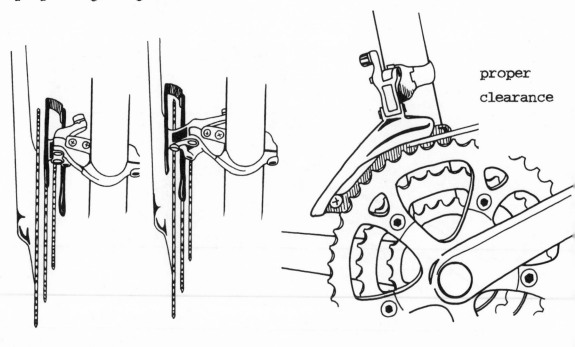

proper
clearance

mounted derailleur, tighten the mounting bolt into the braze-on.

❻ Complete the bottom bracket installation (Chapter 8).

Note: There are no height or twist adjustments on these derailleurs, and they must be used with the chainring size for which they were intended.

Front derailleur and left hand shifter adjustment
I. Position adjustments

With a seat-tube-clamp front derailleur, the position is adjusted with a 5mm Allen wrench on the band clamp bolt. Bottom-bracket face-mounted front derailleurs have no vertical or rotational (twist about the seat tube) adjustments.

❶ Position the height of the front derailleur so that the outer cage passes about 1mm to 2 mm (1/16 to 1/8 inches)

above the highest point of the outer chainring.

❷ Position the outer plate of the derailleur cage parallel to the chainrings when viewed from above. Check this by shifting to the big chainring and sighting from the top.

Note: Height and rotational adjustments of seat tube clamp-on versions of Shimano's new differential-plate XTR front derailleurs are set in the same manner as standard front derailleurs.

II. Limit-screw adjustments

The front derailleur has two limit screws that stop the derailleur from throwing the chain to the inside or outside of the chainrings. These are usually labeled "L" for low gear (small chainring) and "H" for high gear (large chainring). On most derailleurs, the low gear screw is

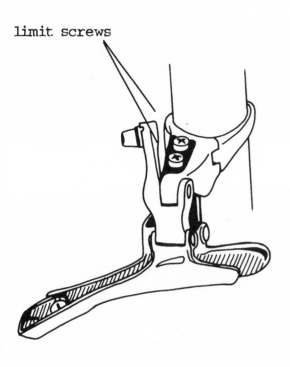

limit screws

closer to the frame; however, the new Shimano differential-plate derailleurs have the limit-screw positions reversed, but their adjustment is the same.

If in doubt, you can determine which limit screw controls which function by the same trial-and-error method outlined above for the rear derailleur. Shift the chain to the inner ring, then tighten one of the limit screws. If turning that screw moves the front derailleur outward, then it is the low-gear-limit screw. If turning that screw does not move the front derailleur, then the other screw is the low-gear-limit screw.

LOW-GEAR-LIMIT SCREW ADJUSTMENT

❶ Shift back and forth between the middle and inner chainrings.

❷ If the chain drops off of the little ring to the inside, tighten the low-gear-limit screw (clockwise) 1/4 turn, and try

shifting again.

❸ If the chain does not drop easily onto the inner chainring when shifted, loosen the low-gear-limit screw 1/4 turn and repeat the shift.

HIGH-GEAR-LIMIT SCREW ADJUSTMENT

❶ Shift the chain back and forth between the middle and outer chainring.

❷ If the chain jumps over the big chainring, tighten the high-gear-limit screw 1/4 turn and repeat the shift.

❸ If the chain is sluggish going up to the big chainring, loosen the high-gear-limit screw 1/4 turn and try the shift again.

II. Cable-tension adjustment

❶ With the chain on the inner chainring, remove any excess cable slack by turning the barrel adjuster on the shifter counterclockwise (or loosen the cable-fixing bolt, pull the cable tight with pliers, and tighten the bolt).

❷ Check that the cable is loose enough to allow the chain to shift smoothly and repeatedly from the middle to the inner chainring.

❸ Check that the cable is tight enough so that the derailleur starts to move as soon as you move the shifter.

Note: This tension adjustment should work for indexed as well as friction shifters. With indexed front shifting, you may want to fine-tune the barrel adjuster to avoid noise from the chain dragging on the derailleur in some cross gears, or to get more precise shifting.

Another note: Certain front derailleurs

V

the transmission

front
derailleur
cable tension
adjustment

have a cam screw at the end of the spring to vary main tension. For quicker shifting to the smaller rings, increase the spring tension by turning the screw clockwise.

THE SHIFT CABLES AND HOUSINGS

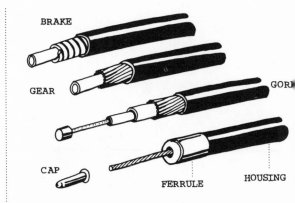

In order for your derailleurs to function properly, you need to have clean, smooth-running cables. Because of all the muck and guck that you encounter on a mountain bike, you also need to regularly replace those cables. Replace any cables that have broken strands, kinks, or fraying between the shifter and the derailleur. You should also replace housings (also called outer cables) if they are bent, mashed, just plain gritty or the color clashes with your bike (this is really important).

CABLE INSTALLATION/REPLACEMENT
Procedure for buying cables

❶ Buy new cables and housing with at least as much length as the ones you are replacing.

❷ Make sure that the cables and housing are for indexed systems. These cables will stretch minimally, and the housings will not compress in length. Under its external plastic sheath, indexed housing is *not* made of steel coil like brake housings; it is made of parallel (coaxial) steel strands of thin wire. If you look at the end, you will see numerous wire ends sticking out surrounding a central Teflon tube (make sure it has this

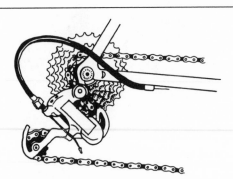

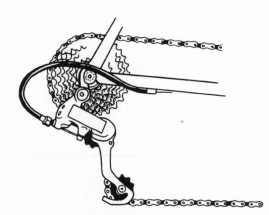

housing length

Teflon liner, too).

❸ Buy two cable crimp ends to prevent fraying, and a tubular cable housing end (ferrule) for each end of every housing section. These ferrules will prevent kinking at the cable entry points, cable stops, shifters and derailleurs.

❹ It is really not a bad idea to buy a bunch of cables, cable ends and ferrules when you first set up your work area.

They're cheap, and you should be changing cables regularly, without having to have to make a special trip to the bike shop every time you need a little cable-end cap.

Cutting the housing to length

❶ Use a special cutter like Shimano's cable/housing cutter (see Chapter 1 tools). Standard wire cutters will not cut index-shift housing.

❷ Cut the housing to the same lengths as your old ones. If you have no old housings to compare with, cut them so that the housing curves smoothly from cable stop to cable stop, and turning the handlebars does not pull or kink them. Allow for enough length at the rear derailleur so that the derailleur can swing forward and backward freely.

❸ With a nail or toothpick, open each Teflon sleeve-end that has been smashed shut by the cutter.

❹ Place a ferrule over each housing end.

Replacing cable in thumb shifters, Rapidfire Plus or Rapidfire levers:

❶ Shift both levers to the gear setting that lets the most cable out. This will be the highest gear position for the rear shift lever (small cog), and the lowest for the front (small ring).

thumb shifter

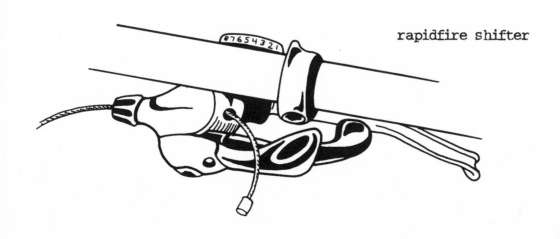

rapidfire shifter

the transmission

cutting cable
housing to
length

75

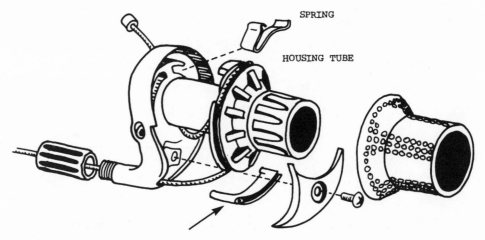

SPRING

HOUSING TUBE

CABLE GOES THROUGH THIS PIECE

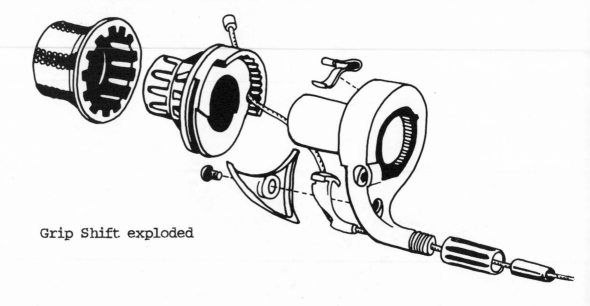

Grip Shift exploded

❷ Pull out the old cable and recycle it.

❸ The recessed hole in the lever body into which the cable head seats should be visible right up against the barrel adjuster. Thread the cable through the hole and out through the barrel adjuster.

❹ Guide the cable through each housing segment and cable stop. Slotted cable stops allow you to slip the cable and housing in and out from the side.

Replacing cable in Grip Shift

The Grip Shift lever must be disassembled to replace the cable.

❶ Disconnect the derailleur cable.

❷ Roll or slide the handlebar grip away from the Grip Shift to allow room for the shifter to slide apart.

❸ With a Phillips screwdriver, remove the triangular plastic cover holding the two main sections together.

❹ Pull the outer shifter section away

from the main body to separate it from the inner housing. Watch for the spring to ensure that it does not fall out. It can be nudged back into place if it does.

❺ Pull the old cable out and recycle it.

❻ Clean and dry the two parts if they are dirty; a rag and a cotton swab are usually sufficient. Finish Line offers a cleaning and grease kit specifically designed for Grip Shift shifters. A really gummed-up shifter may require solvent and compressed air to clean and dry it.

❼ Using a non-lithium grease, lubricate the inner housing tube and spring cavity, all cable grooves, and the indexing notches in the twister. Grip Shift recommends a silicone-based Teflon grease.

❽ Thread the cable through the hole, seating the cable end in its little pocket.

❾ Loop the cable once around the housing tube, and exit it through the barrel adjuster.

❿ Make sure the spring is in its cavity in the housing; hold the spring in with a small amount of grease if need be.

⓫ Slide the outer (twister) body over the inner tube. Be sure that the shifter is in the position that lets the most cable out (on models with numbers, line up the highest number with the indicator mark on rear shifters, lowest number on front shifters).

⓬ Lift the cable loop into the groove in the twister, and push straight inward on it as you pull tension on the cable exiting the shifter. The twister should slide in until flush under the housing edge; you

may have to jiggle it back and forth slightly while pushing in to get it properly seated.

⓭ Replace the cover and screw.

⓮ Check that the shifter clicks properly.

Attach cable to rear derailleur

❶ Put the chain on the smallest cog so the rear derailleur moves to the outside.

❷ Run the cable through the barrel adjuster, and route it through each of the housing segments until you reach the cable clamping point at the derailleur bolt. Make sure that the rear shifter is on the highest setting; this ensures that the maximum amount of cable is available to the derailleur.

❸ Pull the cable taut with a pair of pliers, and pull the cable into its groove under the cable-fixing bolt.

❹ Tighten the bolt. On most derailleurs this takes a 5mm Allen wrench.

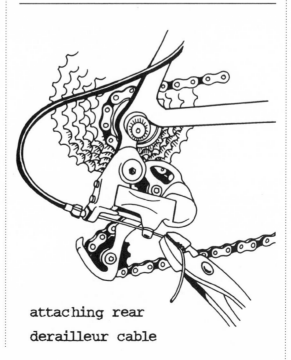

attaching rear
derailleur cable

attaching
cable to rear
derailleur

Attach cable to front derailleur

1 Shift the chain to the inner ring so that the derailleur moves farthest to the inside. This ensures that the maximum amount of cable is available to the derailleur.

2 Connect the cable to the cable anchor on the derailleur while pulling it taut with pliers, using the groove into which the cable is supposed to fit. Make sure you do not hook up a top-pull front derailleur from the bottom, or vice versa. Also note that some older derailleur models require housing to run the full length of cable.

Final touches

A high quality cable assembly includes

attaching front derailleur cables

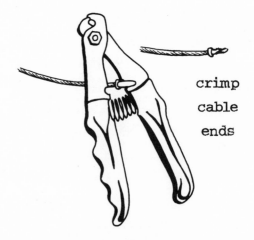

crimp cable ends

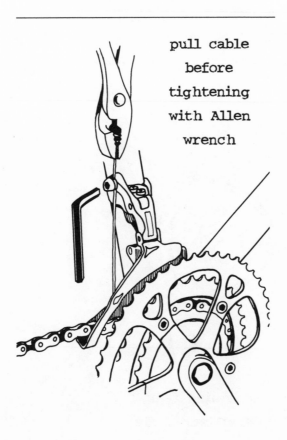

pull cable before tightening with Allen wrench

the cable housing end ferrules throughout, and crimping cable ends, which are clipped about 1-2cm past the cable clamp-bolts. Also, little rubber cable donuts or pieces of thin cable sheathing can be purchased at your local shop and installed to keep the bare cables from scratching the frame's finish.

Gore-Tex cables

If you are using Gore-Tex or some other type of plastic-coated low-friction cable, follow the instructions on the package, since these require very special treatment in order to work properly.

Cable lubrication

New cables and housings with Teflon liners do not need to be lubricated. Old cables can be lubricated with chain lubricant. Grease sometimes slows their movement, but some manufacturers recommend (and supply) their own molybdenum disulfide grease for cables.

1 Pull the housing segments out of their slotted cable stops; there is no reason to disconnect the cable.

2 Coat with lubricant the areas of the cable that will be inside of the cable

reducing
cable
friction

housing segments.

Note: If you do not have slotted cable stops, you might as well replace the cables and housings, since an old cable will have a frayed end and will be hard to put back through the housing after lubrication. Another reason to keep cables, housing ferrules and cable ends in stock.

Easy steps to reduce cable friction

Besides replacing your cables and housings with good quality cables and lined housings, there are other specific steps you can take to improve shifting efficiency.

❶ The most important friction-reducing step is to route the cable so that it makes smooth bends, and that turning the handlebars does not increase the tension on the shift cables.

❷ Choose cables that offer particularly low friction. The best choice is die-drawn cables. These are simply standard cables that have been pulled by a machine through a small hole in a piece of hard steel called a die. This flattens all of the outer strands and smoothes the cable surface. Thinner cables and lined housings with a large inside diameter also reduce friction. Gore-Tex and other companies offer cables coated with Teflon or a similar substance.

❸ Cable friction when moving to smaller cogs can be reduced by increasing the size of the derailleur-return spring. You can buy an after-market stiffer spring designed specifically for your derailleur

liddle rubba donuts

bassworm

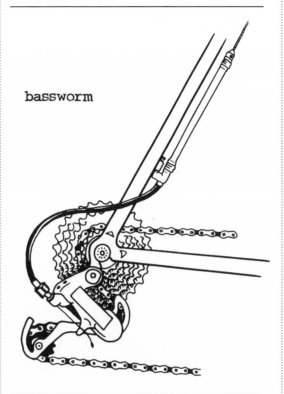

or try Grip Shift's "Bassworm." The Bassworm is simply a piece of surgical tubing that acts as a cable return spring and keeps the cable clean where it enters the housing. It is hooked into the final cable stop and slipped over the cable just in front of the last segment of cable housing, pulled tight, and the set screw on its end is tightened down onto the cable.

❹ Hydraulic shift tubes are available from Safe Systems that eliminate cable-friction problems; however, they are expensive.

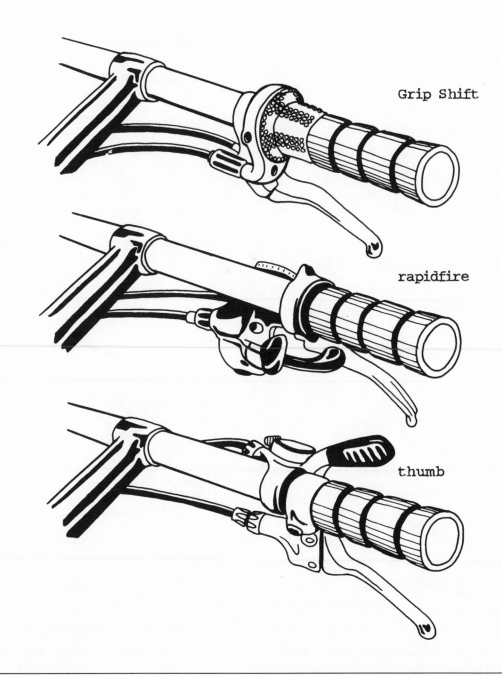

Grip Shift

rapidfire

**shifter
replacement**

thumb

THE SHIFTERS

Twist shifters, thumb shifters and Rapidfire levers all move the derailleurs, but they go about it in very different ways.

Shifter replacement/installation

Replacing shifters requires removing at least grips and bar ends, and often brake levers as well. Shifters are generally labeled right and left, but if you're in doubt, you can tell which is which because the right one has a lot more clicks. Obviously, this is not as big an issue with friction shifters.

❶ Remove bar ends, usually with a 5mm Allen wrench.

❷ Remove grips by peeling them back

thumb
shifter
exploded

at either end, squirting water underneath, and twisting back and forth while sliding them off. If you are planning on replacing them, you can cut the grips off.

❸ Squirt hair spray inside (water is okay, too) when replacing grips. Hair spray acts like a lubricant when its wet, but dries like a glue.

Replacing shifters
with integral brake levers

These shifters are integral with the brake levers. If you are replacing the entire brake lever/shift lever unit:

❶ Remove the old brake lever and shifter.

❷ Slide the new brake lever/shifter onto the bar, making sure that you put the right shifter on the right side and vice versa.

❸ Slide the grip back into position.

❹ Mount the bar end, if you have one.

❺ Rotate the brake lever to the position you like.

❻ Tighten the brake lever fixing bolt.

Replacing the shifter unit
on the same brake lever

❶ After shifting to release the maximum amount of cable, unbolt the old shift lever from the brake lever body.

❷ Position the new shifter exactly like the old one was.

❸ Replace the bolt and tighten it.

❹ Reinstall/replace cable and tighten it.

Replacing Grip Shift

❶ Remove the old shifter, replace the brake lever if you had to remove it to get the old shifter off.

❷ Loosen and slide the brake lever inward to allow room for the Grip Shift.

❸ Slide the appropriate (right or left) Grip Shift on with the cable-exit barrel pointing inward.

❹ Slide on the plastic washer over the bar that separates the grip from the Grip Shift.

❺ Replace the grip (and bar end).

❻ Butt the Grip Shift up against the grip with the plastic washer separating them. Rotate the shifter until the cable-exit barrel is oriented so it will not interfere with the brake lever.

❼ Tighten the Grip Shift to the handlebars with a 3mm Allen wrench.

❽ Butt the brake lever up against the Grip Shift, and rotate the brake lever to the position you like, and tighten it down.

❾ Reinstall/replace cable and tighten it.

Top-mounted thumb shifters

❶ Remove the bar end, grip, brake

replacing
shifter units

lever and old shifter.

❷ Slide on the shifter.

❸ Slide on the brake lever, grip and bar end.

❹ Tighten the bar end and brake lever in the position you want.

❺ Tighten the shifter in the position that is comfortable for you that allows easy access to the cable-barrel adjuster and free cable travel.

❻ Reinstall/replace cable and tighten it.

SHIFTER MAINTENANCE
Grip Shift

Grip Shift requires periodic lubrication. The exploded diagram used in combination with the instructions under **Replacing cable in Grip Shift** details how to take a shifter apart, clean it and grease it. Use only non-lithium grease. As long as you have the shifter disassembled, you might as well replace the cable, since shifter disassembly is required for the task (follow cable replacement steps above).

Rapidfire SL and Rapidfire Plus

Shimano Rapidfire SL and Rapidfire Plus shifters are not designed to be disassembled by the consumer. Squirting a little chain lube in it every now and then is a good idea, though. If a Rapidfire Plus lever stops working, it requires purchasing a new shifter unit. The brake lever does not need to be replaced; just bolt the new shifter to it. Sometimes the gear indicator unit stops working, and it can even jam the lever

and stop it from reaching all of the gears. This was most common in the 1993 and 1994 models. The indicators can be removed from the shifter with a small screwdriver. The indicator's little link arm needs to be stuck back into the hole from whence it came. Once the indicator jams, you can expect it to happen again; eventually, you will want to replace the lever or dispense with the indicator. The 1995 Plus and 1996 SL models have smaller, simpler gear indicators that are less prone to breakage. I know of none that have broken, but they are removable and replaceable.

Original Rapidfire

Shimano's first attempt at a two-lever mountain shifter did not work very well and if you are having trouble with yours, I recommend throwing it out and getting a new system. You know you have original Rapidfire if the thumb operates both the down- and up-shift levers. Newer Rapidfire SL and Plus levers require the thumb only for downshifting; the forefinger reaches back to perform the upshifts.

Thumb shifters

Indexed (click) thumb shifters are not to be disassembled. Periodic (semi-annual or so) lubrication with chain lube is recommended and is best accomplished from the back side once the shifter assembly is removed from its clamp. Frictional (non-clicking) thumb shifters can be disassembled, cleaned, greased,

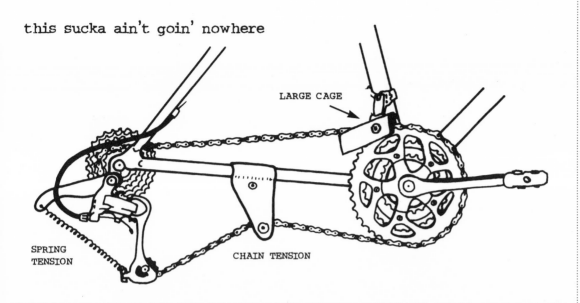

this sucka ain't goin' nowhere

LARGE CAGE

SPRING TENSION

CHAIN TENSION

and reassembled. Put the parts back the way you found them. You can avoid the hassle of disassembly by squirting chain lube in instead.

Special downhill-specific drivetrain adaptations

Internal-gear rear hubs, tension arms, rollers and giant front derailleur cages have become a part of downhill racing, due to the extraordinary demands it places on a chain drive system. These after market products are outside of the scope of this book, but things like the chain tensioners and front derailleur cage extensions are fairly obvious in their function and quite easy to service. Internal planetary-gear hubs are very complex and should not be dismantled unless you really know what you are doing.

Continuously Variable Transmissions (CVTs:)

Continuously Variable Transmissions

regularly appear and disappear from the bike market. They are usually chain or belt driven and are intended to provide the rider with every possible gear combination within the system's range. So far, none of them has made a big splash, so I haven't included any in this book.

Jockey wheel maintenance

The jockey wheels on a derailleur will wear out over time. For best performance, standard jockey wheels should be overhauled every 200-500 miles. That should take care of the guck that the chain and the trail regularly deliver to them. The mounting bolts on jockey wheels also need to be checked regularly. If a loose jockey-wheel bolt falls off while you are riding, you'll need to follow the procedure for a broken rear derailleur on the trail in Chapter 3. Standard jockey wheels have a center bushing sleeve made of either steel or ceramic. Some expensive models have cartridge bearings. A washer with a curved rim facing inward is usually installed on both sides of a standard jockey wheel. Some jockey wheels also have rubber seals around the edges of these washers.

Procedure for overhauling standard jockey wheels

❶ Remove the jockey wheels by undoing the bolts that hold them to the derailleur. This usually takes a 3mm Allen wrench.

❷ Wipe all parts clean with a rag. Solvent is usually not necessary but can be used.

❸ If the teeth on the jockey wheels are broken or worn off, replace the wheels.

❹ Smear grease over each bolt and sleeve and inside each jockey wheel.

❺ Reassemble the jockey wheels on the derailleur. Be sure to orient the cage plate properly (the larger part of the cage plate should be at the bottom jockey wheel).

Cartridge bearing jockey wheel overhaul

If the cartridge bearings in high-end jockey wheels do not turn freely, they can usually be overhauled.

❶ With a single-edge razor blade, pry the plastic cover off one or, preferably, both sides of the bearing.

❷ With a toothbrush and solvent, clean the bearings. Use citrus-based solvent, and wear gloves and glasses to protect skin and eyes.

❸ Blow the solvent out with compressed air or your tire pump and allow the

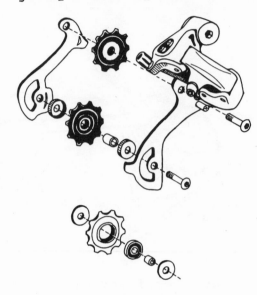

jockey wheel exploded

parts to dry.

❹ Squeeze new grease into the bearings and replace the covers.

Rear derailleur overhaul

Except for the jockey wheels and pivots, most rear derailleurs are *not* designed to be disassembled. If the pivot springs seem to be operating effectively, all you need to do is overhaul the jockey wheels (see above), and clean and lubricate the parallelogram and spring as follows.

Minor wipe and lube

❶ Clean the derailleur as well as you can with a rag, including between the parallelogram plates.

❷ Drip chain lube on both ends of every pivot pin, and put a dab of grease where the spring end slides along the underside of the outer parallelogram plate.

jockey wheel overhaul

84

Upper pivot overhaul

❶ Remove the rear derailleur. It usually takes a 5mm Allen wrench to unscrew it from the frame and to disconnect the cable.

❷ With a screwdriver, pry the circlip off of the threaded end of the mounting bolt. Don't lose it; it will tend to fly when it comes off.

❸ Pull the bolt and spring out of the derailleur.

❹ Clean and dry the parts with or without the use of solvent.

❺ Grease liberally, and replace the parts.

❻ Each end of the spring has a hole that it needs to go into. If there are several holes, and you don't know which one it was in before, try the middle one. (If the derailleur does not keep tension on the chain well enough, you can later try another hole that increases the spring tension.)

❼ Push it all together, and replace the circlip with pliers.

Lower pivot overhaul

❶ Locate and unscrew the small screw with the tall head. It is located near the upper jockey wheel on the derailleur cage. It is designed to maintain tension on the lower pivot spring and is what prevents the cage from springing all of the way around. So once the screw is removed, slowly guide the cage around until the spring tension is relieved.

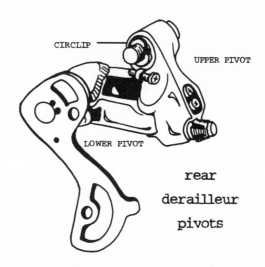

CIRCLIP

UPPER PIVOT

LOWER PIVOT

rear derailleur pivots

❷ Unscrew the lower pivot bolt using a 4mm, 5mm, or 6mm Allen wrench. Be sure to hold the jockey wheel cage to keep it from twisting.

❸ Determine in which hole the spring end has been placed, then remove the spring.

❹ Clean and dry the bolt and the spring with a rag. Solvent may be used if necessary.

❺ Grease all parts liberally.

❻ Replace the spring ends in their holes in either piece. Use the middle hole if you have a choice and aren't certain which it came out of.

❼ Screw the bolt back into the jockey-wheel cage plate.

❽ Twist the jockey wheel-cage plate counterclockwise to tension the spring, and replace the cage stop screw.

Parallelogram overhaul

Very few derailleurs can be completely disassembled, but some can. These have removable pins holding them together.

the transmission

rear derailleur overhaul

The pins will have circlips on the ends which can be popped off with a screwdriver to remove the pins. If you have such a type, disassemble it in a box so the circlips do not fly away. With this type of derailleur, disassemble it carefully. Make note of where each part belongs so that you can get it back together again. Clean all parts, grease them, and reassemble.

**Replacing stock bolts
with lightweight versions**
Lightweight aluminum and titanium derailleur bolts are available as replacement items for many derailleurs. Removing and replacing jockey wheel bolts is simple, as long as you keep all of the jockey wheel parts together and put the inner cage plate back on the way it was. Upper and lower pivot bolts are replaced following the instructions outlined earlier in this chapter.

TROUBLE-SHOOTING

TROUBLESHOOTING REAR DERAILLEUR AND RIGHT-HAND SHIFTER PROBLEMS

Once you have made the adjustments outlined above, your drivetrain should be quiet and have all the gears lined up; the drivetrain should stay in gear, even if you turn the crank backwards. If you cannot fine tune the adjustment so that each click with the right shifter results in a clean, quick shift, you need to check some of the following possibilities.

❶ Check to see if your shifter is compatible with your derailleur. This is especially important if either of them were not original equipment on your bike. Be certain that if the shifter is a different brand than your derailleur, that they are nonetheless designed to work together. The most common example of this is SRAM's Grip Shift, which is specifically designed to work with a Shimano rear derailleur. Of course, SRAM now manufactures it's own SRAM derailleur, which works only with a Grip Shift shifter designed for that model. If your shifter and derailleur are incompatible, you will need to change one of them. Quality being equal, I suggest replacing the less costly item.

❷ Check your derailleur cables to be sure that they run smoothly through the housing. Sticky cable movement will cause sluggish shifting. Lubricate the cable by smearing it with chain lube or a specific lubricant that came with your shifters. If you have slotted cable stops, you need not disconnect the cable to do this; pull each section of housing back out of the cable stop and pull the cable up out of the slot. Lubricate the parts of cable that are inside of the housing sections. If you do not have slotted cable stops, you will need to disconnect the cable. If so, you might as well replace the cables and housings while you are at it.

❸ If lubricating the cable does not help; replace the cable and housing (see **Cable Replacement** earlier in this chapter).

TROUBLESHOOTING FRONT DERAILLEUR AND LEFT-HAND SHIFTER PROBLEMS

If your chain falls off to the inside no matter how much you adjust the low-gear-limit screw, cable tension, and derailleur position:

❶ Check the chain line (the alignment of the front chainrings with the rear cogs.) by placing a long straight edge against the middle chainring and back to the rear cogs. It should come out in the center of the rear cogs.

❷ If the chain line is off, you can adjust it by moving the drive side crankarm inward. This procedure is described in Chapter 8. Some types are moved by moving the bottom bracket inward, others require a new bottom bracket or bottom-bracket spindle. The chain line can also be off if the frame is out of alignment (Chapter 14). If that's the case, it is probably something you cannot fix yourself.

❸ If improving the chain line does not fix your problem, or if you don't want to mess with the chain line, buy a Third Eye Chain Watcher. This is an inexpensive plastic gizmo that clamps around the seat tube next to the inner chainring. Clamp it on and adjust the position so that it nudges the chain back on when it tries to fall off to the inside.

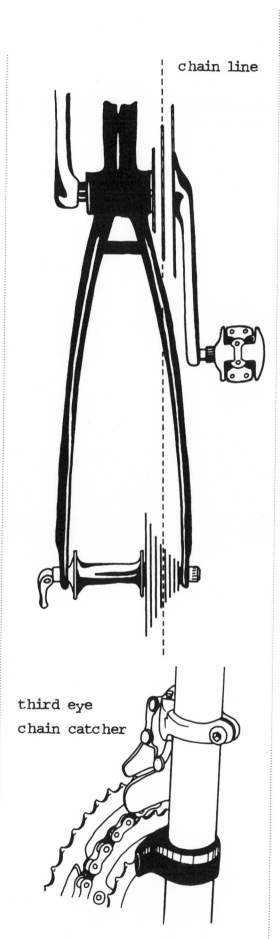

chain line

third eye
chain catcher

the transmission

V

TROUBLE-
SHOOTING

the wheels

tires, rims, hubs and cogs

> "**I**'m just sitting here watching the wheels go round
> and round. I really love to watch them roll."
>
> — JOHN LENNON

tools

spoke wrench
13mm, 14mm,
  15mm, 16mm
  cone wrenches
17mm open-end
  wrench (or an
  adjustable
  wrench)
screwdriver
5mm, 6mm and
  10mm Allen
wrenches
grease
oil
chain whip
cassette lockring
  remover
large adjustable
  wrench
freewheel remover,
  if your bike
  does not have
  a cassette
pump
tire levers
tube patch kit

OPTIONAL
truing stand
wheel-dishing tool
linseed oil
tweezers
cog-wear indicator

arly bicycles may have existed without pedals and steering systems, but they always had wheels. By definition, it is not a bicycle without two wheels.

With the exception of recent molded composites, wheels on mountain bikes are strung together with spokes. The hub is at the center, and its bearings allow the wheel to turn freely around an axle. The rim is supported and aligned by the tension on the spokes. On most bikes, the rim serves as both support for the tire and as a braking surface. On the rear wheel, a cassette freehub or freewheel allows the wheel to spin while coasting and engages when force is applied to the pedals.

The tires provide grip and traction for propulsion and steering. The air pressure in the tire is your first line of suspension and is *the* primary suspension system on most mountain bikes. On virtually all mountain bikes, inner tubes keep the air inside the tires.

This chapter addresses how to: fix a flat or replace a tire or tube, true a wheel, fix a broken spoke or bent rim, overhaul

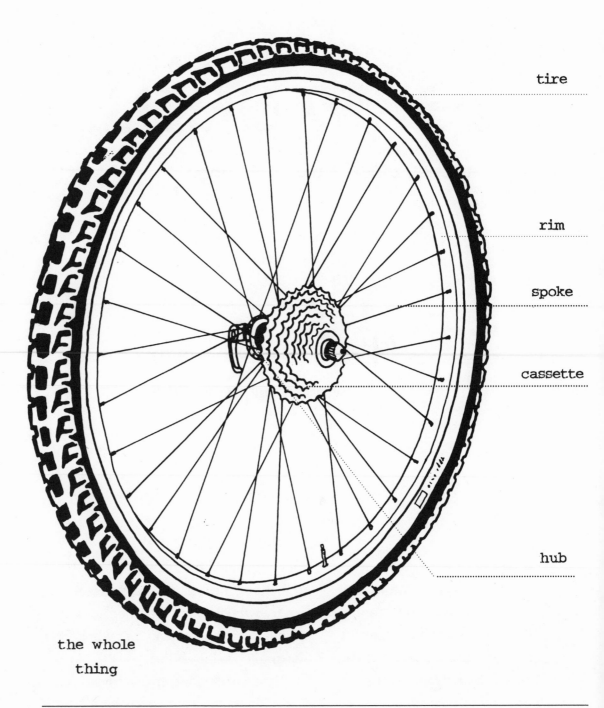

tire

rim

spoke

cassette

hub

tires

the whole
thing

---

hubs, change rear cogs, and lubricate cassettes and freewheels. Have at it.

TIRES

REPLACING OR REPAIRING TIRES
AND INNER TUBES
Removing the tire

❶ Remove the wheel. (See Chapter 2.)

❷ If your tire is not already flat, deflate it. To deflate a Schrader valve (the kind of valve you would find on your car's tire), push down on the valve pin with something thin enough to fit in that won't break off, like a pen cap or a paper clip. Presta, or "French," valves are thinner and have a small threaded

VI

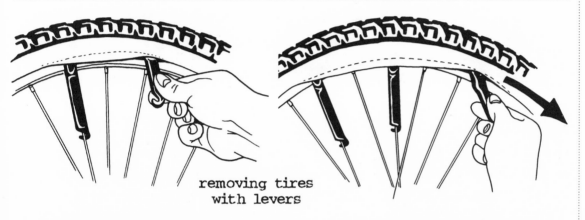

letting air out

PRESTA   SCHRADER

removing tires
with levels

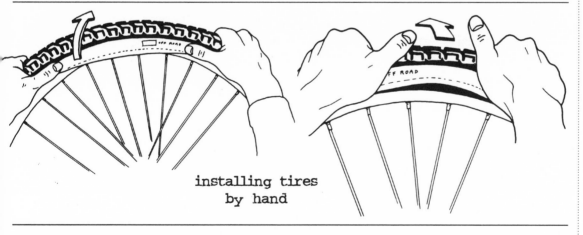

installing tires
by hand

tires 'n tubes

tire
removal

rod with a tiny nut on the end. To let air out, unscrew the little nut a few turns, and push down on the thin rod.

❸ If you can push the tire bead off of the rim with your thumbs without using tire levers, by all means do it, since there is less chance of damaging either the tube or the tire.

If you can't get it off with your hands alone, insert a tire lever, scoop side up, between the rim sidewall and the tire until you catch the edge of the tire bead.

❺ Pry down on the lever until the tire bead is pulled out over the rim. If the lever has a hook on the other end, hook it onto the nearest spoke. Otherwise,

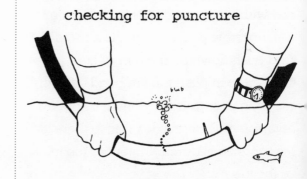

removing inner tube

keep holding it down.

❻ Place the next lever a few inches away, and do the same thing with it.

❼ If needed, place a third lever a few inches farther on, pry it out, and continue sliding this lever around the tire, pulling the bead out as you go. Some people use their fingers under the bead to slide the tire off, but beware of cutting your fingers on sharp tire beads.

❽ Once the bead is off on one side, pull the tube out.

If you are patching or replacing the tube, you do not need to remove the other side of the tire from the rim. If you are replacing the tire, the other bead should come off easily with your fingers. If it does not, use the tire levers as outlined above.

Patching an inner tube

❶ If the leak location is not obvious, put some air in the tube to inflate it until it is two to three times larger than its deflated size. Be careful. You can explode it if you put too much air in.

❷ Listen/feel for air coming out, and mark the leak(s).

❸ If you cannot find the leak by listening, submerge the tube under water. Look for air bubbling out, and mark the spot(s).

Keep in mind that you can only patch small holes. If the hole is bigger than the eraser end of a pencil, a round patch is not likely to work. A slit of up to an inch or so can be repaired with a long oval patch.

Standard patches

❶ Dry the tube thoroughly near the hole.

❷ Rough up and clean the surface about a 1-inch radius around the hole with a small piece of sandpaper (usually supplied with the patch kit). Don't use one of those little metal "cheese graters" that come with some patch kits. They tend to do to your tire what they do to cheese. Do not touch the roughed-up area.

❸ Use a patch kit designed for bicycle tires that have the thin, usually orange, gummy edges surrounding the black patches. Rema

---

checking for puncture

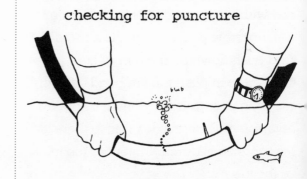

tubes

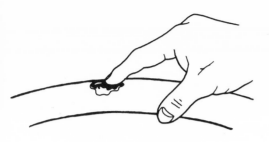

smearing patch glue

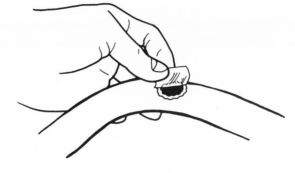

removing cellophane

and Madison are common brands.

4 Apply patch cement in a thin, smooth layer all over an area centered on the hole. Cover an area that is bigger than the size of the patch.

5 Let the glue dry until there are no more shiny, wet spots.

6 Remove the foil backing from the patch (but not the cellophane top cover).

7 Stick the patch over the hole, and push it down in place, making sure that all of the gummy edges are stuck down.

8 Remove the cellophane top covering, being careful not to peel off the edges of the patch. Often, the celophane top patch is scored. If you fold the patch, this celophane will split in the center, allowing you to peel outward and avoid pulling the newly-adhered patch off the tube.

Glueless patches

There are a number of adhesive-backed patches on the market that do not require cement to stick them on. Most often, you simply need to clean the area around the hole with the little alcohol pad supplied with the patch. Let the alcohol dry, peel the backing, and stick on the patch. The advantage of glueless patches is that they are very fast to use, take little room in a seat bag, and you never open your patch kit to discover that your glue tube is dried up. On the downside, I have not found any that stick nearly as well as the standard type. With a standard patch installed, you can inflate the tube without having it in the tire to look for more leaks. If you do that with a glueless patch, it usually lifts the patch enough to start it leaking. Install it in the tire and on the rim before putting air in it after patching.

Installing patched or new tube

Feel around the inside of the tire to see if there is still anything sticking through that can puncture the tube. This is best done by sliding a rag all the way around the inside of the tire. The rag will catch on anything sharp, and saves your fingers from being cut by whatever is stuck in the tire.

patching
inner tubes

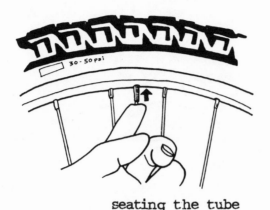

seating the tube

❶ Replace any tire that has worn-out areas (inside or out) where the tread-casing fibers appear to be cut or frayed.

❷ Examine the rim to be certain that the rim tape is in place and that there are no spokes or anything else sticking up that can puncture the tube. Replace the rim tape if necessary.

❸ Put one side of the tire on the rim.

❹ (Optional) Smear baby powder around the inside of the tire and on the outside of the tube, so the two do not adhere to each other.

❺ Put just enough air in the tube to give it shape.

❻ Push the valve through the valve hole.

❼ Push the tube up inside the tire.

❽ Starting at the side opposite the valve stem, push the tire bead onto the rim with your thumbs. Be sure that the tube doesn't get pinched between the tire bead and the rim.

❾ Work around the rim in both directions with your thumbs, pushing the tire onto the rim. Finish from both sides at the valve. You can usually install a mountain bike tire without tools. If you

cannot, use tire levers, but make sure you don't catch any of the tube under the edge of the bead, and finish the same way, at the valve.

❿ Re-seat the valve stem by pushing up on the valve after you have the last bit of bead over the rim edge. You may have to manipulate the tire so that all the tube is tucked under the tire bead.

⓫ Go around the rim and inspect for any part of the tube that might be protruding out from under the edge of the tire bead. If you have a fold of the tube under the edge of the bead, it can blow the tire off the rim either when you inflate it or while you are riding. Both sound like a gun went off next to you, and leave you with a hopelessly unpatchable tube.

⓬ Pump the tire up. Generally, 45-50 psi is a good amount. Much more, and the ride gets harsh. Much less, and you run the risk of a pinch flat or "snake bite."

Patching tire casing (side wall)

Unless it is an emergency, don't do it! If your casing is cut, get a new tire. Patching the tire casing is dangerous. No matter what you use as a patch, the tube will find a way to bulge out of the patched hole, and when it does your tire will go flat immediately. Imagine coming down a steep decent and suddenly your front tire goes complete flat — you get the picture. In emergency situations, you can put layers of non-stretchable material, such as: a dollar bill, an empty energy bar wrapper (or two), even a short section of the exploded tube (double thickness is better) between the tube and tire. (See Chapter 3.)

RIMS & SPOKES

Truing wheel

For more information on truing wheels, see Chapter 12 on wheel building.

If your wheel has a wobble in it, you can fix it by adjusting the tension on the spokes. An extreme bend in the rim cannot be fixed by spoke truing alone, since the spoke tension on the two sides of the wheel will be so uneven that the wheel will rapidly fall apart.

❶ Check that there are no broken

spokes in the wheel, or any spokes that are so loose that they flop around. If there is a broken spoke, follow the replacement procedure **Replacing a broken spoke** later in this chapter. If there is a single loose spoke, check to see that the rim is not dented or cracked in that area. I recommend replacing the rim if it is. If the rim looks okay, mark the loose spoke with a piece of tape, and tighten it up with the spoke wrench until it feels the same tension as adjacent spokes on the same side of the wheel (pluck the spoke and listen to the tone). Then follow the truing procedure below.

❷ Grab the rim while the wheel is on the bike, and flex it side to side to check

tightening and loosening spokes

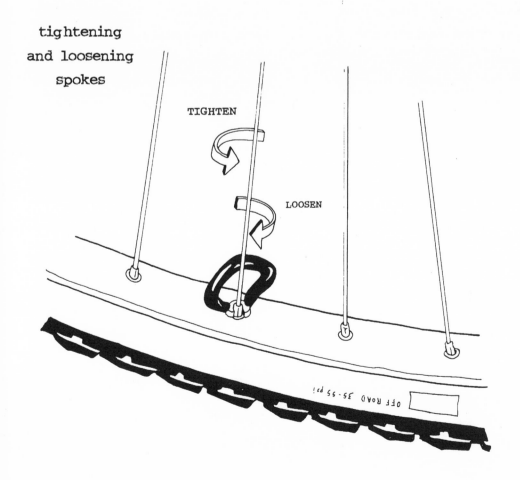

TIGHTEN

LOOSEN

Off Road 35-55 psi

the hub bearing adjustment. If the bearings are loose, the wheel will clunk side to side. The hub will need to be tightened before you true the wheel, since the wheel will behave erratically if you do not. Follow the hub adjustment procedure, Step 31 under **Overhauling hubs** on the following page.

❸ Put the wheel in a truing stand, if you have one. Otherwise, leave it on the bike. Suspend the bike in a bike stand or from the ceiling, or turn it upside down on the handlebars and saddle.

❹ Adjust the truing stand feeler, or hold one of your brake pads so that it scrapes the rim at the biggest wobble.

❺ Where the rim scrapes, tighten the spoke (or spokes) that come(s) to the rim from the side opposite of the bulge. Loosen the spoke(s) that come(s) from the wobble side of the hub. This will pull the rim away from the feeler or brake pad.

When correcting a wheel that is laterally out of true (wobbles side-to-side), always tighten spokes in pairs: one spoke coming from one side of the wheel, the other pair from the opposite side. Tightening spokes is like opening a jar upside down. With the jar right-side up, turning the lid to the left opens the jar, but this reverses when you turn the jar upside down (try it and see). Spoke nipples are just like the lid on that upside-down jar. In other words, counter-clockwise tightens, and clockwise loosens. It may take you a few attempts before you catch on, but you will eventually get it. If you temporarily make

the wheel worse, simply undo what you have done and start over.

It is best to tighten and loosen by small amounts (about ¼ turn at a time), decreasing the amount you turn the spoke nipples as you move away from the spot where the rim scrapes the hardest. If the wobble gets worse, then you are turning the spokes the wrong direction.

❻ As the rim moves more toward center, readjust the truing-stand feeler or the brake pad so that it again finds the most out-of-true spot on the wheel.

❼ Check the wobble first on one side of the wheel and then the other, adjusting spokes accordingly, so that you don't end up pulling the whole wheel off center by chasing wobbles only on one side. As the wheel gets closer to true, you will need to decrease the amount you turn the spokes to avoid over-correcting.

❽ Accept a certain amount of wobble, especially if truing in a bike, since the in-the-bike method of wheel truing is not very accurate and is not at all suited for making a wheel absolutely true. If you have access to a wheel dishing tool, check to make sure that the wheel is centered. (See Chapter 12.)

Replacing a broken spoke

 Go to the bike store and get a new spoke of the same length. **Remember**: the spokes on the front wheel are usually not the same length as the spokes on the rear wheel. Also, the spokes on the drive side

truing a wheel

hubs

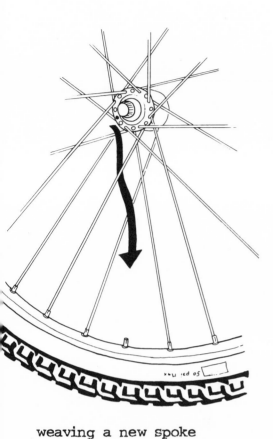

weaving a new spoke

of the rear wheel are almost always shorter than those on the other side.

❶ Make sure you are using the proper-size spoke.

❷ Thread the spoke through the spoke hole in the hub flange. If the broken spoke is on the drive side of the rear wheel, you will need to remove the cassette cogs or the freewheel to get at the hub flange. (See **Changing cassette cogs** or **Changing freewheels** later in this chapter.)

❸ Weave the new spoke in with the other spokes just as it was before. It may take some bending to get it in place.

❹ Thread it into the same nipple, if the nipple is in good shape. Otherwise, use a new nipple; you'll need to remove the tire, tube, and rim strip to do so.

❺ Mark the new spoke with a piece of tape, and tighten it up about as snugly as the neighboring spokes on that side of the wheel.

❻ Follow the steps for truing a wheel as outlined above.

HUBS

Overhauling hubs

 Hubs should turn smoothly and noiselessly. If they are regularly maintained, you can expect them to still be running smoothly when you are ready to give up on the rest of your bike.

There are two general types of hubs: the standard "cup and cone" type, and the "sealed bearing" (or "cartridge bearing") type. All hubs have a "hub shell" that contains the axle and bearings and is connected to the rim with spokes, or in the case of disc wheels, by sheets of composite material.

Standard "cup and cone" hubs have loose ball bearings that roll along very smooth bearing surfaces called the "bearing races" or "cups," with an axle going through the center of the hub. These hubs also have conical-shaped nuts threaded onto the axle called "cones." These cones press the bearings gently inside the cups and guide the bearings as they travel along the bearing races. The cone surface that comes in contact with the bearings has been machined to minimize friction. The operation of the hub depends on the smoothness and lubrication of the cones,

overhauling
hubs

front hub with
cartridge bearing

front hub
with standard
ball bearings

about hubs

ball bearings, and bearing races. Outside of the cones are one or more spacers (or washers) followed by threaded locknuts that tighten down against the cones and spacers to keep the hub in proper adjustment. The rear hub will have more spacers on both sides, especially on the drive side.

The term "sealed-bearing" hub is a bit of a misnomer, since many cup and cone hubs offer better protection against dirt and water than some sealed-bearing hubs. The phrase "cartridge-bearing hub" is more accurate, since the distinguishing feature of these hubs is that the bearings, races and cones are all assembled as a complete unit at the bearing factory, and then plugged into a hub shell machined to accept the cartridge. Cartridge-bearing front hubs have two bearings, one on either end of the hub shell. Rear hubs have at least that, and often come with additional

bearing cartridges to stabilize the rear cassette (the part onto which the rear cogs are attached).

Cartridge-bearing hubs can have any number of axle assembly types. Some have a threaded axle with locknuts quite similar to a cup-and-cone hub. Much more common on mountain bikes are aluminum axles, often very thick with correspondingly large bearings. Their end caps usually snap on or are held on with set screws or circlips. The large diameter axles and bearings are meant to prevent independent movement of the legs of suspension forks or rear suspension assemblies.

All hubs

❶ Remove the wheel from the bike. (See Chapter 2.)

❷ Remove the quick-release skewer or the nuts and washers holding the wheel onto the bike.

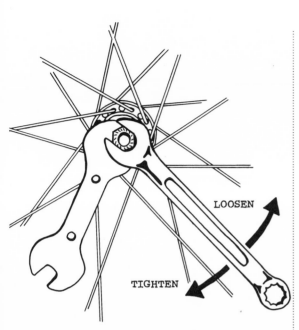

loosening and tightening locknut

LOOSEN

TIGHTEN

Overhaul standard "cup-and-cone" hub, front or rear

DISASSEMBLY:

❶ Set the wheel flat on a table or workbench. Slip a cone wrench of the appropriate size (usually 13mm or 14mm) onto the wrench flats on one of the cones.

❷ Put an appropriately sized cone wrench, standard wrench, or adjustable wrench on the locknut on the same side.

❸ While holding the cone with the cone wrench, loosen the locknut. This may take considerable force, since these are often fastened together very tightly to maintain the hub's adjustment. Make sure that you are unscrewing the locknut counterclockwise ("lefty loosey, righty tighty").

❹ As soon as the locknut loosens, move the cone wrench from the cone on top to the cone on the opposite end of the

axle, in order to hold the axle in place as you unscrew the lock nut. It will generally will unscrew with your fingers; use a wrench on it if necessary to get past any damaged threads.

❺ Slide any spacers off. If they will not slide off, the cone will push them off when you unscrew it. Please note that some spacers have a small tooth or "key" that corresponds to a notch on the axle.

❻ Unscrew the cone off of the axle. Again, you may need to hold the opposite cone with a wrench and use a wrench on this cone. An easy way to keep track of the various nuts, spacers and cones is to lay them down on your work bench in the order they were removed, or you can slide a twist-tie through all the parts in the correct order of orientation. Either method serves as an easy guide when reassembling the hub.

❼ Put your hand over the end of the hub from which you removed the nuts and spacers (to catch any bearings that might fall out), and flip the wheel over. Have a rag underneath the wheel to catch stray bearings.

❽ Pull the axle up and out, being careful not to lose any bearings that might fall out of the hub or that might be stuck to the axle. Leave the cone, spacers, and locknut all tightened together on the opposite end of the axle from the one you disassembled. Make a mental note about which side of the hub axle has the cone assembly still attached.

overhauling
cup–and–cone
hubs

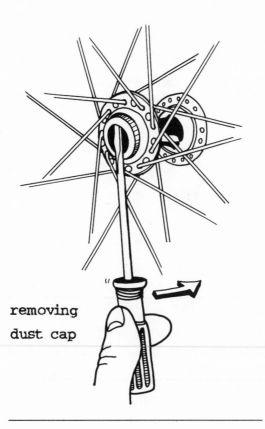

removing
dust cap

**cleaning
cup-and-cone
hubs**

Be sure you install the axle back into the same side of the hub. This is more important on rear hubs, but you may still want to mark your front hub with a rubber band or similar object.

9 Remove all of the ball bearings from both sides of the hub. They may stick to a screwdriver with a coating of grease on the tip, or you can push them down through the center of the hub and out the other side with the screwdriver. Tweezers might also be useful for removing bearings. Put the bearings in a cup, a jar lid, or the like. Count the bearings, and make sure you have the same number from each side.

10 Gently pop off the seals that are pressed into either end of the hub shell with a screwdriver.

CLEANING:

11 Wipe the hub shell out with a rag. Remove all dirt and grease, from the bearing surfaces. Using a screwdriver, push a rag through the hole in the middle of the hub body to clean off any grease or dirt. Wipe off the outer faces of the shell. Finish with a very clean rag on the bearing surfaces. They should shine and be completely free of dirt or grease. If you let your hub go too long between overhauls, the grease may have solidified and glazed over so completely that you will need a solvent to remove it. Use gloves and a citrus-based solvent. If you have a rear cassette hub, take this opportunity to lubricate the cassette. (See **Lubricating cassettes and freewheels** later in this chapter.)

12 Wipe down the axle, nuts and cones with a rag. Clean the cones really well with a clean rag. Again, solvent may be required if the grease has solidified. Get any dirt out of the threads on the disassembled axle end, as the cone will then push this into the hub upon reassembly.

13 Wipe the grease and dirt off of the seals. A rag over the end of a screwdriver is sometimes useful to get inside. Again, glaze-hard grease may have to be removed with a solvent.

Note: It is always better to use new ball bearings when overhauling standard "cup and cone" hubs; however, do not avoid performing an overhaul just because you don't have any new ball bearings. Inspect the ball bearings carefully. If there is even the slightest hint of uneven wear or pitting on the balls, cups or cones, throw the bearings out and complete the overhaul with new bearings. Always err on the side of caution, but if your hubs really need an overhaul, and you're planning a "killer" ride tomorrow, and it's 8:00 PM, and all the bike shops are closed, so you can't get new bearings, by all means, overhaul your hubs with the bearings that are already in there. Just be smart about it.

14 Wipe the bearings off by rubbing all of them together between two rags. This may be sufficient to clean them completely, but small specks of dirt can still adhere to them, so I prefer to take the next step as well.

15 Super clean and polish the bearings either in soap and water or in a citrus solvent. I prefer to wash them in a plugged sink with an abrasive soap like Lava, rubbing them between my hands as if I were washing my palms. This really gets them shining, unless they are caked with glaze-hard grease. Make sure you have plugged the sink drain! This method has the added advantage of getting my hands super clean for the assembly step. It is silly to contaminate your super clean parts with dirty hands. If there is hardened glaze on the bearings, soak them in solvent. If that does not remove it, go buy new bearings at the bike shop. Take a few of the old bearings along so you are sure to buy the right size.

16 Dry all bearings and any other wet parts. Inspect the bearings and bearing surfaces carefully. If any of the bearings have pits or gouges in them, replace all of them. Same goes for the cones. Most bike shops stock replacement cones. If the bearing races (or cups) in the hub shell are pitted, there is not much you can do. Some hubs have removable steel races pressed into the aluminum shell, but you usually need a hydraulic press to get them in and out — and good luck finding the races. You either learn to live with the pits or get a new hub (and, of course, spokes and perhaps the rim, too).

ASSEMBLY AND LUBRICATION:

17 Press the seals in on both ends of the hub shell.

18 Smear grease with your clean finger into the bearing race on one end of the hub shell. I like using white grease so that I can see if it gets dirty, but any bike grease will do. Grease not only lubricates the bearings, it also forms a

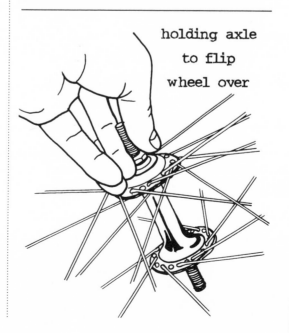

holding axle
to flip
wheel over

assembly and
lubrication of
cup-and-cone
hubs

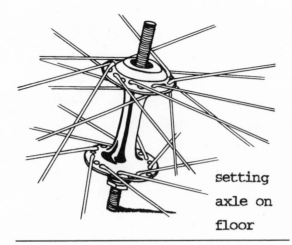

setting
axle on
floor

barrier to dirt and water.

19 Stick half of the ball bearings into the grease, making sure you put in the same number of bearings that came out. Distribute them uniformly around in the bearing race.

20 Smear grease on the cone that is still attached to the axle, and slide the axle into the hub shell. Lift the wheel up a bit (30° angle), so you can push the axle in until the cone slides into position, and keeps all the bearings in place. It is important to replace the axle and cone assembly into the same side of the hub from which it was removed – this is essential for rear hubs. If you fail to do this on a rear hub, you could end up with too many axle threads on one side of the axle and not enough on the other.

21 Holding the axle pushed inward with one hand to secure the bearings, turn the wheel over.

22 Smear grease into the bearing race that is now facing up. Lift the wheel and allow the axle to slide down just enough so that it is not sticking up past the bearing race. Make sure no bearings fall out of the bottom. If the race and

about hubs

bearings are properly greased and the axle remains in the hub shell, they are not likely to fall out.

23 While the top end of the axle is still below the bearing race, place the remaining bearings uniformly around in the grease. Make sure you have inserted the correct number of bearings.

24 Slide the axle into place by setting the wheel down on the table, so that the wheel rests on the lower axle end, seating the cone up into the bearings.

25 Using your fingers, screw the top cone down into place, seating it snugly onto the bearings. Covering the top cone with a film of grease is also a good idea.

26 In correct order, slide on the washer and any spacers. Watch for those washers with the little tooth or "key" that fits into the lengthwise groove in the axle.

27 Use your finger to screw on the locknut. Note that the two sides of the locknut are not the same. If you are

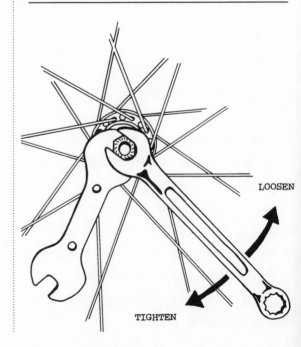

LOOSEN

TIGHTEN

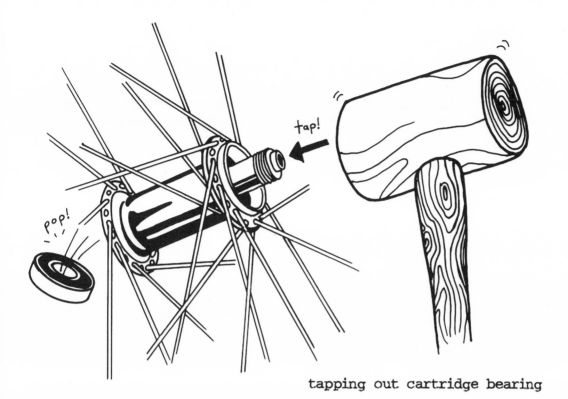

tapping out cartridge bearing

unsure about which way the locknut goes back on, check the orientation of the locknut that is on the opposite end of the axle (this locknut was not removed during this overhaul and is assumed to be in the correct orientation). As a general rule, the rough surface of the locknut faces out so that it can get a better hold on the dropout.

HUB ADJUSTMENT:

28 Thread the cone onto the axle until it rests up against the bearings. The axle should turn smoothly without any roughness or grinding, and there should be a very slight amount of lateral play. The slight looseness will be taken out when the quick-release skewer is tightened down with the wheel in the frame. If the hub is a bolt-on type without a quick-release skewer, you don't want any play in it. Thread the locknut down until it is snug against the cone.

29 Place the cone wrench into the flats of the hub cone wrench. Tighten the locknut with the other wrench. Tighten it about as tightly as you can against the cone and spacers, in order to hold the adjustment. Be aware that you can ruin the hub if you accidentally tighten the cone down against the bearings instead of against the locknut.

30 If the adjustment is off, loosen the locknut while holding the cone with the cone wrench. If the hub is too tight, unscrew the cone a bit. If the hub is too loose, screw the cone in a bit.

31 Repeat Steps 28-30 until the hub adjustment feels right.

Note: You may find that tightening the locknut against the cone suddenly turns your "Mona Lisa" perfect hub adjustment into somthing slightly less beautiful. If this is the case, simply loosen the locknut and turn the cone 1/8 of a turn in the

overhauling
cartridge
bearing hubs

103

appropriate direction (usually tighter), then re-tighten the locknut. It's rare that I get a hub adjustment perfectly "dialed-in" on the first try, so expect that you are going to have to tinker with the adjustment a bit before it's right.

32 Put the skewer back into the hub. Make sure that the conical springs have their narrow ends to the inside.

33 Install the wheel in the bike, tightening the skewer. Check that the wheel spins well without any side play at the rim. If it needs readjustment, go back to Step 31.

34 Congratulate yourself on a job well done! Hub overhaul is a delicate job, and it makes a difference in the longevity and performance of your bike.

Overhaul cartridge-bearing hub

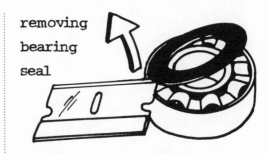

removing bearing seal

Cartridge-bearing hubs generally do not need much maintenance; however, if you ride through water above your hubs, you can expect water and dirt to get through any kind of seal. If the ball bearings inside the cartridges get wet, they should be overhauled or replaced.

There are many types of cartridge-bearing hubs, and it is outside the scope of this book to explain how to disassemble every one of them. Generally, there will be an end cap that can be removed by just pulling it off or by loosening a set screw first. Once the end cap is removed, you can often smack the end of the axle with a soft hammer or on a table, and it will push the opposite bearing out. Pop the other bearing out

the same way. The axle usually has a shoulder on either side, internal to the bearings, which can be used to force the bearings out. Simply tap the axle with a soft hammer and the shoulder should force the bearings out of the hub.

Once the cartridge bearings are out, you can sometimes overhaul them (otherwise you'll need to buy new ones):

1 Gently pop the bearing covers off with a single-edge razor blade.

2 Squirt citrus-based solvent into the bearing under pressure (wear rubber gloves and protective glasses) to wash out the grease, water and dirt.

3 Blow out the bearing with compressed air to dry it out.

4 Pack it with grease and snap the bearing covers back on.

5 Reassemble the hub the opposite way it came apart. Sometimes a light tap on either end of the axle with a soft hammer will free the bearings from a side load (something akin to a pinched cartridge bearing) that will make the hub noticeably hard to turn.

Note: Reassembling the bearings of most new cartridge-bearing hubs is relatively easy: simply press the bearings with your hand, or use the shoulder on the

VI

cassettes n' cogs

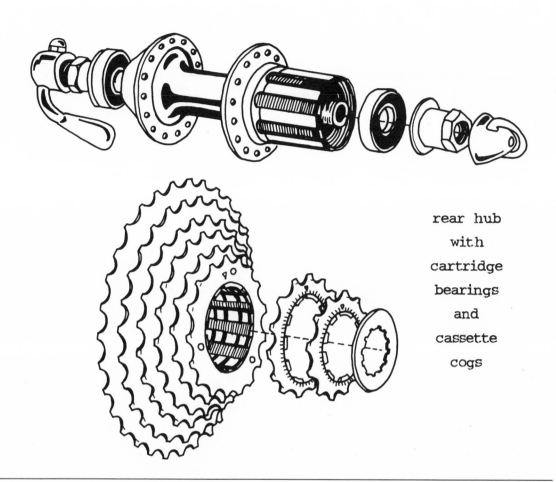

rear hub
with
cartridge
bearings
and
cassette
cogs

rear hub
diagrams

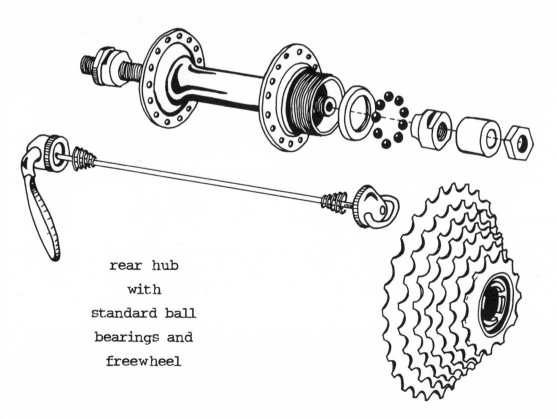

rear hub
with
standard ball
bearings and
freewheel

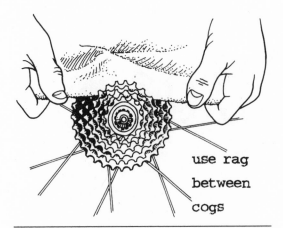

use rag
between
cogs

axle as a punch to press the bearings into place. In most cases, even a soft hammer is not necessary; however, with older model cartridge-bearing hubs (Suntour, Sanshin, Specialized, Shimano, and others), it isn't so easy. The tolerance between the hub cups and the outer surface of the bearing is so tight that these bearings must be pressed in or pounded in with a hammer. A direct blow from a hammer would ruin the bearing, so with these types of hubs, it is best to use either an old cartridge bearing or a similar-sized piece of metal to tap the bearings into the hub.

Grease Guard hubs

Wilderness Trail Bikes, Suntour, and others make high-end hubs, some labeled Grease Guard, that have small grease ports on them that accept a small-tipped grease gun. The tip in this type of grease gun is about the size of the tip of a pencil. Injecting grease into these grease ports forces grease through the bearings from the inside out, squeezing the old grease, and whatever else is in area of the bearing surfaces, out of the outer

cleaning cogsets

end. Grease injection systems do not eliminate the need for overhauling your hubs. Grease injection merely extends the amount of time between overhauls; furthermore, these systems are only as good as you are about using them.

CASSETTES, FREEWHEELS AND COGS

Both freehub cassettes and freewheels are freewheeling mechanisms, meaning that they allow the rear wheel to turn freely while the pedals are not turning.

A freehub cassette is an integral part of the rear hub. The cogs slide onto the cassette, engaging longitudinal splines on the cassette body.

A freewheel is a separate unit with the cogs attached to it. The entire freewheel

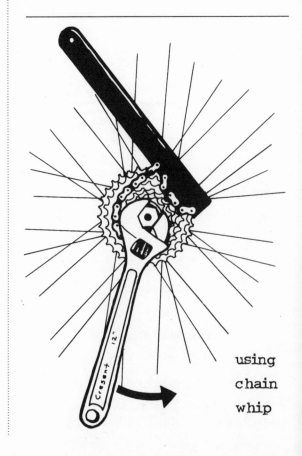

using
chain
whip

threads onto the drive side of the rear hub. Thread-on freewheels are rapidly falling out of fashion relative to cassettes, since they are heavier, less versatile with respect to cog interchangeability, and leave the drive side of the hub axle unsupported.

Most cassettes and freewheels rely on a series of pawls that engage when pressure is applied to the pedals, but allow the bike to freewheel when the rider is coasting.

Most cassettes can be lubricated without removing them from the hub. Changing gear combinations is accomplished by removing the cogs from the cassette body and putting on different ones.

Freewheels can be removed easily with a freewheel tool. Entire freewheels with different gear combinations can also be switched this way to adapt the bike to different terrain or for a special event.

Cleaning rear cogs

The easiest way to clean the rear cogs is to slide a rag back and forth between each pair of cogs. The other way is to remove them (See **Changing cassette cogs** below) and wipe them off with a rag.

Changing cassette cogs

❶ Get out a chain whip, a cassette lock-ring remover, a wrench (adjustable or open) to fit the remover, and the cog(s) you want to install. (Some very old cassettes have a threaded smallest cog

instead of a lockring. These require two chain whips and no lockring remover.)

❷ Remove the skewer.

❸ Wrap the chain whip around a cog at least two up from the smallest cog, wrapped in the drive direction to hold the cassette in place.

❹ Insert the splined lock-ring remover into the lock-ring. It is the metallic ring holding the smallest cog in place. Unscrew it in a counterclockwise direction, while using the chain whip to keep the cassette from turning.

❺ Pull the cogs straight off. Some cassette cogsets are all single cogs separated by loose spacers, and some cogsets are all bolted together.

❻ Clean the cogs with a rag, a toothbrush, and perhaps some solvent.

❼ Inspect the cogs for wear. If the teeth are hook-shaped, they may be ripe for replacement. Rohloff also makes a cog wear indicator tool. If you have access to one, use it following the accompanying instructions.

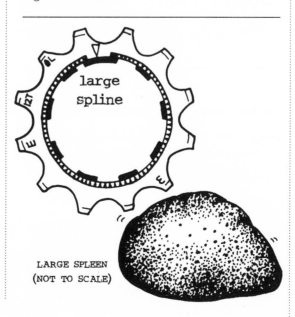

large spline

LARGE SPLEEN
(NOT TO SCALE)

8 a. If you are replacing the entire cogset, just slide the new one on. Note that one spline is usually wider than the others.

b. If you are replacing some individual cogs within your cogset, be certain that they are of the same type and model. For example, not all 16-tooth Shimano cogs are alike. Most cogs have shifting ramps, differentially shaped teeth, and other asymmetries. They differ with model as well as with sizes of the adjacent cogs, so you need to buy one for the exact location and model.

Bolt-together cogsets must be disassembled and put back together. There are two kinds of bolt-together cogsets: one with three long thin bolts holding the stack of cogs and spacers together, and one with cogs bolted to an aluminum spider that has internal splines to fit on the cassette body. For the type with the three bolts, just unscrew the bolts, take it apart, and put in the replacement cogs.

To save time and trouble in the future, you can put the cogs back on the cassette body separately and throw out the bolts.

9 Tighten the lockring back on with the lockring remover and wrench. If you have the old type with the thread-on first cog, tighten that on with a chain whip instead. Make sure that all of the cogs are seated and can't wobble side to side, indicating that the second cog is sitting against the ends of the splines. If they are loose, loosen the lockring, turn the second cog until it falls in place, and

tighten the lockring again.

Changing freewheels

If you have a freewheel and want to switch it with another one, follow this procedure. Replacing individual cogs on an existing freewheel is beyond the scope of this book, and is rarely done these days.

1 Get out the appropriate freewheel remover for your freewheel, a big adjustable wrench to fit it, and the freewheel you are replacing it with.

2 Remove the quick-release skewer, and take the springs off of it.

3 Slide the skewer back in from the non-drive side, place the freewheel remover into the end of the freewheel so that the notches or splines engage, and thread the skewer nut back on, tightening it against the freewheel remover to keep it from popping out of its notches.

4 If you have access to a vise, tighten the freewheel remover in the vise and place the wheel on top of the freewheel remover so that the notches of the remover fit into slots on the freewheel. While exerting downward pressure on the wheel, turn the wheel counterclockwise (to your left). You may have to rock the wheel back-and-forth slightly before it breaks free. If you don't have access to a vise, put the big adjustable wrench onto the flats of the freewheel remover, and loosen it (counterclockwise). It may take considerable force to free it, and you may even need to put a large pipe on the end of the wrench for

more leverage. Have the tire on the ground for traction as you do it. Once the freewheel pops loose, be careful to not keep unscrewing it without loosening the skewer nut since you will snap the skewer in two.

❺ Loosen the skewer nut a bit, unscrew the freewheel a bit more, etc., until it spins off freely and there is no longer any danger of having the freewheel remover pop out of the notches it engages.

❻ Remove the skewer and spin off the freewheel.

❼ Grease the threads on the hub and the inside of the new freewheel.

❽ Thread on the new freewheel by hand. Tighten it either with a chain whip, the freewheel remover and a wrench, or by putting it on the bike and pedaling.

❾ Replace the skewer with the narrow ends of its conical springs facing inward.

Lubricating cassettes and freewheels

 Lubricating cassettes and freewheels can usually be accomplished simply by dripping chain lube into them.

If yours is the kind of cassette with the teeth on the faces of the hub shell and cassette, just drip oil into the crease between the cassette and the hub shell as you turn the cassette counterclockwise.

IF IT IS THE STANDARD KIND OF CASSETTE:

❶ Disassemble the hub axle assembly. (See **Overhauling hubs** on page 99.)

❷ Wipe clean the inside of the drive-side bearing surface.

❸ With the wheel laying flat and the cassette pointed up toward you, flow chain lube in between the bearing surface and the cassette body, as you spin the cassette counterclockwise. You will hear the clicking noise smooth out. Keep it flowing until old black oil flows out of the other end of the cassette.

❹ Wipe off the excess oil, and continue with the hub overhaul.

IF IT IS A FREEWHEEL:

❶ Wipe dirt off of the face of the fixed part of the freewheel surrounding the axle.

❷ With the wheel lying flat, and the cogs facing up toward you, drip lubricant into the crease between the fixed and moving parts of the freewheel or cassette as you spin the cogs in a counterclockwise direction. You will hear the clicking noise inside get smoother as you get lubricant in there. Keep the flow of lubricant going until old, dirty oil flows out the back side around the hub flange.

❸ Wipe off the excess oil.

Once you have the freehub on freewheel reassembled, go ride your bike!

brakes

"**W**ell, I predict that if you think about it long enough you will find yourself going round and round and round and round until you finally reach only one possible, rational, intelligent conclusion. The law of gravity and gravity itself did not exist before Isaac Newton. No other conclusion makes sense."

— ROBERT M. PIRSIG, from *Zen and the Art of Motorcycle Maintenance*

Oh, well. We came after Newton, so we need a good set of brakes.

tools

2.5mm, 3mm, 4mm, 5mm, 6mm Allen wrenches
9mm and 10mm open-end wrenches
small adjustable wrench
pliers
grease

TYPES OF BRAKES

As of 1996, by far the most common brake for mountain bikes is the cable-actuated cantilever brake. However, it looks as though Shimano's V-brake will certainly gain a large following in the next few years. Cantilever brakes have been around for a long time because they work very effectively. They are light, simple, offer good mud clearance and above all, they stop your bike. Cantilevers pivot on bosses attached to the frame and fork. A cable actuates the brake by pulling on another cable attached to both cantilever arms.

There are several other options when it comes to mountain bike brakes as well. For rear-suspension frames, linkage brakes that mount on the cantilever bosses offer the advantage of operating without a cable stop, making them useful for a part of the bike that is constantly in motion. These models rely on an articulated linkage that pulls both brake arms toward one another.

Some hydraulic brakes mount on the cantilever bosses and are also useful on rear-suspension bikes. On these brakes, the pads are driven straight toward the rim by hydraulic pressure.

Roller cams and U-brakes also mount on bosses attached to the frame and fork. You should know that the brazed-on bosses for these brakes are not quite the same as those used for standard cantilevers, so it's quite a hassle to make the switch on a bike equipped with standard bosses. Roller cams and U-brakes peaked in popularity in the late 1980s, but there are still quite a few around. They do offer superb clearance and braking power.

Unlike most other brakes that use the edge of the rim as a braking surface, disc brakes have hydraulically-driven pads that pinch a hub-mounted disc — much like those on a motorcycle or a car. As these units have become lighter and simpler, their popularity has grown.

CABLES & HOUSINGS

cables and housings

Given that cables transfer braking force from the levers to the brakes, their proper installation and maintenance are critical to good brake performance. If there is excess friction in the cable system, the brakes will not work properly, no matter how well the brakes, calipers and levers are adjusted. Each cable should move freely and be replaced if there are any broken strands.

Cable tensioning

As brake pads wear and cables stretch, the cable tension drops. The barrel adjuster on the brake lever offers about enough tension adjustment to mitigate these kind of changes. When adjusting cable tension, tighten the cable enough that the lever cannot contact the grip, no matter how hard you brake. And it

should be loose enough that the brakes (assuming they are centered and the wheels are true) are not dragging on the rims. There is still some latitude within that range, so set them as you prefer.

Increasing cable tension:

❶ Back out the barrel adjuster by turning it counterclockwise to tighten the cable.

❷ Adjust the tension so that the brake lever does not hit the grip when the brake is applied. Lock in the tension by holding the barrel adjuster while

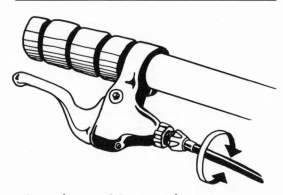

changing cable tension

tightening the locknut down against the lever body.

❸ You may find that you need to tighten the cable more than by simply fiddling with the barrel adjuster. If you need to take up more slack than the barrel adjuster allows you to, tighten the cable at the brake. First, screw the barrel adjuster most of the way in. This leaves some adjustment in the system for brake setup and cable stretch over time. Loosen the bolt clamping the cable at the brake. Check the cable for wear. If there are any frayed strands, replace it. (See **Cable installation** below.) Otherwise, pull the cable tight, and re-tighten the clamping bolt. Tension the cable as needed with the barrel adjuster.

Reducing cable tension:

❶ Back out the locknut on the barrel adjuster a few turns (counterclockwise).
❷ Tighten the barrel adjuster by turning it clockwise until your brake pads are properly spaced from the rim.
❸ Tighten the locknut by turning it clockwise against the lever body to lock in the adjustment.
❹ Double-check that the cable is tight enough so that the lever cannot be squeezed all the way to the grip.

Cable maintenance

❶ If the cable is frayed or kinked or has any broken strands, replace it. (See **Cable installation** in next column.)
❷ If the cable is not sliding well, lubricate it. If you have it, use molybdenum disulfide grease; otherwise, try a chain lubricant. Standard greases can gum up on cables and eventually restrict movement.

To lubricate, open the brake (via the quick release), and pull each section of cable housing out of each slotted cable stop. If your bike does not have slotted cable stops, you will have to pull out the entire cable. Slide the housing up the cable, rub lubricant with your fingers on the cable section that was inside the housing, and slide the housing back into

place. If the cable still sticks, replace it.

Cable installation

❶ Remove the old cable, making sure not to lose any parts of the cable clamps or straddle-cable holders.

When installing a new cable, it is a good idea to replace the housings as well, even if you don't think they need to be. Daily riding in particularly dirty conditions means that cables and housings may have to be replaced as often as once a month.

❷ Purchase good quality cables and lined housings. Try using die-drawn cables: They have been pulled through a constricting die and will pull with less friction, because the exterior strands have been flattened. Some even come coated in Teflon. When properly installed, Gore-Tex cables and housings can reduce friction significantly. Be sure to follow the instructions, because, if not installed properly, the coating can get completely wadded up and prevent cable movement.

Most cable housing is spiral-wrapped to prevent splitting under braking pressure. Newer housings have straight strands to prevent compression under braking pressure and are also spiral-wrapped to prevent splitting. Teflon liners reduce friction and are of great benefit on a mountain bike.

❸ Cut the housing sections long enough to reach the brakes, and route them so that they do not make any sharp bends. If you are replacing existing housing, look

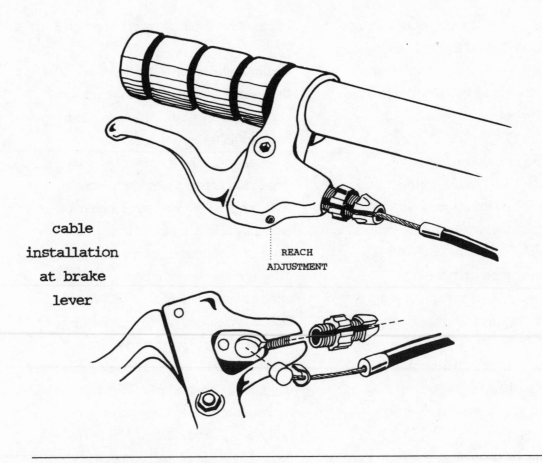

cable
installation
at brake
lever

REACH
ADJUSTMENT

**cable
installation**

at the bends before removing it. If the bends are smooth and do not bind when the wheel is turned, cut the new housings to the same lengths. If not, cut each new segment longer than you think necessary and keep trimming it back until it gives the smoothest path possible for the cable, without the cable tension being affected by steering. Use a cutter specifically designed for cutting housings, or a large, sharp sided-cutter.

❹ After cutting, make sure the ends are flat. If not, flatten them with a file or a clipper.

❺ If the end of the Teflon liner is mashed shut after cutting, open it up with a sharp object like a nail or a toothpick.

❻ Slip an end cap over each housing

end for support and to prevent it from pinching the cable.

❼ Decide which hand you want to control which brake (the standard is the right hand controlling the rear brake).

❽ Rotate the barrel adjuster and locknut so that their slots line up with those on the lever and lever body. Tighten the adjusting barrel to within one turn of being screwed all of the way in.

❾ Insert the round end of one cable into the appropriate lever.

❿ Pull the cable down into the lined-up slots on the barrel and nut. Once the cable is in place, it's a good idea to turn the barrel and nut so that the slots are offset to prevent the cable from slipping back out. If your lever is not slotted, you

brakes

will have to feed the entire length of the cable through the hole in the lever body.

11 Hopefully, you have slotted cable stops on your bike. They sure make installation a lot easier. Assuming that you do, slide the cable through the housing sections and then route the cable and housing from the brake lever to the brake. If you don't have slotted stops, go ahead and install the various sections of housing in the appropriate slots. Then slide the cable through the already-installed housing.

Note: With new cables and lined housing, it is usually best not to use a lubricant on the cable. It can gum up inside the housing and attract dirt. Some manufacturers; however, supply lubricants specifically for this purpose with their cables and housings.

12 With a suspension fork, end the front brake housing at the stop on the brake arch. Without suspension, you may have a cable stop that is integral to the stem or one attached to the headset. I recommend bypassing any integral cable stop on the stem or stem through-hole, as these require readjustment of the front brake with any change in stem height. Instead, use a collar that slips around the stem above the headset, or one that slips into the headset stack between locknuts.

13 Attach the cable to the brake. (See section on your type of brake.) Pull it taut and tighten the cable-clamping bolt.

14 Adjust cable tension with the lever barrel adjuster (as in **Cable tensioning**).

15 Cut off cable ends about an inch past the cable-fixing bolts. Crimp end caps on all exposed cable ends to prevent fraying.

Note: Once the cable has been properly installed, the lever should snap back quickly when released. If it does not, re-

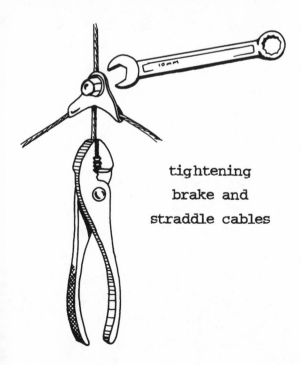

tightening
brake and
straddle cables

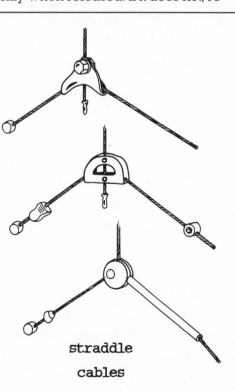

straddle
cables

straddle
cables

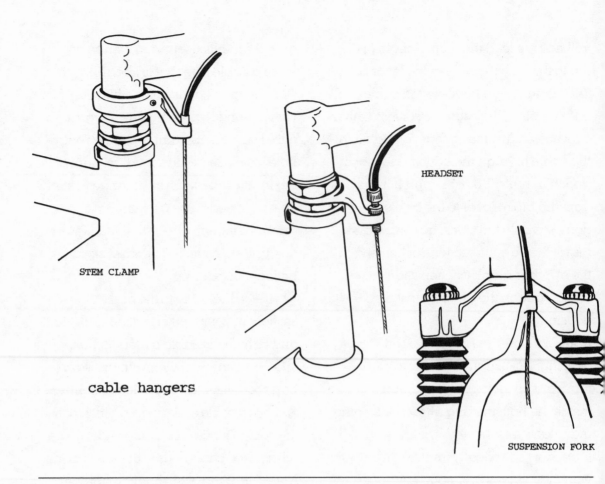

STEM CLAMP

HEADSET

SUSPENSION FORK

cable hangers

cable hangers

check the cables and housings for free movement and sharp bends. Release the cable quick release, and check the levers for free movement. With the cable still loose, check that the brake pads do not drag on the tire as they return to the neutral position; make sure the brake arms rotate freely on their pivot bosses, and check that the brake arm return springs pull the pads away from the rims. Follow brake-adjustment instructions for your particular type of brake.

BRAKE LEVERS

The levers must operate smoothly and be set up so that you can easily reach them while riding.

Lubrication/service

Lubricate all pivot points in the lever with grease or oil. Do this frequently. Check return spring function for levers that have them.

Make sure that the lever or lever body is not bent in a way that hinders movement. Check for stress cracks, and if you find any, replace the lever.

Lever removal, installation, and positioning

Levers mount on the bar inboard of the grip and bar end. They are also mounted inboard of twist shifters and outboard of thumb shifters. Some manufacturers offer integrated systems that include both lever and shifter in a single unit.

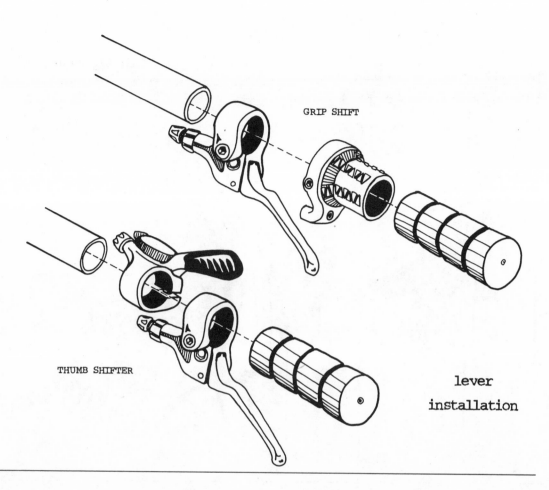

GRIP SHIFT

THUMB SHIFTER

lever

installation

brakes

❶ If installed, remove the bar end, by loosening the mounting bolt and sliding it off.

❷ Remove the handlebar grip by lifting the edges on both ends, squirting water underneath, and twisting it until it becomes free and slides off.

❸ If installed, remove the twist shifter by loosening the mounting bolt and sliding it off.

❹ Loosening the mounting bolt with an Allen wrench and slide the lever off.

❺ Slide the new lever on, and replace the other parts in the order in which they were installed. Slide the grips on using water or hair spray inside as a lubricant.

❻ Make certain the levers do not extend beyond the ends of the bars, and then position them it according to preference.

❼ Tighten all mounting bolts on levers, shifters, and bar ends.

Reach and leverage adjustments

Some levers have a reach adjustment set screw (usually on the lever body just under the barrel adjuster). If you have small hands, you may want to tighten the reach set screws so the levers are closer to the bars when fully open.

Some brakes also have a leverage adjustment, which moves the cable end holder in or out relative to the lever pivot. Some use a a rotating notched eccentric disc for this adjustment, while others use a screw or insert. The closer the cable end is to the pivot, the higher the

brake levers

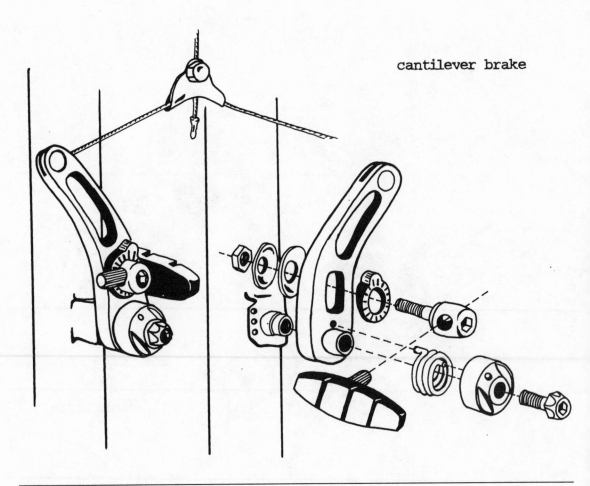

cantilever brake

leverage, but the less cable the lever pulls over the stroke.

BRAKE CALIPERS
Cantilever brakes
Removal
Disconnect cables. Take the brakes off by unscrewing the mounting bolts on the front of each cantilever arm. Be careful not to lose any parts, and keep them in the order they were removed.

Installation
❶ Grease all threads and pivot points.
❷ Follow the installation directions that came with your brakes, if you have them. If not, follow the general installation instructions below.
❸ Make sure you install the brakes with all of the parts in the order in which they were packaged together. In particular, the springs will often be of different colors, and they are not interchangeable from left to right.
❹ If the brake has a separate inner sleeve bushing to fit over the cantilever boss, install that first. Slip the brake and return spring over it.
❺ Determine what sort of return system your brakes use. If the brake arms have no spring-tension adjustment, or a set screw on the side of one of the arms for adjusting spring tension, go to Step 6. Such brakes utilize the hole in the cantilever boss to anchor the bottom end of the spring. If the brake arms have a large nut for adjusting spring tension,

skip to Step 8. These brakes do not use the hole in the cantilever boss as a spring anchor.

❻ Slip the brake onto the boss, inserting the lower end of the spring into the hole in the cantilever boss (if the boss has three holes, try the center one first). You also want to make sure that the top end of the spring is inserted into its hole in the brake arm as well.

❼ Install and tighten the mounting bolt into the cantilever boss.

❽ Slip the brake (with any included bushings) onto the cantilever boss.

❾ Install the spring so that one end inserts into the hole in the brake arm and the other inserts into the hole in the adjusting nut.

❿ Install and tighten the mounting bolt while holding the adjusting nut with the appropriate open-end wrench (usually 15mm) so that the pad is touching the rim. This facilitates pad adjustment later.

Pad replacement and installation

❶ Remove the old pad, if making a replacement.

❷ Install the pad. Most cantilevers rely on an eye bolt with an enlarged head and a hole through it to accept the pad post. Some brakes (Avid, for example), have a slotted clamp with a hole for the pad post. A few brakes still use a threaded pad post that passes through a slot in the brake arm.

❸ If your brake spring can be adjusted so that it holds the pad against the rim, set it up that way now. It will make the

pad adjustments much easier. If not, you will have to push each arm toward the rim as you adjust the pad.

Pad adjustment

There are five separate adjustments that must be made for each pad. These adjustments are quite easy with some brakes and a real pain in the rear with others.

The adjustments are:

(1) offset distance of the pad from the brake arm;

(2) vertical pad height;

(3) pad swing in the vertical plane for mating with the rim's sidewall angle;

(4) pad twist to align the heel and toe of the pad with the rim's curvature;

(5) pad swing in the horizontal plane to set toe-in.

Brakes that feature a cylindrical brake arm are by far the easiest to adjust. Pad adjustment is simple because the pad is held to the cylinder with a clamp that offers almost full range of motion. Avid, OnZa, Gravity Research Pipe Dreams, and Dia Compe VC900 all rely on this type of system. All other cantilevers employ a single bolt to hold all five adjustments. It requires a bit of manual dexterity to hold all of these adjustments simultaneously while tightening the pad eye bolt.

WITH ALL TYPES OF CANTILEVERS:

❶ Loosen the pad clamping bolt and set the pad offset by sliding the post in or out of the clamping hole. The farther the pad is extended away from the brake arm,

brakes

brake pad
alignment

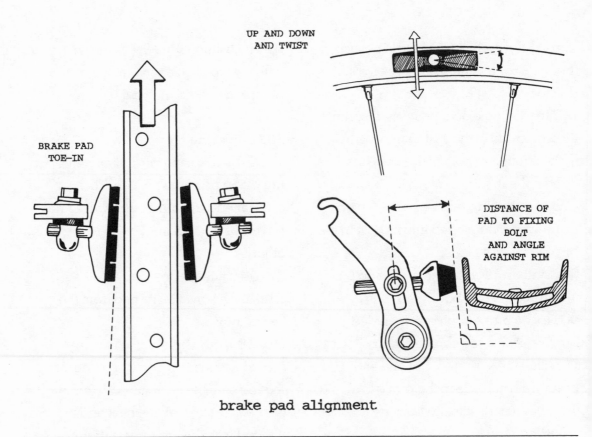

BRAKE PAD
TOE-IN

UP AND DOWN
AND TWIST

DISTANCE OF
PAD TO FIXING
BOLT
AND ANGLE
AGAINST RIM

brake pad alignment

brake pad alignment

the greater the angle of the brake arm will be from the plane of the wheel. A benefit of this is that leverage is increased. Drawbacks are: the brake feels less firm, since less lever pull force is required; and heel clearance can be an issue if the rear brake arms stick out farther, particularly for small frames. A good way to start off is with the post clamped in the center of its length. With threaded pad posts, pad offset is set by placing spacers between the brake arm and the pad.

❷ Roughly adjust the vertical pad height. This consists of sliding the clamping mechanism that holds the pad up and down the slot on the brake arm. With cylindrical-clamp brakes, loosen the bolt clamping the pad holder to the brake arm, and snug the bolt back up,

once the rough adjustment is reached. With all other types, leave the pad bolt just loose enough so that you can move the pad easily and continue.

❸ Adjust pad swing in the vertical plane so that the face of the pad meets the rim flat with the top edge of the pad face 1mm to 2mm below the top of the rim. Fine tune this adjustment by sliding the pad up or down, to get the ideal combination of height and angle.

❹ Adjust the pad twist so that the top edge of the pad is parallel to the top of the rim. Modern pads are quite long and require precision with this adjustment. With cylindrical-clamp brakes, the pad-securing bolt may now be tightened.

❺ Finally, adjust the toe-in of the pad. The pad should either be adjusted flat to the rim, or toed in so that when the

brakes

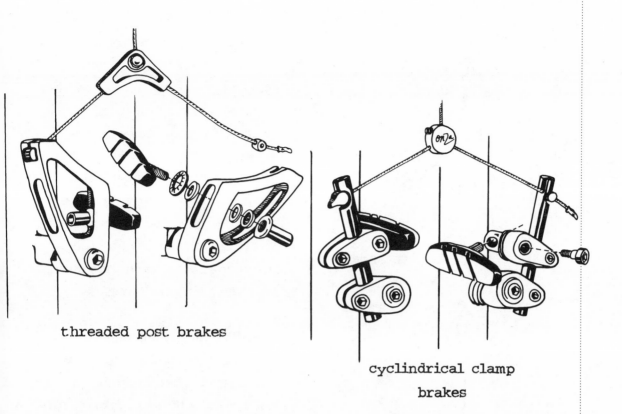

threaded post brakes

cyclindrical clamp
brakes

forward end of the pad touches the rim the rear end of it is 1mm to 2mm away from the rim. If the pad is toed out, the heel of it will catch and tend to chatter, making an obnoxious squealing noise. If the brake arms are not stiff, or they fit loosely on the cantilever boss so that there is play in them, the same thing will happen with a flat pad adjustment, so toe-in is a requirement. Over time, the pad will wear until it is flat to the rim. If you find the noise objectionable, this type of brake will require very frequent readjustment.

For cylindrical-arm brakes with two fixing bolts, toe-in is adjusted by again loosening the bolt that holds the vertical height adjustment of the pad. Since you have already tightened the other bolt that holds the pad in place, you simply loosen this second bolt and swing the pad horizontally until you arrive at your preferred toe-in or flatness setting. Tighten the bolt again, and you are done with pad adjustment.

With any brake using a single bolt to hold the pad to the arm and to control the pad's rotation, you have a tricky task of holding all of the adjustments you have made and simultaneously tightening the nut. Most eye-bolt systems are tightened with a 10mm wrench on the nut on the back of the brake, while the front is held with a 5mm Allen wrench. Help from someone else — to either hold or tighten — is useful here. Probably the trickiest brake to adjust has a big toothed or notched washer between the head of the eye bolt and the flat brake arm. The washer is thinner on one edge than the

**brake pad
alignment**

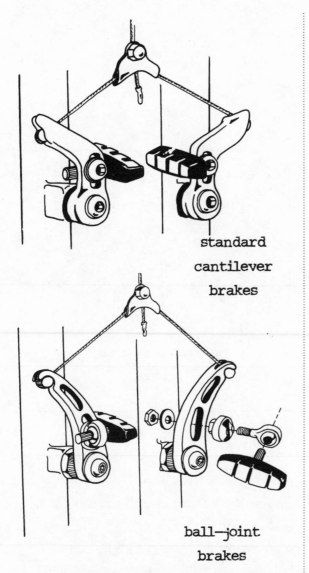

standard
cantilever
brakes

brake pad
alignment

ball—joint
brakes

Paul, etc.). The concave/convex surfaces allow the necessary swivel and tightening the bolt secures everything. Again, you may not get it right on the first try. Threaded posts also employ such washers.

Brakes with a cylindrical arm and a clamp around it, with only a single eye bolt holding the pad and pinching the clamp around the arm (WTB, SRP, etc.), are adjusted functionally the same as the ones with the cupped washers.

Straddle-cable adjustment

The straddle cable should be set so that it pulls on the brake arms in such a way that it provides the best braking. This is not always the adjustment that produces the highest leverage, since sometimes brake feel is improved when leverage is slightly reduced. In general, I recommend setting up the brakes with the highest leverage and then reducing it if you want to change the feel.

With any lever arm, the mechanical advantage is highest when the force is applied at right angles to the lever arm. There is an esoteric argument that I will go into later as to what actually constitutes the brake's lever arm, but, for general purposes, if you set the straddle cable so that it pulls as close to 90 degrees to the brake arm as you can, this will work very well. With the low-profile brake arms so common now, this will result in the straddle cable being very short and set very low and close to the tire. Make sure that you allow at least an

other, so rotating it (by means of the tooth or notch) toes the pad in or out. With this type, you must hold all of the pad adjustments as you turn this washer, and then keep it and the pad in place as you tighten the nut. It's not an easy job, and the adjustment usually doesn't work on the first try. Trial and error is necessary.

The other common type has a convex or concave shape to the brake arm, and convex/concave washers separate the eye-bolt head and nut from the brake arm (Shimano, most Dia Compe, Ritchey,

inch of clearance over the tire to prevent mud or a bulge in the tire from engaging the brake.

The straddle cable usually has a metal blob on one end, and the other end is clamped to one brake arm by a bolt. The blob fits into the slotted brake arm and acts as a quick release for the brake.

With Shimano cantilevers built since 1988, the brake cable connects directly to the cable clamp on one brake arm, and a single link wire with a blob on either end replacing the straddle cable. After 1993, Shimano changed the closure so that the link-wire holder holds not only the link wire but a fixed length of cable housing as well. The link-wire holder is slipped onto the brake cable, which is passed directly through the housing to the cable clamp on the brake arm. The mechanic has no need to change straddle-cable settings, as its length is predetermined. Between 1988 and 1993,

Shimano brakes did not have the length of housing on the link wire holder, the holder was instead clamped to the brake cable shifter. Its position set by a plastic gauge. Without the gauge, simply make the length of cable from link-wire holder to brake arm the same on both sides. It will work well.

Some brakes do not have a cable clamp on either brake arm; both arms are slotted to accept the blob on the end of a straddle cable or link wire. In this case, either a small cylindrical clamp is installed on the opposite end of the straddle cable; or a link-wire holder that holds two link wires must be used.

To set the length of any straddle-cable, loosen the bolts or set screws that hold the straddle-cable holder onto the end of the brake cable, and slide it up on the brake cable. Then tighten it in place. It is set properly when the brake engages quickly, and the lever cannot be pulled

brakes

straddle—
cable
adjustment

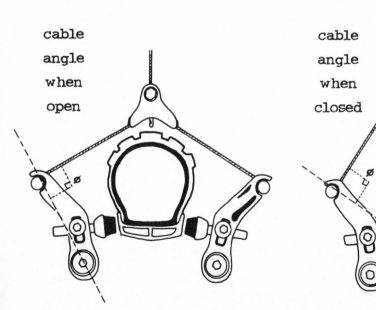

cable
angle
when
open

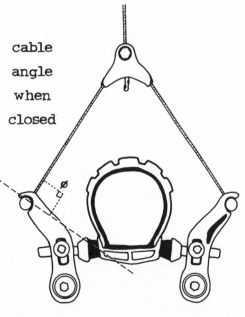

cable
angle
when
closed

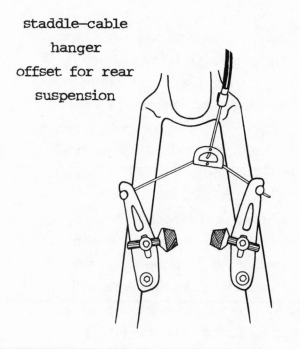

staddle—cable hanger offset for rear suspension

spring
tension
adjustment

closer than a finger's width from the bar. Small adjustments can be taken up with the barrel adjuster on the brake lever.

The lateral position of the straddle-cable holder can be changed with set screws, as well. The holder should generally be centered on the straddle cable. In some cases, as with very small frames, the brake cable pulls asymmetrically as it comes around the seat tube. In these cases, the straddle-cable holder may need to be offset slightly for the brakes to work.

Spring tension adjustment

The spring tension adjustment centers the brake pads about the rim and also determines the return spring force. With brakes that have a single set screw on the side of one brake arm, there is only one adjustment to make. Turn the screw until the brakes are centered and the pads hit the rim simultaneously when

the brakes are applied. If the boss has more than one hole, higher spring tensions can only be achieved by moving the spring to a lower hole in the brake boss (or vice versa).

Some brakes rely on large tensioning nuts and do not utilize the holes in the brake bosses as anchors. On these, the tensioning nuts may be turned on both arms until you get the combination of return force and centering you prefer. You must loosen the mounting bolt while holding the tensioning nut with a wrench. Turn the nut to the desired tension, and, while holding it in place with the wrench, tighten the mounting bolt again.

On brakes without a tension adjustment, centering is accomplished by removing the brake arm and moving the spring to another hole on the boss. It is a rough adjustment at best, and some bosses do not have more than a single hole. When this adjustment fails, you can twist the arm on the boss to tighten or loosen the spring a bit. That, of course, is an even rougher adjustment.

Lubrication/service

The only lubrication necessary on cantilever brakes is on the cables, levers, and brake arms. This should be performed whenever braking feels sticky. Lever and cable lubrication is covered above, and cantilevers can only be lubricated by removing them, cleaning and greasing the pivots, and replacing them.

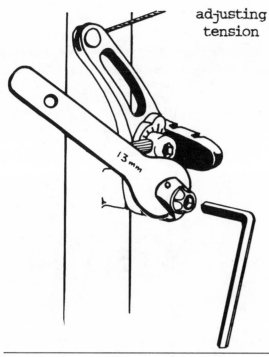

adjusting
tension

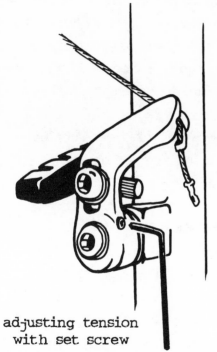

adjusting tension
with set screw

SHIMANO V-BRAKES

These brakes are extremely powerful
and can be very grabby if used with a
standard brake lever. So it is important
that you use the levers that were
designed for use with the brake.

Installation

Lever installation to the bars is the same
as others. (See page 116.)

Leverage adjustment

The levers allow a certain amount of
adjustment to vary the distance between
the lever pivot and the head of the cable.
To start with, set it at the position that
offers the weakest leverage. That places
the head of the cable farthest from the
pivot. Only increase the leverage if you
become very confident in using the
brakes. On XTR, a threaded adjuster
performs the adjustment. On XT and
below, leverage is adjusted by installing
or removing a series of inserts.

V-brake installation and adjustment

❶ Grease the cantilever boss on your
frame or fork, then insert the spring pin of
each brake arm in the center hole of the
boss. Tighten each brake arm with the
brake pivot bolt.

❷ Adjust the amount of pad offset from
the brake arms by holding the pads
against the rim and measuring the space
between the end of the cable guide pipe
on the left brake arm and the cable-fixing
bolt on the right brake arm. This length
should be at least 39mm. The pad offset
from the brake arm is adjusted by
interchanging concave washers of
different thicknesses on the threaded pad
post. There is a convex washer on either
side of the brake arm whose flat side
contacts the arm and whose curved side
nests with a concave washer. The

VII

brakes

v–brakes

125

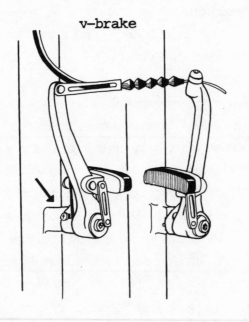

v–brake

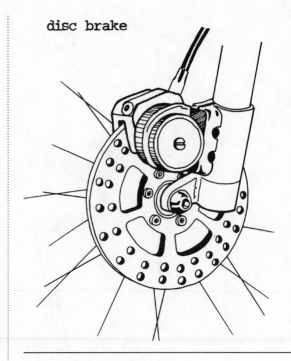

disc brake

disc brakes

concave washer on one side is 6mm thick, and 3mm thick on the other. Interchange these washers from side to side to achieve the proper brake-arm spacing.

❸ Adjust the pad-rim contact by loosening the pad-fixing nut and holding the pad flat against the rim. The pad's top edge should be about 1mm below the edge of the rim. Tighten the pad-fixing nut. The V-brake linkage keeps the pad moving straight as it contacts and leaves the rim surface. Therefore there is no toe-in on V-brakes, so the pad should be parallel to the rim.

❹ Connect the cable to the brake. The cable housing stops at the end of the cable-guide pipe on the left brake arm, and the cable runs through the pipe and the rubber bellows-shaped tube to the fixing bolt on the right arm. Set the cable length so that there is 1mm of space between the pads and the rim. Tighten

the cable-fixing bolt.

❺ Center the brake pads by turning the spring-tension-adjustment screws on each brake arm. A clockwise turn pulls the arm farther from the rim, and vice versa.

❻ Squeeze the brake lever a number of times to seat the cable. Readjust if necessary.

DISC BRAKES
Adjustment

Disc brakes need to be adjusted so that the disc turns parallel to the pads without rubbing, or just rubbing lightly, in the case of floating systems. They also need to be adjusted to stop quickly well before the lever pulls to the grip. It is beyond the scope of this book to go into great detail about each individual type. Instead, you should refer to the instruction manual on the particular brake.

In general, cable-activated disc brakes

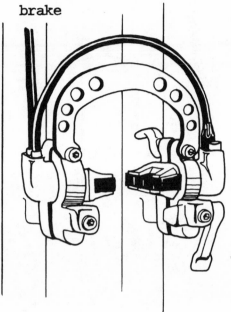

hydraulic brake

can be adjusted by tensioning the cable the same way as you would on a cantilever brake. On such brakes, only the caliper is hydraulic. The rest operates on the same principle as a cantilever brake.

The pads can usually be moved closer to the disc by turning a bolt that reduces the fluid volume in the caliper.

On fully hydraulic systems, volume in the entire system can often be adjusted at either the lever or at the caliper. If the brakes feel spongy, bleeding the air out of the system may be necessary. Unless your brakes have specific bleeding instructions, have the factory or a manufacturer-certified shop perform this service.

To perform anything other than what is outlined in these admittedly general statements, refer to the instruction manual included with your braking system.

HYDRAULIC RIM BRAKES

This refers to brakes that are fully hydraulic and are mounted on the cantilever bosses.

Installation of levers and hoses

Hydraulic levers are installed identically to cable-actuated levers. The hoses are not to be cut or routed through cable stops. Generally, you secure these to the frame by means of plastic draw clamps. Make sure there are no kinks in the hoses and that they do not stick out from the bike enough to hit your legs or hook on obstacles as you ride.

Pad replacement

On most models, pad replacement is quite simple, requiring only that you pop them out and install new ones. Refer to the instructions for the specific brake.

Installation of brakes

This is beyond the scope of this book. Follow the instructions that come with the brakes.

Adjustment and Bleeding

Most systems have a simple Allen screw adjustment for fluid volume which adjusts pad-to-rim spacing. Follow the manufacturer's recommendations. If you do something to cause hydraulic fluid to leak out, you will immediately lose braking.

Sponginess of brakes usually indicates the need for bleeding air from the lines.

VII

brakes

hydraulic and linkage brakes

Some are relatively simple to bleed, and others are not. Do not attempt to bleed bicycle hydraulic systems yourself without a manual from the manufacturer. Have the brake factory or a shop certified to perform such service do this.

LINKAGE BRAKES

There are so many vastly different linkage brakes on the market that it would not be possible to include them all in detail here. Linkage brakes are often quite similar to cantilevers and are adjusted, centered and mounted in much the same way.

It is preferable to refer to instructions from the specific manufacturer.

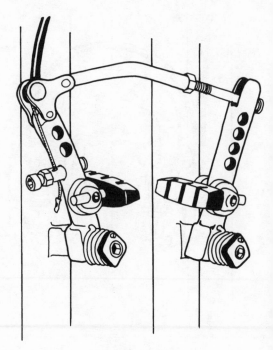

linkage brake

U-brakes

U-BRAKES

Removal and Installation

U-brakes mount on the same bosses as roller-cams do. They **cannot** be mounted on cantilever bosses, which are too close to the hub.

Remove the brake by unscrewing the mounting bolts. Grease the pivots, and replace them.

Attach the straddle-cable yoke to the brake cable, and attach the straddle cable to the cable clamp on one arm. An easy way to set the position of the straddle cable yoke on a chainstay-mounted U-brake is to squeeze the lever to the grip, after slipping the yoke up against the bottom-bracket cable guide. Then tighten it in place. This is the highest it could be set on the cable and

allows the longest possible straddle cable.

Adjustment

❶ Set the rear straddle-cable-yoke position on the brake cable as outlined above. On a front brake, set it about 2 inches above the brake.

❷ Tighten the straddle cable while pulling it tight with a pair of pliers and squeezing the pads against the rim with your hand. Make sure you have tightened the anchor bolts enough that the cables do not slip.

❸ Check that you cannot pull the lever closer than a finger's width from the grip. Tension the cable as needed with the straddle-cable yoke or the lever-barrel adjuster.

❹ Set the spring tension by releasing the straddle cable, loosening the

128

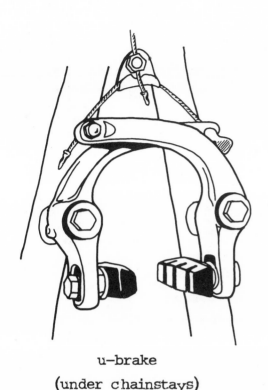

u–brake
(under chainstays)

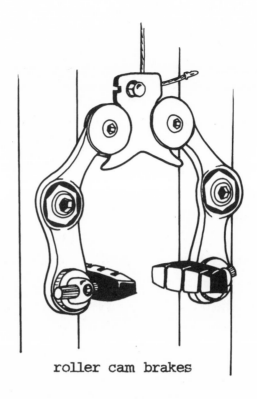

roller cam brakes

roller cam
brakes

mounting bolt and swinging the pad away from the rim. Then tighten the mounting bolt. Center the brake by setting the spring tension on one arm first, followed by the other arm in the same fashion. If your brake has a small Allen set screw on the side of one arm, use it to make fine spring-tension adjustments.

Pad replacement and positioning
U-brakes rely on brake pads with threaded posts. Install them with the original spacers in their original orientation. The pads should hit the center of the braking surface and have a small amount of toe-in. There is no adjustment for spacing from the brake arm. Hold the pad in place with your hand while tightening the nut with a

wrench. As the pads wear, they tend to slide up on the rim and hit the tire, so check this adjustment frequently. You should also regularly clear hardened mud filling inside of the brake arms against the tops of the pads. It can build up here on U-brakes and abrade the tire sidewalls.

ROLLER-CAM BRAKES
Removal and Installation
Roller-cams mount on bosses attached to the fork and either the chainstays or the seatstays, the same as U-brakes. These are mounted farther from the hub than cantilever bosses and, like U-brakes, they *will not*, work on standard cantilever bosses.

Roller-cams are removed by first pulling the cam plate out from between the rollers on the ends of the arms. Remove the mounting bolt and pull the arms off of the bosses.

Installation is performed in reverse. Grease the bosses and the inside of the pivots, as well as the edges of the cam plate and the mounting bolts.

Adjustment

Check that the pulleys spin freely, and loosen them with a 5mm Allen wrench on the front, and an open-end wrench on the back. The pulleys should rest on the narrow portion of the cam, which gives the greatest mechanical advantage when the brakes are applied. You change pad spacing by changing the location of the cam on the cable.

Use a 17mm wrench on the nut surrounding the mounting bolt to center the brake or to adjust spring tension. Loosen the mounting bolt, make *small* adjustments to the 17mm nut, and tighten the mounting bolt down again.

Once the adjustments are set, tighten the cam onto the cable so it will not slip.

Pad positioning and replacement

The pad eye bolt is held on the front with a 5mm Allen wrench. The bolt in the back is adjusted using a 10mm open wrench. The pads should be toed in slightly. As the pads wear, they tend to slide up the rim and rub the tire, so check this adjustment periodically.

TROUBLE-SHOOTING

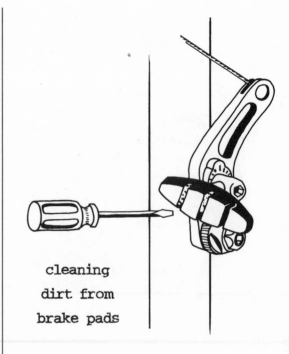

cleaning
dirt from
brake pads

BRAKE TROUBLESHOOTING —NOISE

The first thing to check with any brake is that it stops the bike!

❶ While the bike is stationary, pull each lever and see that it firmly engages the brake while the lever is still at least a finger's width away from the handlebar grip. If not, skip to **Cable adjustment** earlier in this chapter (or to **Hydraulic systems** if that is what you have).

❷ Move at 10 mph or so, and apply each brake one at a time. By itself, the rear brake should be able to lock up the rear wheel and skid the tire, and the front brake alone should come on hard enough that it will cause the bike to pitch forward. Careful. Don't overdo it.

If you can't stop the bike quickly, you must make some adjustments and, perhaps, do a little cleaning. A brake

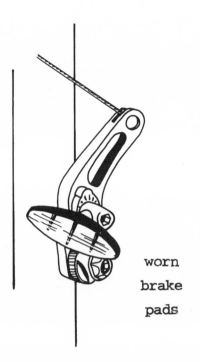

worn
brake
pads

TROUBLE-
SHOOTING

works by forcing the brake pads into contact with the rim (or disc) to create friction. Anything that reduces the ability of these surfaces to generate friction against each other compromises braking. With this in mind, it should be obvious that these surfaces need to be clean and dry, that they should line up well with each other, and that the mechanism to pull them into contact should move freely and pull at an angle that offers high mechanical advantage.

That said, you can probably generate this **brake inspection list** to perform frequently:

❶ Check that the cables have enough tension to pull the pads against the rims without the levers contacting the grips, and that they are loose enough to allow the wheels to turn without dragging on the pads when centered between them. See **Adjusting cable tension** below to adjust.

❷ Check for and remove any grease or glaze buildup on rims and pads. Grease can be removed with rags or solvent, and lightly buffing surfaces with sandpaper will remove glaze. Solvent residues on pads and rims cause brake squeal. You can remove such residues with soap and water.

❸ Check that the pads are not excessively worn (if they have grooves, make sure these are not worn off) and that they contact the rims effectively. Dig out any rocks or pieces of aluminum that are embedded in the pads to prevent rim damage. Replace or adjust pads as needed, and adjust the brake (see section under your brake) to get the desired response.

❹ Check the cables for fraying, wear, and free movement, and that the angle the cable meets each cantilever brake arm is close to 90 degrees (pulling at right angles generates the most leverage). If replacing, see **Cable installation**. Recognize that cables, housings, and pads are maintenance items; replace them frequently with good quality ones. Even new, poor quality, pads can require more than twice as much distance to stop as good ones!

❺ Check that the brakes are centered (the pads don't rub the rim) and that they apply and return easily. Readjust as needed (see adjustment section for your brake).

6 If the brakes squeal, try cleaning the rims and pads as in (2) above. If they still squeal, toe the pads in so that the forward corner of each pad touches the rim while the trailing corner is a millimeter or so away from it (see pad adjustment under your brake type).

TROUBLE-SHOOTING

VIII

cranks and bottom brackets

"If you don't have time to do it right,
you must have time to do it over."

— ANONYMOUS

tools

5mm and 8mm Allen wrenches
pliers
file
crank puller
crank bolt wrenches (Allen & socket)
chainring nut tool
Shimano splined bottom-bracket cup tool
3/8-inch drive socket
screwdriver
adjustable pin tool
lockring spanner
pin spanner

OPTIONAL
shop-style fixed- cup installation tool

1. CREAKING NOISES

Those mysterious creaking noises can be enough to drive you nuts. Just as you think you have your bike tuned to perfection, a little noise comes along to ruin your ride. What's worse is these annoying little creaks, pops and groans can be a bear to locate. Pedaling-induced noises can originate from almost anything connected to your crankset, starting with the cleats on your shoes all the way down to the spot where your crankarms join up with the bottom-bracket spindle, loose chainrings or poorly adjusted bearings. Of course, they could also originate from seemingly unrelated components like your seat or your handlebars.

Before spending hours overhauling your drivetrain, spend some time trying to isolate the source of the noise. Try different pedals and shoes, pedaling out of the saddle and try to avoid flexing the handlebars. If the source of the creak turns out to be one of those components, turn to the appropriate chapter for directions on how to correct the problem.

If the creaking is in the crank area:

❶ Check to make sure that the chainring bolts are tight, and tighten them if they are not.

❷ If that does not solve the problem, make certain that the crankarm bolts

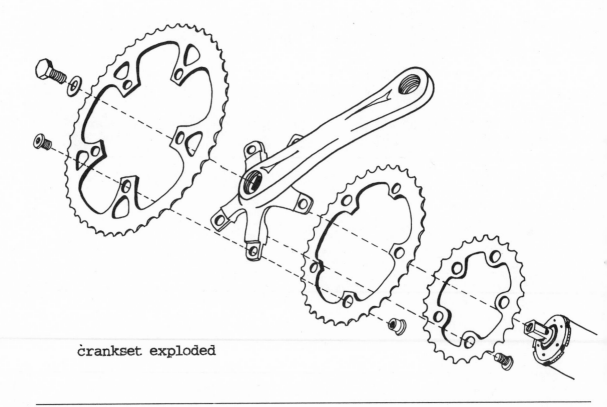

crankset exploded

creaks

are tight. If they are not, the resulting movement between the crankarm and the bottom-bracket spindle is a likely source of noise. If you are using cranks and a bottom-bracket of different brands, check with the manufacturers or your local shop to make sure that the bottom-bracket spindle has the same taper as the inside of the hole in the crank, and that they are recommended for use together. Incompatible cranks and spindles will never properly join and are a potential problem area.

❸ The bottom bracket itself can creak due to improper adjustment, lack of grease, cracked bearings, worn parts, or loose cups. All of these things require adjustment or overhaul procedures, outlined later in this chapter.

❹ Now for the bad news. If creaking persists, the problem *could* be rooted in your frame. Creaks can originate from cracks in and around the bottom-bracket shell, so be sure to check for that. The threads in your bottom bracket shell could also be worn to the point that they allow the cups to move slightly. Neither of these is a good sign, unless, of course, you were hoping for a good excuse to buy a new frame.

2. CLUNKING NOISES

❶ Grab the crankarm, and push on it side-to-side. If there is play, see **Adjusting the bottom bracket** later in this chapter.

❷ Grab each pedal and wobble them to check for play. See **Pedal adjustment** in Chapter 9 if they are loose.

134

3. HARD-TO-TURN CRANKS

If the cranks are hard to turn, you really ought to overhaul your bottom bracket — unless you want to continue boosting the egos of your cycling companions. The steps are outlined later in this chapter.

CRANKARMS AND CHAINRINGS

Crank removal and installation

Depending on the crankset, you will either need a socket wrench or a large Allen wrench to remove the crank bolt and a crank puller to take off the crankarms.

Most cranks these days take either a 14mm or 15mm socket wrench or a 7mm or 8mm Allen wrench. You may still run across a few of those old French TA cranks with bolts that take a 16mm socket.

REMOVAL:

❶ Remove the dust cap, if it's there. Depending on the type, use a 5mm Allen wrench, a two-pin dust cap tool, or a screwdriver.

❷ Remove the crank bolt, using the appropriate wrench.

❸ Back-out the center bolt of the crank puller so that the two parts of the tool are flush.

❹ Thread the crank puller into the hole in the crankarm. Be sure that you thread it in as far as it can go; otherwise, you will damage the threads when you begin to turn the push bolt in the center.

❺ Tighten the crank-puller bolt

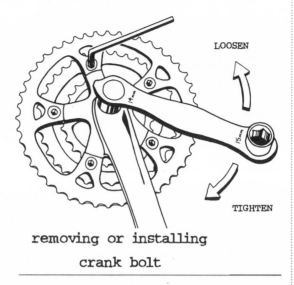

LOOSEN

TIGHTEN

removing or installing
crank bolt

clockwise, either with the socket wrench or the included handle until the crankarm pulls off of the spindle. Unscrew the puller from the crankarm.

INSTALLATION:

❶ Slide the crankarm onto the bottom bracket spindle. **DO NOT** apply grease to either part. Grease allows the crank to slide on too far and could deform it.

❷ Install the crank bolt. Apply grease to the threads, and tighten. Here is where a torque wrench comes in handy. I recommend tightening it down to about 35 to 45 foot-pounds. If you're not using a torque wrench, make sure the bolt is

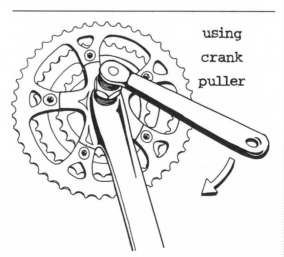

using
crank
puller

cranks and
bottom brackets

crank arm
removal and
installation

quite snug, but don't muscle it into submission.

❸ Removing and reinstalling the right crank arm could affect shifting, so check the front derailleur adjustment. (See Chapter 5.)

❹ You're done. Go ride your bike.

Chainrings

You should get into the habit of checking your chainrings regularly. They do wear out and need to be replaced. It's hard to say how often, so include your chainrings as part of your regular maintenance checklist. Check your chainrings for wear, when you replace your chain.

The chainring teeth should be checked periodically for wear; the chainring bolts should be checked periodically for tightness; the chainrings themselves should be checked for trueness.

❶ Wipe the chainring down and inspect each tooth. The teeth should be uniform in size and shape. Check for side-to-side bends as well. With newer chainrings, it is easy to mistake some built-in shift-enhancing asymmetries for wear. Shifting ramps on the sides, meant to speed chain movement between the rings, often look like cracks. On some chainrings, teeth vary in height to assist shifting.

If the teeth are wave- or hook-shaped, the chainring needs to be replaced. The chain should probably be replaced as well (see Chapter 4), since this tooth

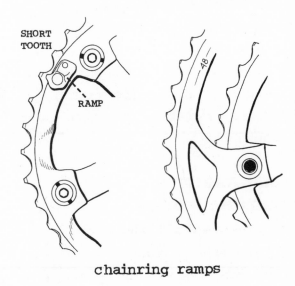

SHORT TOOTH

RAMP

48

chainring ramps

shape effectively changes the spacing between teeth and accelerates wear on the chain.

❷ Remove minor gouges in the chainrings with a file.

❸ If an individual tooth is bent, try carefully bending it back with a pair of pliers or a Crescent wrench.

❹ While turning the crank slowly, watch where the chain exits the bottom of the chainring. See if any of the teeth are reluctant to let go of the chain. That can cause chain suck. Locate any offending teeth and see if you can correct the problem. If the teeth are really chewed up or cannot be improved with pliers and a file, the chainring should be replaced.

Chainring bolts

Check that the bolts are tight by turning them clockwise with a 5mm Allen wrench. If, as you try to tighten the bolt, the nut on the back side turns, hold it with a two-pronged chainring tool designed especially for this purpose. A screwdriver will work in a pinch.

Warped chainrings

❶ Looking down from above, turn the crank slowly and see whether the chainrings wobble back and forth relative to the plane of the front derailleur.

❷ If they do, make sure there is no play in the bottom bracket. If there is play, adjust your bottom bracket by following the directions outlined later in this chapter. There is usually a little bit of chainring wobble and flex when you pedal hard, but excessive wobbling will compromise shifting. Small, localized bends can be straightened with a Crescent wrench. If it's *really* bent, replace it.

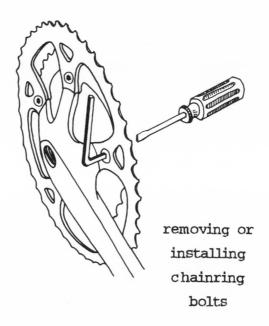

removing or
installing
chainring
bolts

Bent crankarm spiders

If you installed a new chainring and are still seeing serious back-and-forth wobble, chances are good that the spider arms on your crank are bent. If the crank is new, this is a warranty item, so take it to your bike shop.

Chainring replacement

Replacing either of the two largest chainrings is easy. Simply unscrew the five Allen bolts holding them on the chainring. (See illustration on page 134.) You may need to hold the nut on the backside with either the specially-made tool I mentioned before or a thin screwdriver. Install the new rings and tighten the bolts.

To replace the inner chainring, you must first pull off the crankarm (see procedure outlined earlier in this chapter). Remove the Allen bolts holding the chainring on. They are threaded directly into the crankarm.

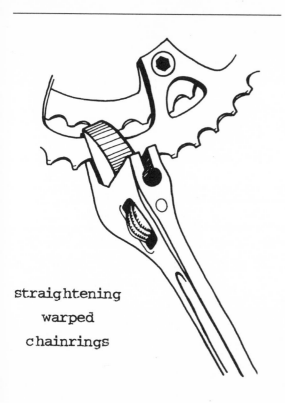

straightening
warped
chainrings

warped
and bent
chainrings

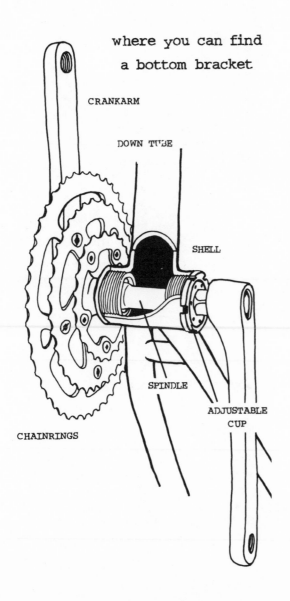

where you can find a bottom bracket

CRANKARM

DOWN TUBE

SHELL

SPINDLE

ADJUSTABLE CUP

CHAINRINGS

bottom brackets

Install the new ring and tighten the bolts. Replace the crankarm (outlined earlier in this chapter). Then ride your bike.

Note: Since the start of 1996, Shimano XTR cranks rely on a thread-on cassette system that allows you to spin off all three chainrings from the crankarm as a single unit. You can then replace individual chainrings or simply pop on a whole new set.

BOTTOM BRACKETS

Most bottom brackets thread into the frame's bottom bracket shell. Simple enough, but it's important to remember that not all of these threads are the same.

Almost all mountain bikes use English standard threads. That translates into a 1.370-inch diameter and a thread pitch of 24 threads per inch. These numbers are usually engraved on the bottom bracket cups. If you are replacing a bottom bracket, make sure that the new cups have the same threads. It is important to remember that the threads on the drive side of an English standard bottom bracket are left-hand threads. In other words, the right-hand cup is tightened by turning *counter*clockwise. Meanwhile, the threads on the left cup are right-hand threads and are, therefore, tightened *clockwise*.

Other threads you may run across are Italian (with a 36mm diameter), French and Swiss (both of these come in 35mm diameter, but use different thread directions). These thread patterns are particularly rare on mountain bikes.

There are bottom-bracket spindle/bearing combinations that do not rely on threaded cups. Some utilize a sealed bearing connected to the frame using a snapring fitted in a groove into an unthreaded bottom bracket shell. Others rely on a threaded cartridge. That cartridge fits into the threaded bottom bracket shell.

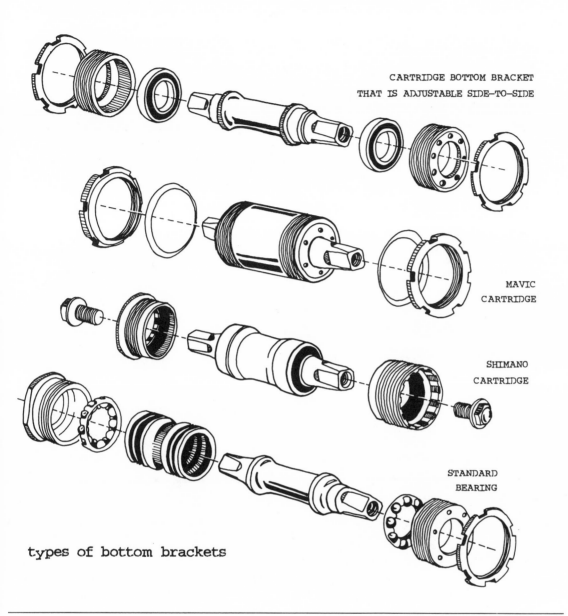

CARTRIDGE BOTTOM BRACKET
THAT IS ADJUSTABLE SIDE-TO-SIDE

MAVIC
CARTRIDGE

SHIMANO
CARTRIDGE

STANDARD
BEARING

types of bottom brackets

Lockrings thread onto the cartridge itself and then tighten against the ends of the bottom bracket shell.

BOTTOM-BRACKET INSTALLATION

Installation of Shimano cartridge-sealed bottom brackets

 As of this writing, most mountain bike bottom brackets come in sealed cartridge units (Shimano style) that are installed with a splined tool attached to a 3/8-inch socket wrench.

❶ Slide the cartridge into the bottom-bracket shell, paying particular attention to the right and left markings on the cartridge. The cup with the raised lip and left-hand thread is the right-hand cup.

❷ Using the splined cup tool with either an open-end wrench on it or a 3/8-inch drive socket wrench, tighten the right (the drive side) cup until the lip seats against the face of the bottom bracket shell.

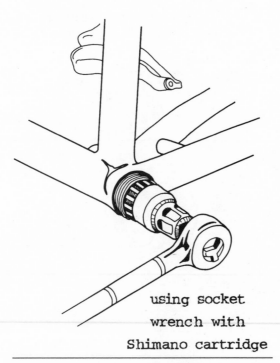

using socket
wrench with
Shimano cartridge

Note: Almost all mountain bikes have English threads, so you will probably be tightening this cup *counter*clockwise. ❸ Insert the non-drive side cup, and, with the same tool, turn it clockwise until it fits tightly against the cartridge. (See Appendix for recommended torque.) There is no adjustment of the bearings to be done; you can put on the crank now.

Installation of cup-and-cone bottom brackets

The old-style cup-and-cone bottom brackets are still fairly common. They use ball bearings that ride between cone-shaped bearing surfaces on the spindle and cup-shaped races in the threaded cups. One cup, called the fixed cup, has a lip on it and fits on the drive side of the bike. The other, called the

adjustable cup, has a lockring that threads onto the outside of the cup and snugs up against the face of the bottom bracket shell. The individual ball bearings are often held together by a retaining cage, though a lot of folks prefer to do without the retainer. They work fine either way.

In order for this type of system to turn smoothly, it is important that the bearing surfaces of the cups are parallel. Since they thread into the bottom bracket shell, the threads on both sides of the shell must be lined up with each other. The end faces of the shell must also be parallel. If you have any doubts about your frame and are installing an expensive cup-and-cone bottom bracket, it is a good idea to have the bottom bracket shell tapped (threaded) and faced by a qualified shop possessing the proper tools.

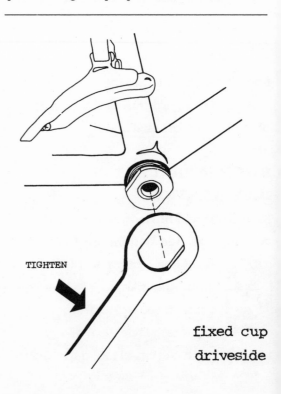

TIGHTEN

fixed cup
driveside

VIII

❶ Unless you have a high-quality fixed cup tool, have a shop install the fixed cup for you. Your shop probably has the type of tool that ensures the fixed cup threads in straight, and holds the wrench flats so that it can be properly tightened. If you do have such a tool and will be installing the fixed cup, remember that English threaded fixed cups are tightened *counter*clockwise.

❷ Wipe the inside surface of the fixed cup with a clean rag, and put a layer of clean grease on to the bearing surfaces.

❸ Wipe the inside of the other cup clean and coat it with grease as well.

❹ Wipe the axle down with a clean rag.

❺ Figure out which end of your bottom bracket spindle (or axle) is the drive side. The drive side will either be marked with an "R," or you can simply tell by choosing the side with the longer end (when measured from the bearing surface). If there is no marking and no length difference, the spindle orientation is irrelevant.

Slide one set of bearings onto the drive side end of the axle. If you're using a retainer cage, make sure you put it on right. The balls, rather than the retainer cage, should rest against the axle bearing surfaces. If you're still confused, there is one easy test: If it's right it'll turn smoothly; if it's wrong it won't.

If you have loose ball bearings with no retainer cage, stick them into the greased cup. Most rely on nine balls; you can confirm that you are using the correct number by inserting and

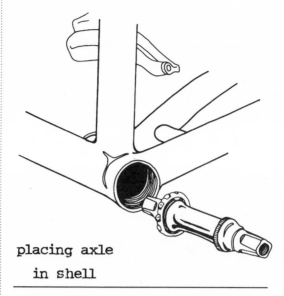

placing axle in shell

removing the axle and checking to make sure that they are evenly distributed in the grease with no extra gap for more balls.

❻ Slide the axle into the bottom bracket so it pushes the bearings into the fixed cup. You can use your pinkie to stabilize the end of the axle as you slide it in.

❼ If the bottom bracket has a protective plastic sleeve, insert it in the shell against the inside edge of the fixed cup. These sleeves are used to keep dirt and rust from falling from the frame tubes into the bearings.

❽ Now turn your attention to the other cup. Drop the bearing set into the adjustable cup. If you are using a bearing retainer, make sure it is properly oriented.

❾ Without the lockring, thread the adjustable cup (clockwise) by hand into the shell over the axle. If you can do it by hand, screw it all the way until the bearings seat between the axle and cup.

cranks and bottom brackets

cup-and-cone bottom-bracket installation

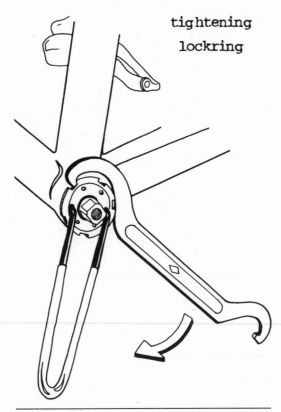

tightening lockring

❿ Locate the appropriate tool for tightening the adjustable cup. Most cups have two holes that accept the pins of an adjustable cup wrench (called a "pin spanner"). The other common type of adjustable cup has two flats for a wrench. On this type you may use an adjustable wrench.

⓫ Carefully tighten the adjustable cup against the bearings, taking great care not to overtighten. Turn the axle periodically with your fingers to ensure that it moves freely. If it binds up, you have gone too far, back it off a bit. The danger of overtightening is that the bearings can force dents into the bearing surfaces of the cups, and the bottom-bracket axle will never turn smoothly again.

⓬ Screw the lockring onto the adjustable cup, and select the proper tool for your lockring. Lockrings come in different shapes, and so do lockring spanners; make sure yours mate properly with each other.

⓭ Tighten the lockring against the face of the bottom-bracket shell with the lockring spanner, while holding the adjustable cup in place with a pin spanner. This is best done with the bicycle upside down, so you can pull down hard on the wrenches.

⓮ As you snug the lockring up against the bottom-bracket shell, check the bottom-bracket spindle periodically. It should turn smoothly without free play in the bearings. I recommend installing the drive-side crankarm at this time (outlined earlier in this chapter). Now you can grasp the crank and wobble it side to side to see if there is free play.

⓯ Adjust the cup so that the axle play is just barely eliminated. While holding the cup in place, tighten the lockring as tightly as you can so the bottom bracket does not come out of adjustment while riding. You may have to repeat this step a time or two until you get the adjustment *just* right.

Installation of other types of bottom brackets

The two bottom-bracket types mentioned earlier in this chapter probably represent about 95 percent of the mountain bikes in circulation. There are, however, a few variations worth mentioning.

Cartridge-bearing bottom brackets

with adjustable cups are reasonably easy to install. These come with a pair of adjustable cups for both ends. With this type, you simply install the drive-side cup and lockring, slide the cartridge in (or if it is a type with the bearings pressed into the cups, slide the axle in) and then install the other cup and lockring. The advantage of having two adjustable cups is that you can center the cartridge by moving it side-to-side in the bottom-bracket shell. If the chainrings end up too close or too far away from the frame, you can move one cup in and one out to shift the position of the entire cartridge.

If you have an unthreaded bottom bracket with snap-ring grooves, set the cartridge bearings against the stops on either end of the spindle. Install one snap-ring with snap-ring pliers, and install the entire assembly of axle and two bearings from the open side of the bottom-bracket shell. Install the other snap-ring and you're done.

Some cartridge-bearing bottom brackets bind up a bit during adjustment and installation and do not seem to want to free up. Sometimes a light tap on each end of the axle will do the trick.

Since there are so many different variations out there, you may have to rely on the instructions included with your bottom bracket, if I haven't covered the type you own.

OVERHAULING
THE BOTTOM BRACKET

 A bottom-bracket overhaul consists of cleaning or replacing the bearings, cleaning the axle and bearing surfaces, and re-greasing them. With any type, both crankarms must be removed.

Overhauling Shimano cartridge-sealed bottom brackets

Standard sealed Shimano-style cartridge bottom brackets are sealed units and cannot be overhauled. They must be replaced when they stop performing properly. Remove them by unscrewing the cups with the splined cup tool. Follow the directions outlined earlier in this chapter.

Overhauling cup-and-cone bottom brackets

❶ Remove the lockring with the lockring spanner.

❷ Remove the adjustable cup with the tool that fits yours.

❸ Leave the fixed cup in place.

❹ Clean the cups and spindle with a rag. There should be no need for a solvent unless the parts are really glazed. If one is required, I always recommend using a citrus-based solvent.

❺ Clean the bearings without removing them from their retainer cages with a citrus-based solvent. A simple way to do it is to shake the bearings about in a plastic bottle with solvent in it. A

overhauling
bottom
brackets

toothbrush may be required, and a solvent tank is certainly handy if you have access to one. Unless your bearings are in perfect shape, go ahead and replace them.

❻ Wash the bearings in soap and water to remove the solvent and any remaining grit. Towel them off thoroughly, and then let them dry completely.

❼ Follow the installation procedure described earlier in this chapter.

Overhauling other types of bottom brackets

If a cartridge-bearing bottom bracket becomes difficult to turn, the bearings must be replaced. If they are pressed into the cups, then you may also have to buy new cups. Be doubly sure to get the correct size.

overhauling
bottom
brackets

Read the installation procedure outlined above and then follow the steps in reverse to remove your crankset.

Replace the bearings. Reinstall your bottom bracket and crankarms.

You're done. Go ride your bike.

pedals

tools

15mm pedal wrench
small and large
 adjustable
 wrenches
3mm, 4mm, 5mm,
 and 6mm
 Allen wrenches
screwdriver
pliers
knife
grease
oil (chain lubricant)

FOR OVERHAULING
PEDALS:
7mm, 8mm, 9mm,
 10mm, 17mm or
 18mm open end
 wrenches
Shimano splined
 pedal tool
 - or - Look splined
 pedal tool
13mm cone wrench
8mm socket wrench
bench vise

*"*F*or everything, turn, turn, turn..."*

— THE BYRDS

To best serve its purpose, a bicycle pedal needs only to be firmly attached to the crankarm, and provide a stable platform for the shoe. A simple enough task, but you'd be amazed at the different approaches people have taken to acheive this goal. Still, for the purpose of our discussion, there are two basic types of mountain-bike pedals. One, the standard cage-type pedal with a toeclip and strap, which is the simplest and cheapest. The second or "clipless" type, with spring-loaded retention, has gained popularity over the last five years and is probably the most common version used on mid- to high-end mountain bikes.

Cage-type pedals are fairly common on lower-end bikes. They are relatively unintimidating for the novice rider, and the frame (or "cage") that surrounds the pedal provides a large, stable platform. Without a toeclip, the top and bottom of the pedal are the same and you can use just about any type of shoe. If you mount a toeclip without a strap, it can at least keep your foot from sliding forward and still allow easy release in almost any direction. When you add a toe strap, the combination works well to keep your foot on the pedal while riding even the roughest of single-track. The strap also allows you to pull on the upward part of your pedal stroke, giving you more power when you need it. Of course, as you add clips and straps, the pedal

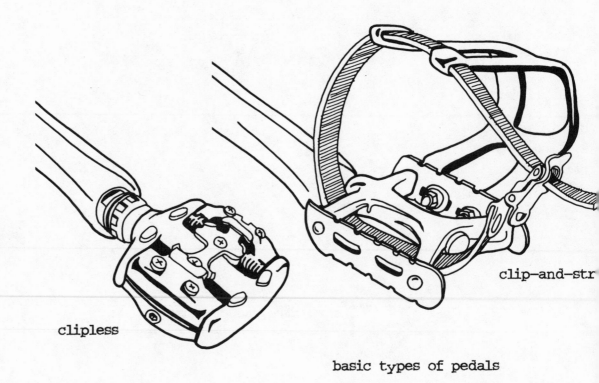

clipless

clip-and-str

basic types of pedals

becomes harder to enter and to exit, and boots or shoes with aggressive shoe tread designs become increasingly difficult to use.

Clipless models offer all of the advantages of a good clip-and-strap combination, yet allow easy entry and exit from the pedal. These pedals are more expensive and require special shoes and accurate mounting of the cleats. Your choice of shoes is, of course, limited to those models that offer stiff soles and accept the cleats necessary for your particular pedal. But once you have them dialed in, you will find that clipless pedals waste less energy through flex and slippage, and allow you to transfer more power directly to the pedals. This greater efficiency explains their almost universal acceptance among cross-country mountain bike racers.

This chapter explains how to remove and replace pedals, how to mount the cleats and adjust the release tension with clipless pedals, how to troubleshoot pedal problems, and how to overhaul and replace spindles on almost all mountain-bike pedals. Incidentally, I use the terms "axle" and "spindle" interchangeably.

PEDAL REMOVAL
AND INSTALLATION

Note that the right pedal axle is right-hand threaded and the left is left-hand threaded. Both unscrew from the crank in the pedaling direction. There's an interesting bit of history behind what led to the decision to thread pedal axles this way. In the early days of cycling, fixed gear bikes were common. It was decided that if the pedal bearings were to seize up on a fixed-gear bike, the pedal should unscrew from the crank rather than tear up the rider's feet and ankles. This isn't much of a concern on a modern road or mountain bike since the freewheel keeps seized pedal bearings from becoming anything more than an inconvenience.

Removal:

❶ Slide the 15mm pedal wrench onto the wrench flats of the pedal axle. Or, if the pedal axle is designed to accept it, you can use a 6mm Allen wrench from the back side of the crank arm. This is particularly handy on the trail, since you probably won't be carrying a 15mm wrench anyway. But, if you are at home and the pedal is on really tight, it'll probably be easier to use the standard pedal wrench. Some pedals, like the Time TMT, have no wrench flats

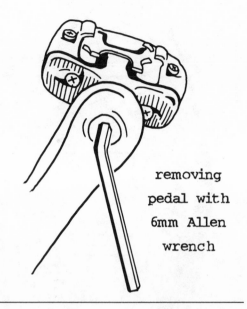

removing
pedal with
6mm Allen
wrench

and can only be removed with a 6mm Allen wrench.

❷ Unscrew the pedal in the appropriate direction. The right, or drive-side, pedal unscrews counterclockwise when viewed from that side. The left-side pedal is reverse threaded, so it unscrews in a clockwise direction when viewed from the left side of the bike. Once loosened, either pedal can be unscrewed quickly by turning the crank forward with the wrench engaged on the pedal spindle.

Installation:

❶ Use a rag to wipe the threads clean on the pedal axle and inside the crankarm.

❷ Grease the pedal threads.

❸ Start screwing the pedal in with your fingers, clockwise for the right pedal, *counter*clockwise for the left.

❹ Tighten the pedal with the 15mm pedal wrench or a 6mm Allen wrench. This can be done quickly by turning the cranks backward with the wrench

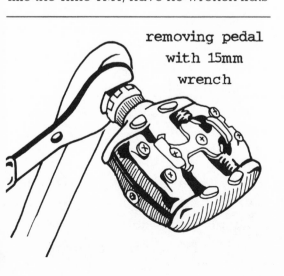

removing pedal
with 15mm
wrench

IX

pedals

removing
and
installing
clipless
pedals

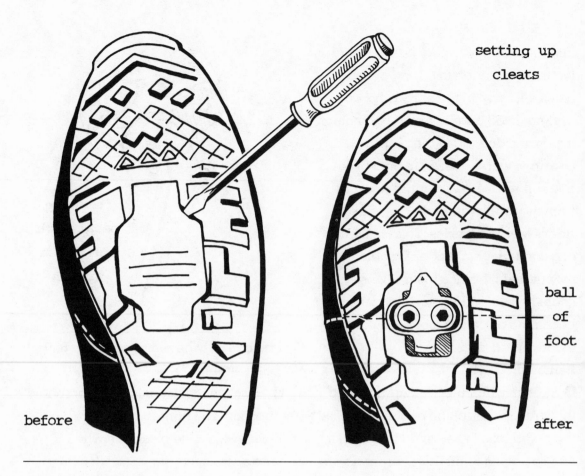

before

ball
of
foot

after

engaged on the pedal spindle.

SETTING UP CLIPLESS PEDALS

Installing and adjusting pedal cleats on the shoes.

The cleat is important because its position determines the fore-aft, lateral (side-to-side), and rotational position of your foot. If your pedals aren't properly oriented, it could eventually cause hip, knee or ankle problems.

❶ If your shoe has a pre-cut piece of rubber covering the cleat-mounting area, remove it. Pry an edge up with a screwdriver, and yank it off with some pliers. It is sometimes helpful to trim the edges with a knife before you try prying off the rubber cover. Warming it up with

a hair dryer also softens the glue.

❷ Put the shoe on, and mark the position of the ball of your foot (the big bump behind your big toe) on the outside of the shoe. You need to line up the ball of your foot over the pedal spindle. This will help you position the cleat. Take the shoe off, and continue drawing the line straight across the bottom of the shoe.

❸ Install the backing plate and threaded cleat plate inside the shoe. You will need to remove the shoe's sock liner. Grease or oil the cleat screw threads.

❹ In order to orient the cleat and set its fore-aft position, take the cleat that came with your pedals and attach it to your shoe. This usually requires a 4mm

Allen wrench. Orient the cleat in the appropriate direction. Some cleats have an arrow indicating forward; if not, the instructions accompanying your pedals probably specify which direction the cleat should point. Position the cleat in the middle of its lateral- and rotational- adjustment range. Center it using the mark you made in Step 2. Snug the bolts down enough that the cleat won't move when clipped in or out of the pedals, but don't tighten them down fully yet. Follow the same steps with your other shoe.

❺ In order to set the lateral position, put the shoes on, sit on the bike, and clip into the pedals. Ride around a bit. Notice the position of your feet. Pedaling is more efficient the closer the feet are to the plane of the bike, but you don't want to turn them in so far that you end up bumping your cranks. So check the position to ensure that your feet are not so close to the crankarms that your shoes or ankles rub on the cranks, or so far from the cranks that your feet are inefficiently or uncomfortably splayed out. Take the shoes off and adjust the cleats if necessary and get back on the bike and clip in again.

❻ In order to set the rotational position, ride around some more. Notice if your feet feel twisted and uncomfortable. You may feel pressure on either side of your heel from the shoe. If necessary, remove your shoes and correct the cleat position. Some pedals offer free-float, allowing the foot to rotate freely for a

few degrees before releasing. Precise cleat adjustment is less important if the pedal is free-floating.

❼ Once your cleat position feels right, trace the cleats with a pen so that you can ensure the cleat stays put and you can find the position again. While holding the cleat in place, tighten the bolts down firmly. Hold the Allen wrench close to the bend so that you do not exert too much leverage and strip the bolts. From the inside of the shoe, place a waterproof sticker over the opening. Replace the sock liner.

❽ When riding, bring the Allen wrench along, since you may want to fine-tune this adjustment over the course of a few rides.

Adjusting release-tension on clipless pedals

If you find the factory release-adjustment setting to be too loose or too restrictive, adjust the release tension.

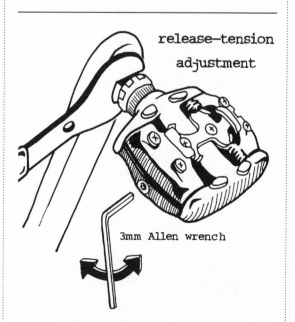

release-tension adjustment

3mm Allen wrench

bumper

OnZa clipless pedal

Most clipless pedals allow you to adjust the spring tension. The adjusting screws are usually located at the front and rear of the pedal. The screws affect the tension of the nearest set of clips. The adjusters are usually operated with a small (usually 3mm) Allen wrench. OnZa and Look pedals are adjusted differently, so see **Other types** below.

1. Locate the tension-adjustment screws.

2. To loosen the tension-adjustment, turn the screw counterclockwise, and to tighten it, turn it clockwise. It's the classic "lefty loosey, righty tighty" approach. There usually are click stops in the rotation of the screw. Tighten or loosen one click at a time (1/4-1/2 turn), and go riding to test the adjustment. Many types include an indicator that moves with the screw to show relative adjustment. Make certain that you do not back the screw out so far that it comes out of the spring plate.

Note: With Ritchey clipless pedals, you will decrease the amount of free-float in the pedal as you increase the release tension.

Other types: Current Look mountain pedals have a single 5mm bolt that adjusts both sides. It has a large window like a ski binding with a pointer to show the relative adjustment. The older, one-sided Look models have a small slotted screw in the center to adjust the tension.

Onza clipless pedals rely on elastomer bumpers to provide release tension. You can adjust OnZas by changing the elastomer. Bumpers of varying hardness are included with the pedals and are available from dealers. Onza's black bumpers are the hardest, and the clear ones the softest. There are several grades in between. The harder the bumper, the greater the release tension. To replace bumpers, unscrew the two Allen bolts holding each bumper on. Pull the old bumper out, put in the new one. While you are at it, make sure that the Phillips screws that hold in the cleat guides are tight, since they have a tendency to loosen up and fall out.

Time pedals have no tension adjustment, so adjustment is a real breeze.

OVERHAULING PEDALS

 Just like a hub or bottom bracket, pedal bearings and bushings need to be cleaned and re-greased regularly. Most pedals have a lip seal around the axle where it enters the pedal. Pedals without one get dirty inside very quickly.

No matter what type you have, you need to remove the pedal from the bike for an overhaul. There is a wide

pedals

variation in mountain-bike pedal designs. This book is not big enough to go into great detail about the inner workings of every single model. Speaking in general terms, pedal guts fall into two broad categories: assemblies that install into the pedal as a unit, and those that use standard cups and cones. Most modern pedals have a nut surrounding the axle on the end adjacent to the crank. You must undo this nut to remove the axle assembly. This type of pedal is closed on the outboard end. The axle assemblies on older pedal designs — and a few newer models — are accessed from the outboard end by removing a dust cap.

Before you start, spend some time figuring out how the axle assembly is put together. This way you will know how to approach disassembly. In a few cases, you may have to do this after you complete step one in the overhaul process. Either way, you need to know how your pedal is put together in order to overhaul it. Some examples are listed below.

A few rare pedals have a pressed-in axle and are not serviceable at home. Older Grafton pedals are an example of this. Even if you remove the cage, there is no access on either side of the pedal; the axle is pressed into Teflon or Nylon bushings.

Some pedals — even expensive clipless models (Tioga comes to mind) — have no bearings at all. Instead, they just use bushings inside a plastic

axle sleeve. If you see no ball bearings or cartridge bearings at the small end of the axle, you probably have such a pedal.

Some pedals use a combination of bushings and bearings. Scott, for example, relies on a bushing on the inboard side of the pedal and a cartridge bearing on the outboard end.

Shimano pedals usually have two sets of loose bearings — one set at the outboard end and another in the middle. These are combined with a bushing on the inboard end. You will see the tiny ball bearings at the small end of the axle.

There are two versions of Look clipless mountain pedals. The older models, marketed under the Look and Campagnolo names, accept a large plastic cleat and clip in on one side only. They closely resemble Look's road pedal in design and function. The newer Look models resemble the design approach taken by Shimano, utilizing a small steel SPD-style cleat on the shoe. Axle assemblies in the older models are accessed with an 18mm open-end wrench. The newer Looks require a special splined tool. Both types have a needle-bearing cartridge pressed deep into the pedal body, and a standard cartridge bearing on the inboard end of the axle. If you have this system, there are no nuts on the thin end of the axle so you can skip Step 2 in the overhaul procedure.

The Look axle system tends to stay

overhauling
clipless
and standard
pedals

very clean. If dirt *does* get in, it usually just gets into the inboard cartridge bearing. No problem, because that can be easily replaced. If, in the unlikely event that the needle bearings get dirty, you can clean out the pedal body with solvent and a clean toothbrush. Dry it, and then regrease it. Reassemble it, and you are done.

OVERHAULING CLIPLESS AND STANDARD PEDALS WITH A NUT ON THE INBOARD SIDE

Level 2. Shimano, Tioga, Scott and Look are good examples.

❶ With the tool designed for your pedal, remove the axle assembly by unscrewing the nut surrounding the axle where it enters the inboard side of the pedal. See note below regarding thread direction. Shimano supplies a plastic splined tool with its pedals. Use a large adjustable wrench to turn the tool. Most other pedals simply take a 17mm open-end wrench. Recent Look pedals use their own, proprietary splined tool (which conveniently has not been supplied with the pedal. However, *it is* sold separately). Older Look pedals usually just need an 18mm open-end wrench. **Note:** The threads *inside* the body are exactly the reverse of those that screw into the crankarm. So, the internal threads on the right (drive-side) axle are left-hand threaded. That means the right axle assembly unscrews clockwise. On the left side, the threads are right-hand threaded, and its axle assembly unscrews counterclockwise. It's confusing, but unlike the crankarm threads, pedal axles are threaded so that pedaling forward *tightens* the assembly in, rather than loosens it. The axle assembly housing is often plastic and can crack if you turn it the wrong way, so be careful. You can usually hold the pedal body with your hand while you unscrew the assembly. If it *is* too tight, you can hold the pedal body with a vise. The threads are small and numerous; expect it to take many turns.

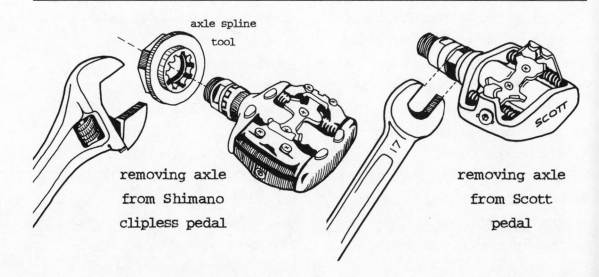

axle spline
tool

removing axle
from Shimano
clipless pedal

removing axle
from Scott
pedal

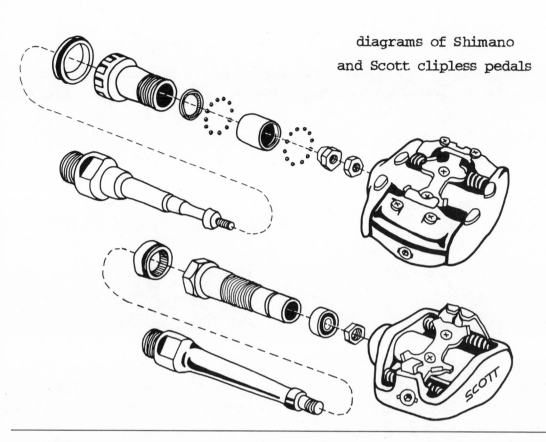

diagrams of Shimano
and Scott clipless pedals

pedals

❷ Once you have removed the pedal body, take a look at the axle/bearing/bushing assembly. You will notice either one or two nuts on the thin end of the axle. These nuts serve to hold the bearings and/or bushings in place. Remove the nuts.

If the axle has just a single nut on the end, you can simply hold the axle's large end with the 15mm pedal wrench and unscrew the little nut with a 9mm wrench (or whatever fits it). The nut will be very tight, since it has no locknut.

If the axle has two nuts on the end, they are tightened against each other. To remove them, hold the inner nut with a wrench while you unscrew the outer nut with another. Shimano and Tioga pedals both use two nuts in this fashion. On the Shimano pedals, the inner nut

acts as a bearing cone. Be careful not to lose the tiny ball bearings as you unscrew the cone.

❸ Now that you have it all apart, clean everything you can get your hands on.

If it is a loose-bearing pedal, use a rag to clean the ball bearings, the cone, the inner ring that the bearings ride on at the end of the plastic sleeve (it looks like a washer), and the bearing surfaces on either end of the little steel cylinder. Clean the axle, and the inside of the plastic axle sleeve as well. If you want to get the bearings really clean, wash them in the sink in soap and water with the sink drain plugged. The motion is the same as washing your hands, and results in both the bearings and your hands being clean for a sterile reassembly. Blot dry.

overhauling
clipless
and standard
pedals

If, on a pedal using a cartridge bearing, the cartridge is dirty or worn out, just replace it. These usually have steel bearing covers that cannot be pried off without damaging them. If you do pry the covers off, the bearing can only be used without the cover. So why not just go ahead and replace the whole thing?

On a bushing-only pedal, like Tioga, just wipe down the axle and the inside of the axle sleeve.

❹ Grease everything and reassemble it as it was.

overhauling loose-bearing pedals

With a loose-bearing pedal, you have some exacting work to do. On a Shimano, grease the bushing inside the plastic axle sleeve, and slide the axle into the sleeve. Slide the steel ring, on which the inner set of bearings rides, down onto the axle, and against the end of the sleeve. Make sure that the concave bearing surface faces out, away from the sleeve. Coat the ring with grease, and stick half of the bearings onto the outer surface of the ring. Slip the steel cylinder onto the axle

so that one end rides on the bearings. Make sure that all of the bearings are seated properly and none are stuck inside of the sleeve. To prevent the bearings from piling up on each other, and ending up inside the sleeve instead of on the races, grease the cone and start it on the axle a few threads. Place the remaining half of the bearings on the flanks of the cone. Being careful not to dislodge the bearings, screw the cone in until the bearings come close to the end of the cylinder but do not touch it. While holding the plastic sleeve, push the axle inward until the bearings seat against the end of the cylinder. Make sure that the first set of bearings is still in place. Screw the cone in. Tighten it with your fingers only, and loosely screw on the locknut.

❺ Adjust the axle assembly.

Pedals like the Scott, with only a bushing and a cartridge bearing, simply require that you tighten the nut against the cartridge bearing, while holding the other end of the axle with the 15mm pedal wrench. This secures

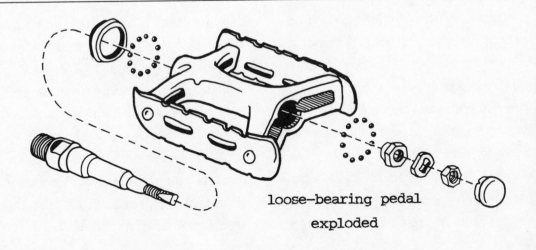

loose-bearing pedal
exploded

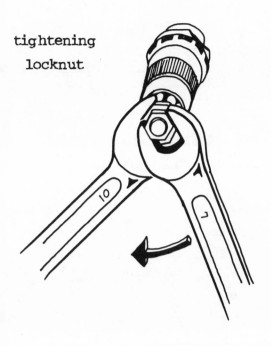

tightening
locknut

the inner ring of the cartridge bearing against the shoulder on the axle, and proper adjustment is assured.

With a bushing-only pedal, tighten the inner nut until the axle turns stiffly or not at all. Then just back the nut off slightly, until the assembly turns freely. With a wrench on each nut, tighten the outer nut against the inner. Check for freedom of motion and no play. Readjust as necessary.

With a Shimano loose-bearing assembly, hold the cone with a 10mm wrench and tighten the outer locknut down against it. Check the adjustment for freedom of rotation, and be sure there is no play. Readjust as necessary.

❻ Replace the axle assembly in the pedal body.

Smear grease on the outside of the assembly and on the inside of the pedal hole. This will act as a barrier to dirt and water. Screw the sleeve back

in place with the same wrench you used to remove it. Remember: Pay attention to proper thread rotation. Be careful; it is easy to overtighten and crack the plastic sleeve.

❼ Put the pedals back on your bike and you're done. Go ride your bike.

OVERHAULING LOOSE-BEARING PEDALS WITH A DUST CAP ON THE OUTBOARD END

❶ Remove the dust cap with the appropriate tool. This could be a pair of pliers, a screwdriver, an Allen wrench or a splined tool made especially for your pedals. It's pretty easy to figure out which one is needed to remove the cap.

❷ As if you were overhauling a hub, hold the cone on the outboard end of the axle with a cone wrench, and unscrew the locknut that secures it in place.

❸ Holding the pedal over a rag to catch the bearings, unscrew the cone. Keep the bearings from the two ends separate in case they differ in size or in number. Count them so you can put the right numbers back in when you reassemble the pedal.

❹ With a rag, clean the bearings, cones and bearing races. Clean the inside of the pedal body by pushing the rag through with a screwdriver. If there is a dust cover on the inboard end of the pedal body, you can pop that out with a screwdriver and clean it as well.

❺ If you want to get the bearings really clean, wash them in a plugged sink with

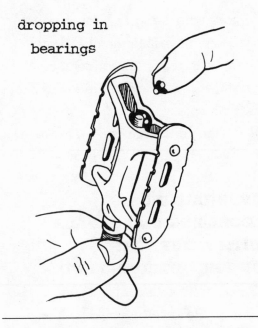

dropping in
bearings

soap and water. The motion is the same as washing your hands, and results in both the bearings and your hands being clean for a sterile reassembly. Blot dry.

❻ If you removed it, press the inboard dust cover back into the pedal body. Smear grease in the inboard bearing cup, and replace the bearings. Once all of the bearings are in place, there will be a gap equal to about half the size of one bearing.

❼ Drop the axle in, and turn the pedal over so that the outboard end is up. Smear grease in that end, and replace the bearings.

❽ Screw the cone in by hand until it almost contacts the bearings. This will help you avoid the hassle of chasing loose bearings across the floor.

❾ If there is a toothed washer on your pedal, slide it on and screw on the lock nut. While holding the cone with a cone wrench, tighten the lock nut.

❿ Check that the pedal spins smoothly

without play. Readjust as necessary.

⓫ Replace the dust cap.

⓬ Put the pedals back on your bike and you're done. Go ride your bike.

OVERHAULING CARTRIDGE BEARING PEDALS WITH OUTBOARD DUSTCAP

OnZa and Ritchey and a few other pedals use a brass bushing on the inboard (crank) end, and a sealed cartridge bearing on the outboard end. There is no internal sleeve to the pedal; the end nut is accessed from the outboard end by removing the dustcap.

❶ Take off the dustcap. Ritcheys take a 6mm Allen wrench, current OnZas take a screwdriver, and older OnZas use a 5mm Allen wrench.

❷ Hold the crank end of the axle with a 15mm pedal wrench, and unscrew the nut on the outboard end with an 8mm socket wrench.

❸ Push the axle out the inboard end, freeing the outboard cartridge bearing.

removing locknut
on OnZa—type pedals

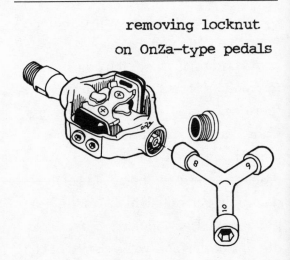

156

OnZa—type clipless
pedal exploded

❹ Clean and regrease the axle and the inside of the pedal body hole. Replace the cartridge bearing if necessary. On Ritcheys, the brass bushings inside the pedal body are also replaceable.

❺ Push the axle back into the pedal body, slip the cartridge bearing onto the outboard end of the axle, and thread on the end nut.

❻ While holding the crank end of the axle with a 15mm pedal wrench, tighten the little nut down against the cartridge bearing.

Note: Ritcheys will still have side play at this point; the dustcap is an integral part of the assembly. Once it is tightened down, the play goes away.

❼ Replace the dustcap.

❾ Put the pedals back on your bike and you're done. Go ride your bike.

LIGHTEN YOUR BIKE WITH AN AFTERMARKET TITANIUM SPINDLE

 Many manufacturers offer aftermarket titanium axles for high-end pedals. Some manufacturers offer only a titanium axle that is installed into the same sleeve, bushings, and bearings as the one it replaces. Other manufacturers sell a complete assembly, including the sleeve, bushings, and bearings.

If you are going to install a lightweight aftermarket axle or axle assembly into your pedals, make sure that you purchase one intended for your pedal brand and model. If all you are doing is replacing the axle, go ahead and follow the overhaul procedures outlined earlier in this chapter. If you bought the

lightening
your bike
with a
titanium
spindle

entire assembly, just take out your old assembly. Again (I obviously feel the need to say this often), pay attention to the direction of the threads. Using the procedures I outlined earlier in this chapter, install the new assembly.

Reinstall your pedals. You'll be amazed how much lighter your bike feels.... Or is that your wallet?

TROUBLESHOOTING

TROUBLESHOOTING PEDAL PROBLEMS

❶ Creaking noise while pedaling

a. The shoe cleats are loose or they are worn and need to be replaced (see cleat mounting and adjustment in this chapter).

b. Pedal bearings need cleaning and lubrication (see **Overhauling pedals** in this chapter).

c. The noise is originating from somewhere other than the pedals (see Chapter 8).

❷ Release or entry with clipless pedals is too easy or too hard

a. Release tension needs to be adjusted (see **Adjusting pedal release tension** in this chapter).

b. Pedal-release mechanism needs to be cleaned and lubricated. Clean off mud and dirt, and drip chain lubricant on the springs and spring contacts.

c. The cleats themselves need to be cleaned and lubricated. Clean off dirt and mud and put a dry chain lubricant or a grease like pure Teflon on the contact ends of the cleats.

d. The cleats are worn out: replace them.

e. The knobs on the sole that contact the pedal might be so tall that they prevent the cleat from engaging. Locate where the pedal edges contact the sole, and trim some of the rubber with a knife.

f. The clips on the pedal are bent down. Straighten them if you can, or replace them. If you can't repair or replace the clips, you may have to replace the

pedals

orthotics to correct the problem.

c. Fatigue and improper seat height can also contribute to joint pain. Pain right behind the kneecap can indicate that your saddle is too low. A pain in the back of the leg behind the knee suggests that your saddle is too high.

If any of these problems result in chronic pain, consult a specialist.

lubing release mechanism

entire pedal.

g. If it is hard to clip into your pedals, check the cleat guide at the center of the pedal. It is held on with two Phillips screws, and they may be loose or have fallen out.

❸ **You experience knee and joint pain while pedaling**

a. Cleat misalignment often causes pain on the sides of the knees, (see cleat adjustment instructions above).

b. If your foot naturally rolls inward (pronates), and your shoe and cleat are not allowing it to do so, then there is likely to be an increase in the tension on the iliotibial (I-T) band. That will eventually cause pain on the outside of the knee. You need to see a specialist because you will probably need

TROUBLE— SHOOTING

saddles and seatposts

"**Y**our view of the world pretty much depends on where you're sitting."

— C. P. ELLKEY

tools

**4mm, 5mm, 6mm
Allen wrenches
open-end wrenches
of various sizes
adjustable wrench
grease**

After a few hours on the bike, I can pretty much guarantee that you will be most aware of one component on your bike: the saddle. It is the part of your bike with which you are most ... uh ... *intimately* connected. Nothing can ruin a good ride faster than a poorly positioned or bad saddle.

The seatpost connects it to the frame. Some have shock absorbing systems that cushion the ride. Some bikes, like the Softride, employ a flexible beam attached to the front of the frame instead of a seatpost.

SADDLES

Most bike saddles are simply made up of a flexible plastic shell, some padding, a cover and a pair of rails. There are countless variations on (and a few notable exceptions to) this theme: Some have extra thick or high-tech padding; some have rails made of titanium, cro-moly or even carbon fiber; others have synthetic covers, covers made from Kevlar or covers made from the finest full-grain leather money can buy. You can expect to spend anywhere from $20 to $200 for a decent saddle, and price may not be the best indicator of what makes a saddle really good — namely comfort.

You have a lot of choices when you decide to pick a saddle. My best advice is to ignore weight, fashion and looks, and choose a saddle that is comfortable. I could go on for pages about hi-zoot gel padding, scientifically designed shells

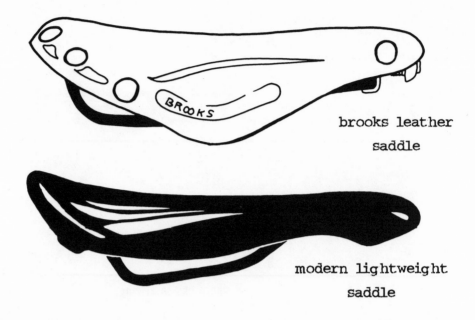

brooks leather
saddle

modern lightweight
saddle

that flex in just the right places at just the right moment, and all sorts of factors that engineers consider when designing a saddle. None of it would count for squat if, after reading it, you ran out and bought a saddle that turned out to be a giant pain in the rear. People are different and saddles are different. Try as many as you can before buying one.

Determine which saddle shape and design is the most comfortable for your body and then — and *only* then — start looking at things like titanium rails, fancy covers and all of the other things that improve a saddle. I know a lot of people who need 300- or 400-gram saddles with tons of thick padding to feel comfortable on even a short ride. I know others who can ride for hours on a skinny little 200-gram Selle Italia Flite. It's a matter of preference. Any decent bike shop worth its weight in titanium should let you try a saddle for a while before locking you into a sale.

Brooks and Ideale saddles have no plastic shell, foam padding or cover. They are simply constructed from a single piece of thick leather attached to a steel frame with large brass rivets. This was the main type of saddle up until the 1980s. Brooks still makes them. They even offer them with titanium rails these days. This sort of saddle requires a long break-in period and frequent applications of a leather-softening compound that comes with the saddle or from a shoe store. Like a lot of old bike parts, you either love 'em or you hate 'em. If you're not familiar with them by now, you'll probably hate 'em, so go out and buy a nice comfortable modern saddle.

A saddle with a plastic shell and foam padding requires little maintenance, except to keep it clean; and check that the rails are not bent or cracked (a good sign that you need to replace your saddle).

SADDLE POSITION

Even if you have found the perfect saddle, it can still feel like some medieval torture device if it isn't properly positioned. Saddle placement is the most important part of finding a comfortable riding position. Not only does saddle position affect how you feel on the bike, but with the saddle in the right place you suddenly become a much better rider. There are three basic elements to saddle position: tilt, fore-and-aft and saddle height.

The most common cause of numb crotch and butt fatigue is an improperly tilted saddle. The general rule of thumb is that you should keep the saddle level when you first install it. After a while, some people find that they prefer a slight upward or downward tilt to their saddles. I strongly recommend against making that tilt much more than a 1/4 inch. Too much upward tilt and you place too much of your body weight on the nose of the saddle. Too much downward tilt will cause you to scoot down the saddle as you ride. That puts unnecessary pressure on your back, shoulders and neck.

Fore-and aft-position determines where your butt sits on the saddle, the position of your knees relative to the pedals, and how much of your weight is transferred to your hands. Regardless of manufacturer, all saddles are designed to have your butt centered over the widest part. If this is not the case, reposition the saddle. You want to

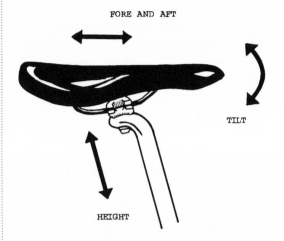

FORE AND AFT

TILT

HEIGHT

saddle adjustments

position the saddle so that you have a comfortable amount of bend in your arms, without feeling too cramped or stretched out. If you find that your neck and shoulders feel tighter than usual and your hands are going numb, then redistribute your weight by moving the saddle back. Fore-and-aft saddle position also affects how your legs are positioned relative to the pedals. Ideally, your fore and aft position should be such that your knee pushes straight down on the forward pedal when your crankarms are in a perfectly horizontal position.

Proper saddle height is key to transferring good power to the pedals. The ideal road-bike saddle height places your leg in a 90- to 95-percent extension when you're riding; however, you may find that this position to be too high for riding single-track. In order to improve your balance and center of gravity, I recommend bringing the

saddle
position

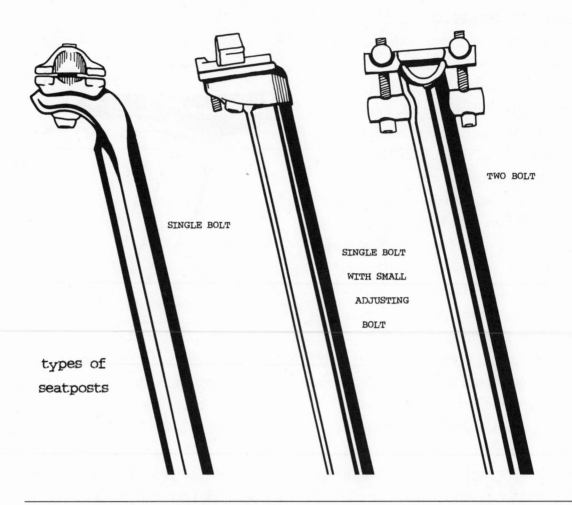

SINGLE BOLT

TWO BOLT

SINGLE BOLT
WITH SMALL
ADJUSTING
BOLT

types of
seatposts

saddle height down— how far depends on you and the kind of riding you do. Pro downhillers prefer very low saddle heights when compared to pro cross-country riders.

SEATPOST MAINTENANCE

A standard seatpost requires little maintenance other than removing it from the frame every few months. When you do that, wipe it down, regrease it and the inside of the frame's seat tube, and then reinstall it. This should prevent the seatpost from getting stuck in the frame (a very nasty and potentially serious problem). I have outlined the procedures for installing a new seatpost and for removing a stuck seatpost later in this chapter.

Suspension seatposts require periodic tune-ups. I have outlined the steps further on in this chapter.

Regularly check any seatpost for cracks or bends so that you can replace it before it breaks with you on it.

INSTALLING A SADDLE

Most seatposts have either one or two bolts for clamping the saddle. The single-bolt systems have either a vertical bolt or a horizontal bolt.

saddles and seatposts

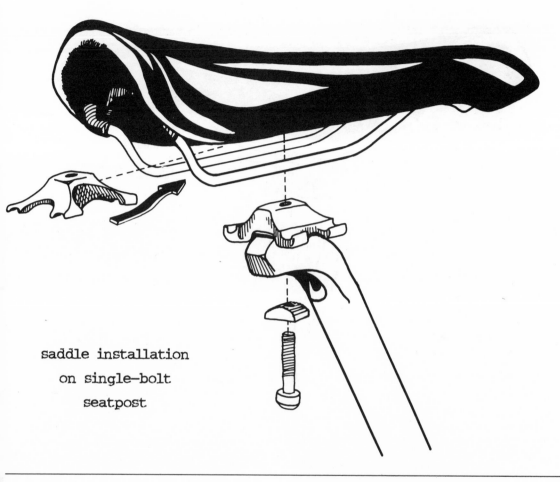

saddle installation
on single—bolt
seatpost

seatpost
installation

Remember those complicated heavy things on your first cheap bike? Those steel seatposts had the single horizontal bolt, which pulled together a large number of washers with ears to hold the saddle rails. Fortunately, most of us don't have to mess with that type of post anymore. The two-bolt posts can rely on one of two systems. In one, the two bolts work together by pulling the saddle into the clamp. On others, a smaller second bolt works to offset the force of the main bolt. No matter what type you have, it is reasonably easy to figure out how to remove, install and adjust the saddle.

SADDLE INSTALLATION ON SEATPOST WITH A SINGLE VERTICAL CLAMP BOLT

Systems with a single vertical bolt usually have a two-piece clamp that fastens onto the saddle rails. On most single-bolt models, saddle tilt is controlled by moving the clamp and saddle across an arc covered with small teeth. Before you tighten the clamp bolt, make sure there is not a second, much smaller bolt (or "set screw") that adjusts seat tilt. If it does, skip to the next section. ❶ Loosen the bolt until there are only a couple of threads still holding onto the

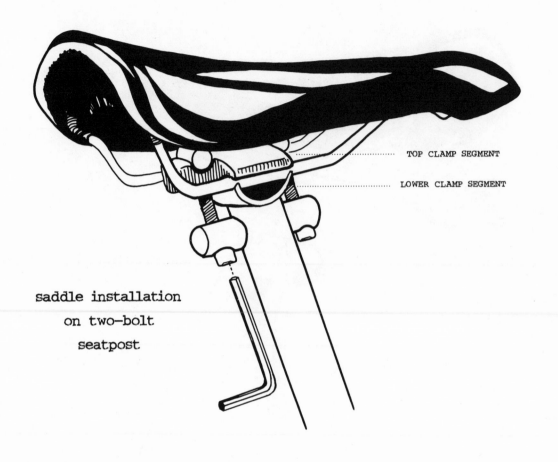

TOP CLAMP SEGMENT

LOWER CLAMP SEGMENT

saddle installation
on two—bolt
seatpost

upper clamp.

❷ Turn the top half of the clamp 90 degrees and slide in the saddle rails. Do it from the back where the space between the rails is wider. You might need to remove it completely from the bolt if the clamp is too large. If you do disassemble the clamp, pay attention to the orientation of the parts so you can put it back together the same way.

❸ Set the seat rails into the grooves in the lower part of the clamp, and set the top clamp piece on top of the rails. Slide the saddle to the desired fore-aft position.

❹ Tighten the bolt and check the seat

tilt. Readjust if necessary.

SADDLE INSTALLATION ON SEATPOST WITH LARGE CLAMP BOLT AND SMALL SET SCREW

❶ Loosen the large bolt until the top part of the clamp can either be removed or moved out of the way, so that you can slide the saddle rails into place.

❷ Set the saddle rails between the top and bottom sets of grooves in the seat clamp. Slide the saddle to the desired fore-aft position. Tighten the large bolt.

❸ To change saddle tilt, loosen the

large clamp bolt, and adjust the set screw as needed. Repeat until the desired adjustment is reached.

Note: On these types of seatposts, the set screw can be placed either vertically or horizontally. On those with a vertical set screw, the screw is usually just the large bolt. On those using a horizontal set screw, it is usually placed on the front portion of the seatpost. With a horizontal set screw, push down on the back of the saddle with the large bolt loose, to make sure the clamp and set screw are in contact.

INSTALLING SADDLE ON SEATPOST WITH TWO EQUAL-SIZED CLAMP BOLTS

❶ Loosen one or both of the bolts, so that the saddle rails slide into their grooves between the two sides of the clamp.

❷ Move the top part of clamp (note: some posts have two upper pieces) out of the way by turning it, or by removing it. Set the saddle rails into the grooves in the lower part of the clamp. Install the top clamp piece (or pieces) on top of the saddle rails.

❸ Slide the saddle to the desired fore-aft position. Tighten down one or both of the clamp bolts completely.

❹ Loosen one clamp bolt and tighten the other to change the tilt of the saddle. Repeat as necessary and tighten both bolts.

SEATPOST INSTALLATION INTO THE FRAME

❶ Grease the seatpost and the inside of the seat tube. Grease the seat lug binder bolt. If the seatpost comes with a sleeve that allows a thin, one-size-fits-all post fit your frame, grease it inside and out, and insert it.

❷ Insert the seatpost, and tighten the seat binder bolt. Some binder bolts are tightened with a wrench (usually a 5mm Allen), and some have a quick-release lever. To tighten a quick release, flip the lever open so that it is directly in line with the body of the bolt — in other words, about halfway open. Finger-tighten the adjusting nut, and then close the lever. It should be fairly snug, about tight enough to leave an impression in

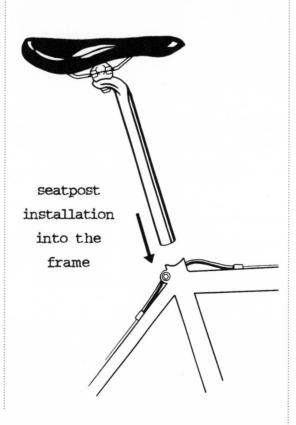

seatpost installation into the frame

closing quick release

the heel of your hand for a few moments. Adjust if necessary.

3 After the saddle is attached, adjust the seat height to your desired position. It is a good idea to mark this height on the post with an indelible marker or a

piece of tape. This way, if you remove it, you can just slide it right back into the proper place.

INSTALLING A SOFTRIDE SUSPENSION BEAM ONTO FRAME

The frame must be built to accept the beam, or you must purchase a retrofit kit from Softride to install it on a standard frame.

1 Attach the beam to the front frame mount with a steel pin. The underside of the beam's nose has a small steel eyelet that fits between two tabs on the bracket. These tabs are located on the top of the frame's top tube. With a soft hammer, tap the included pin through the bracket, through the eye on the bottom of the beam, and out through the hole in the other side of the bracket.

2 Attach the beam to the rear frame

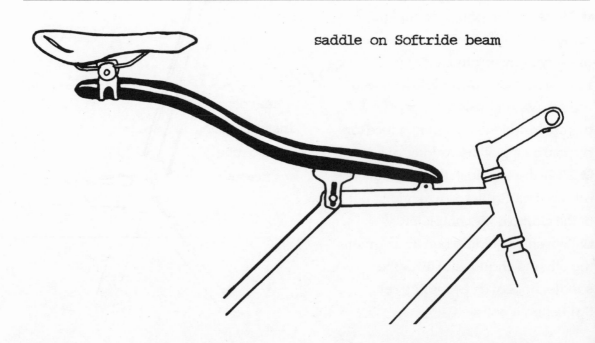

saddle on Softride beam

mounting bracket, located a few inches behind the front eyelet. It has two curved tabs that extend down on both sides of the beam. Long, curved slots in each tab are used to adjust the saddle height. Pass the bolt through one of the rectangular washers (with its knurled side pointing inward) and into the slot of one tab. Then pass it through the round end cap of the cylindrical frame mount and the frame mount itself. Then pass it through the second end cap, the other oval tab hole and the other rectangular washer, and then screw on the nut.

Note: The holes in the aluminum end caps of the frame mount are probably offset. Rotate them so that they are in line.

❸ Swing the beam up to the desired height, with the fixing bolt loose. For starters, set it about an inch higher than what your normal seat height would be. That should offset the, beam's flex. If you reach the end of the adjustment in the bracket tab slots and the seat is still not as high as you need it to be, rotate the rear frame-mount end caps. The caps' offset holes offer two height positions for this very reason.

❹ Tighten the fixing bolt. Readjust saddle height as needed.

SUSPENSION SEATPOSTS

Shock-absorbing seatposts come equipped with some sort of spring — either a steel coil, an elastic polymer ("elastomer"), or an air cushion. The

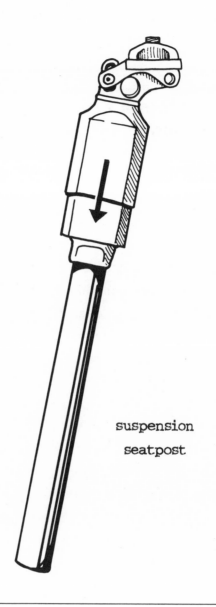

suspension
seatpost

elastomer spring is probably the most common, and air shocks are the rarest. There are a number of different suspension-seatpost designs out there and it is difficult — if not impossible — to write instructions that apply to all of them without being so general that those instructions become useless. Fortunately, most shock-absorbing seatposts are an aftermarket item and come with extensive instructions. I strongly recommend following the

suspension
seatposts

same regular maintenance schedule you would use for a standard seatpost.

REMOVING A STUCK SEATPOST

 This is a Level 3 job because of the risk involved. This may be a job best done by a shop, because if you make a mistake you run the risk of destroying your frame. If you're not 100-percent confident in your abilities, go to some one who is — or at least someone you can blame if they screw it up.

❶ Remove the seat binder bolt. Sounds easy enough.

❷ Squirt penetrating oil around the seatpost, and let it sit overnight. To get the most penetration, remove the bottom bracket (Chapter 8), turn the bike upside down, squirt the penetrating oil in from the bottom of the seat tube and let it sit overnight.

❸ The next day, stand over the bike and twist the saddle.

❹ If Step 3 does not free the seatpost, you will need to move into the difficult and risky part of this procedure.

You will now sacrifice the seatpost. Remove the saddle and all of the clamps from the top of the seatpost. With the bike upside down, clamp the top of the seatpost into a large bench vise that is bolted to a very secure workbench. Congratulations, you have just ruined your seatpost. Don't ever ride it again. Grab the frame at both ends, and begin to carefully apply a twisting pressure.

Be aware that you can easily apply enough force to bend or crack your frame, so be careful. If the seatpost finally releases, it often makes such a large "pop" that you will think that you have broken many things!

5. If step 4 does not work, you need to go to a machine shop and get the post reamed out of the seat tube.

If you still insist on getting it out yourself, you should really sit down and think about it for a while. Will the guy at the machine shop really charge you so much money that is now worth the risk of completely trashing your frame?

Have you thought about it for a while? And *still* you insist on doing this yourself? Okay, but don't say I didn't warn you.

Take a hacksaw and cut your seatpost off a little more than an inch above the seatlug on your frame. (Now you really *have* destroyed your seatpost, so, I don't have to warn about riding it again.) Remove the blade from the saw and wrap a piece of tape around one end. Hold on to the taped end and slip the other end into the center of the post. Carefully (no, make that *very* carefully) make two outward cuts about 60 degrees apart. Your goal is to remove a pie-shaped wedge from the hunk of seatpost stuck in your frame. Be careful, this is where many people cut too far and go right through the seatpost into the frame. Of course, *you* wouldn't do that, now would you? Once you've made the cut, pry or pull this piece out with a large screwdriver or a pair of pliers. Be careful here, too. A lot of over-enthusiastic home mechanics have damaged their frames by prying too hard here. But *you* wouldn't do that, would you?

Once the wedge is out, work the remaining piece out by curling in the edges with the pliers to free more and more of it from the seatpost walls. It should eventually work its way out.

Now, once your seatpost is out of the frame, remember to go back and re-read that part of this chapter outlining the regular maintenance procedures required for a seatpost. In other words, take out and apply grease every once in a while. You don't want to have to do this again, do you?

TROUBLESHOOTING PROBLEMS IN THE SEAT AND SEATPOST

❶ Loose saddle.

Check the bolts. They are probably loose. Tighten the bolts. If you need help, look up the instructions that apply to your seatpost. Go ride your bike.

❷ Stuck seatpost.

It can be a serious problem. Follow the instructions carefully or you might risk damaging your frame.

❸ Saddle squeaks with each pedal stroke.

Put up with it or get a new saddle.

❹ Creaking noises from the seatpost.

A seatpost can creak from moving back and forth against the sides of the seat tube while you ride. A dry seatpost can creak, so grease it.

Some frames use a collar to change the seat tube to a standard diameter. Remember that the internal diameter of the seat tube is larger below the collar. I have seen bikes that creaked because the bottom of the seatpost rubbed against the sides of the seat tube below the extension of the collar. You can solve that problem by trimming the seatpost back a little. If you do saw off the seatpost, make sure that you still have at least 3 inches of seatpost below the clamp.

If the creaking originates from the seatpost head where the saddle is clamped, you should check the clamp bolts. Lubricate the bolt threads and you will be able to tighten them a bit more.

Shock-absorbing seatposts can

X

saddles and seatposts

TROUBLE-SHOOTING

squeak as they move up and down. Try greasing the sides of the inner shaft. Grease the elastomers inside, too.

❺ Seatpost slips down.

Tighten the frame binder bolt. If the seat-binder lug is pinched closed, and you still can't get it tight enough, you may be using a seatpost with an incorrect diameter, or the seat tube on your bike has been stretched. Double check the seat-tube diameter with a pair of calipers. Your local shop may have one.

Try putting a larger seatpost in the frame, and replace yours if you find one that fits better. If the next size up is too big, you may need to "shim" your existing post. Cut a 1-inch x 3-inch piece of aluminum from a pop can. Pull the seatpost out grease it and the pop can shim, and insert both back into your frame. You may need to experiment with various shim sizes. Go ahead, they're cheap.

TROUBLE–SHOOTING

handlebars, stems and headsets

tools

metric Allen
  wrenches
headset wrenches
  sized for your
  particular
  headset
grease
hair spray
scissors, tin snips,
  or knife
soft hammer
hacksaw
round file
flat file
bike stand

OPTIONAL
bench vise
headset cup
  remover
star nut
  installation tool
headset fork
  crown race
  slide hammer
Shimano
  or Chris King
  tool to protect
  fork crown race
  when setting
headset press
Chris King headset
  press inserts to
  protect bearings
  during
  installation
torque wrench

"**I**f you don't change direction, you're liable to end up where you're headed."

— ANONYMOUS

On a bike you, either maintain or change your direction by applying force to your handlebars. If everything works properly, variations in that pressure will result in your front wheel changing direction. Pretty basic, right? Right, but there *is* a series of parts between the handlebars and the wheel that makes that simple process possible. In this chapter, we'll cover most of that system by going over handlebars, stems and headsets. This chapter is designed to start at the outside of the handlebars and move toward the middle.

BAR ENDS

Installation of bar ends

❶ Slide the shifters, brake levers and grips inward to make room at the end of the bar for the bar end. See **Grip removal** in this chapter for how to move the grip, and Chapters 5 and 7 about shifters and brake levers.

❷ Loosen the bolt on the bar-end clamp; it usually accepts a 5mm Allen wrench. Slide the bar end onto the bar.

❸ Tighten the clamp bolt enough that it just holds the bar ends in place. Rotate the bar ends to the position you like.

❹ Tighten the clamp bolt. Make sure it is snug.

Notes: The ends of some super-light handlebars can be damaged by bar ends. These bars come equipped with small cylindrical aluminum inserts that support the bar under the bar end. Similarly, some composite bars have an aluminum reinforcement at the end to support them under the bar end. These

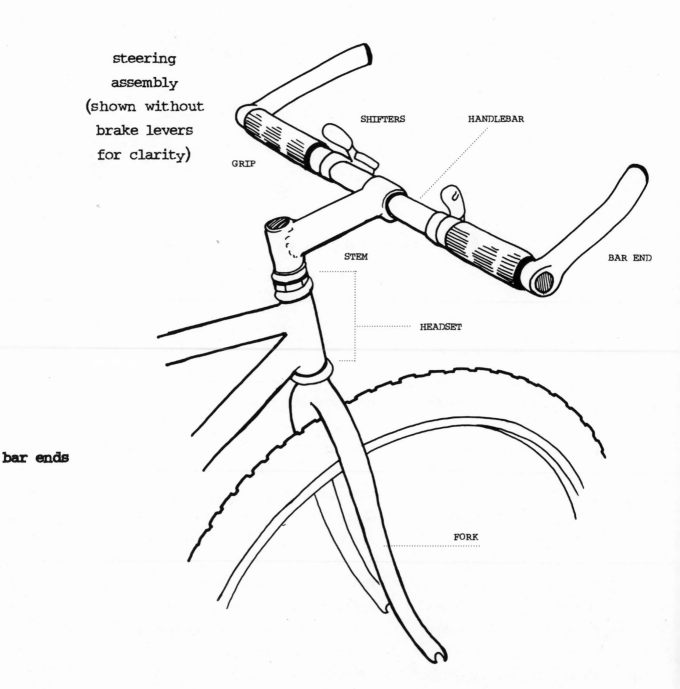

steering assembly (shown without brake levers for clarity)

SHIFTERS

HANDLEBAR

GRIP

STEM

BAR END

HEADSET

FORK

bar ends

bars cannot be shortened, since the bar ends will not have the support they need.

• Bar ends are meant to provide a powerful hand position while climbing, as well as an alternative stretched-out position while riding on smooth roads. They are *not* meant to be positioned vertically to provide a higher hand position. If you want your hands higher, get a taller, more vertical stem and perhaps bars that have a double bend to elevate the ends. This way you still have easy access to the brake levers.

• Some bar ends have features to provide adjustment in more planes than just rotationally about the bars.

174

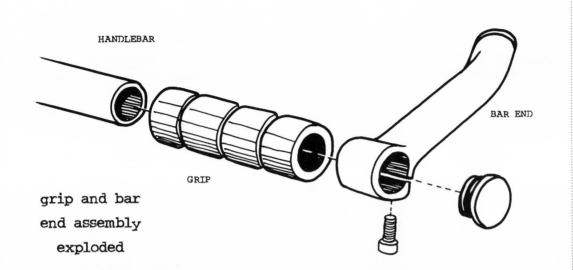

grip and bar
end assembly
exploded

Some (Profile) use a ball joint that fits
over the end of the bar with one bolt for
all adjustments and fixing to the bars.
Other types (Syntace), use a second
bolt that allows the bar end to twist
about its axis.

Remove bar ends

❶ Loosen bolt on bar-end clamp; it
usually accepts a 5mm Allen wrench.

❷ Pull the bar end off.

GRIPS

Grip removal

❶ Remove bar ends and bar-end plugs.

❷ Roll back an edge of the grip on itself.

❸ Squirt water on the bar and the
exposed grip underside. Flip the rolled-
up edge back down, and repeat Steps 2
& 3 on the other end of the grip.

❹ Starting at the ends, twist the grip back
and forth as you pull outward on it. The
wet sections will slip easily, and the dry
middle section will get moving as the
ends twist.

Grip installation

❶ Squirt hair spray or water inside

using water
to remove grip

the grip.

❷ Twist it onto the bar.

Notes: Some grips have a closed end. If
you are going to use bar ends, you will
need to cut off the closed end. Some of
these grips have a marked groove where
they are meant to be cut with a pair of
scissors. Otherwise, you can cut them off

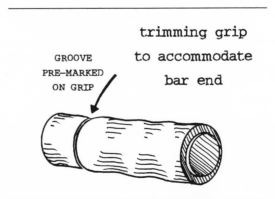

trimming grip
to accommodate
bar end

GROOVE
PRE–MARKED
ON GRIP

grips

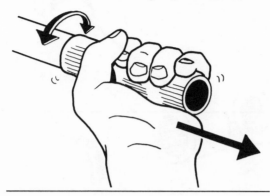

grip removal

anywhere you wish with scissors, tin snips, or a knife. If you have a thin, lightweight handlebar you can also just hit the end of the grip with a soft hammer after it is installed. The bar will cut a nice hole in the grip end like a cookie cutter.

• Grips used alongside Grip Shift and other twist shifters are shorter than standard grips, since part of the hand is sitting on the twist grip. Grips specifically designed for Grip Shift shifters are readily available in bike shops. If you can't find them, just cut yours down to the proper length.

HANDLEBARS

Handlebar removal

❶ Remove the bar ends and grips, at least from one side. It is easier to remove grips when the bar is clamped into the stem than when it is sitting on a workbench, so, if you are moving the parts to another bar, remove them while the bar is still on the bike. For instructions for removing bar ends, see above.

❷ Remove brake levers and shifters. (Turn to Chapter 7 for information on brake levers and Chapter 5 for shifters.)

❸ Loosen the bolt on the stem clamp surrounding the bar. This usually takes a 5mm Allen wrench.

❹ Pull the bar out.

Handlebar installation

❶ Remove the stem-clamp bolt, grease its threads, and replace it. Grease the inside of the stem clamp, and grease the clamping area in the center of the bar.

❷ Twist the bar to the position you find most comfortable. I prefer rotating the bar to the point that the bends point up and back toward me, but it's all a matter of preference.

Handlebar maintenance and replacement schedule

A bike cannot be controlled without handlebars, so you never want one to break on you. *Do not look at your bars as a permanent accessory on your bike.* All aluminum bars will eventually fail. If titanium, steel or carbon-fiber bars are repeatedly stressed above a certain level, they will eventually fail as well. What that level is depends on the particular bar. The trick is not to be riding them when they fail.

Keep your bars clean. Regularly inspect the bars for cracks, crash-induced bends, corrosion, and stressed areas. If you find any sign of wear or cracking, replace the bars. *Never straighten a bent handlebar. Replace it!* If you crash hard on your bike, consider replacing your bars even if they look

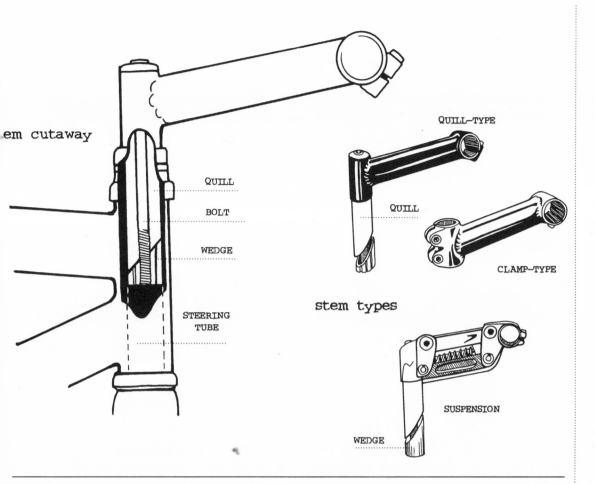

em cutaway

QUILL

BOLT

WEDGE

STEERING
TUBE

QUILL-TYPE

QUILL

CLAMP-TYPE

stem types

SUSPENSION

WEDGE

handlebars, stems
and headsets

fine. If you have had a crash and see no problems with the bars, remove the bar ends and check whether the bar is bent at the edges of the bar end. A carbon-fiber bar can be broken internally and the damage may not be visible from the outside. If your bars have taken an extremely hard hit, its a good idea to replace them rather than gamble on their integrity.

The Italian stem and bar manufacturer, 3T, recommends replacing stems and bars every four years. As with a stem, if you rarely ride the bike, this is overkill. If you ride hard and ride often, every four years may not be frequent enough. Do what is appropriate for you, and be aware of the risks.

STEMS

The stem connects to the fork-steering tube and clamps around the handlebar. Stems come in one of two basic types: for threaded, or unthreaded fork-steering tubes. Some stems have shock-absorbing mechanisms with pivots and springs to provide suspension.

Stems for threaded steering tubes have been the most common historically. They have a vertical "quill," which extends down into the steering tube of the fork and binds to the inside of the steering tube by means of a wedge-shaped plug pulled up by a long bolt that runs through the quill.

Stems for unthreaded fork-steering tubes have a clamping collar in place of the quill. Since the steering tube has no

stems

installation
and
adjustment
of standard
stem

threads, the top headset cup slides on and off. In this case, the stem plays a dual role. It clamps around the steering tube to connect the handlebars to the fork, and it also keeps the headset in proper adjustment by preventing the top headset cup from sliding up the steering tube.

Suspension stems are made for both threadless and threaded steering tubes. Some, like the Softride, use a parallelogram system with four pivots to prevent the handlebar from twisting as it moves up and down. Others, like the Girvin, have a single pivot around which the bar swings in an arc. Both incorporate some sort of a spring for suspension, usually a steel coil or an elastic polymer ("elastomer"). Some suspension stems also come with a hydraulic damper to control the speed of movement.

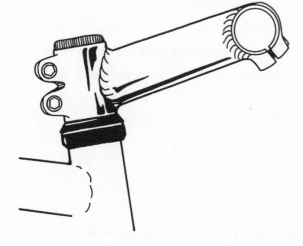

**threadless headset cup held
in place by stem**

REMOVE STANDARD QUILL-TYPE STEM FROM THREADED FORK

❶ Unscrew the stem-fixing bolt on the top of the stem. It should take three turns or so. Most stem bolts take a 6mm Allen wrench.

❷ Tap the top of the bolt down with a soft hammer to disengage the wedge or plug from the end of the quill. If the head of the bolt is recessed down in the stem so that a hammer cannot get at it, leave the Allen wrench in the bolt and tap the top of the Allen wrench until the wedge is free.

❸ Pull the stem out of the steering tube. If the stem will not budge, see **Removing stuck stem** later in this chapter.

INSTALL AND ADJUST HEIGHT OF STANDARD STEM IN THREADED FORK

❶ Grease the stem quill, the bolt threads, the outside of the wedge or conical plug, and the inside of the steering tube. Thread the bolt through the stem and into the wedge or plug until it pulls it into place, but not so far as to prevent the stem from inserting into the steering tube.

❷ Slip the stem quill into the steering tube to the depth you want. Make sure the stem is inserted beyond its height-limit line. Tighten the bolt until the stem is snug but can still be turned.

❸ Line up the stem with the front wheel, and tighten the bolt. It needs to be tight, but don't overdo it. You can over-tighten the stem bolt to the point

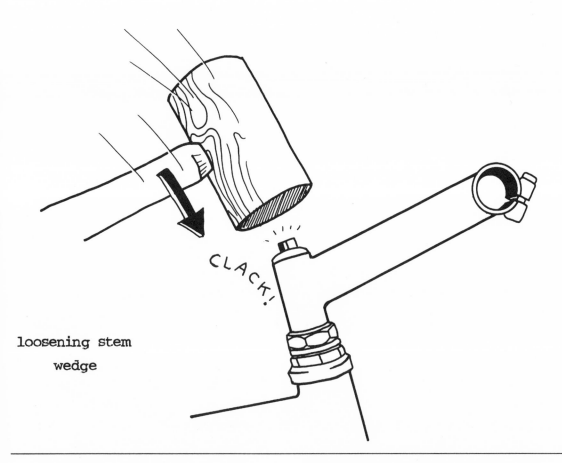

loosening stem
wedge

that you bulge out the steerer tube on your fork, so be careful.

REMOVE CLAMP-TYPE STEM FROM THREADLESS STEERING TUBE

❶ Loosen the horizontal bolts clamping the stem around the steering tube. Again, this should take about two or three turns.

❷ With a 5mm Allen wrench, unscrew and remove the adjusting bolt in the top cap covering the top of the stem clamp and steering tube. The fork can now fall out, so hold the fork as you unscrew the bolt.

❸ With the bike standing on the floor, or while holding the fork to keep it from falling out, pull the cap and the stem off of the steering tube. Leave the bike standing until you replace the stem, or

slide the fork out of the frame, keeping track of all headset parts.

If the stem will not budge, see **Remove ❹ stuck stem** later in this chapter.

INSTALL AND ADJUST HEIGHT OF STEM ON THREADLESS STEERING TUBE

Installing and adjusting the height of a stem on a threadless fork is much more complicated than installing and adjusting the height of a standard stem in a threaded fork. That's why this step is listed with a Level 2 designation. Because the stem is an integral part of the headset, any change to the stem position alters the headset adjustment.

❶ Stand the bike up on its wheels, so

installation
and
adjustment
of stem
height
on threadless
steering tube

the fork does not fall out. Grease the top end of the steering tube. Remove the stem clamp bolts, and grease their threads. With the stem-clamp bolts loose, slide the stem onto the fork-steering tube.

❷ Set the stem height to the desired level. If you want to place the stem in a position higher than directly on top of the headset, you must put some spacers between the bottom of the stem clamp and the top piece of the headset. No matter what, there *must* be contact (either directly or through spacers) between the headset and the stem. Otherwise, you risk an accident or damage to your fork and stem.

Note: Some manufacturers produce a pinch-binding headset adjustment holding ring with which you can raise or lower your stem without affecting the adjustment of your headset. You slide the ring onto the steering tube on top of the headset and below the stem. Once the headset position is set, you tighten the pinch bolt on the ring. After that is in place, you can raise the stem without throwing the headset out of adjustment.

❸ Check the steering tube length: In order to adjust the threadless headset, the top of the stem clamp (or spacers placed above it) should overlap the top of the steering tube by 3-6mm (1/8"-1/4").

Steering tube too short: If the top of the stem clamp overlaps the top of the steering tube by more than 6mm (1/4"), the steering tube is too short to set the stem height where you have it. If you

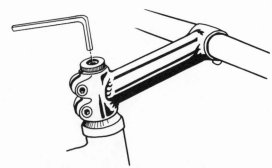

loosening and tightening bolt on threadless-style headset

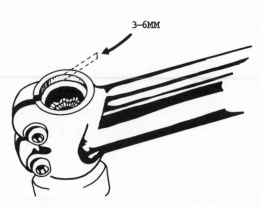

measuring distance between stem clamp and top of steering tube

have spacers below the stem, remove some until the top edge of the stem clamp overlaps the top of the steering tube by 3-6mm. If you do not wish to, or cannot lower the stem any further, you either need a longer steering tube or a stem with a smaller clamp. Stems for threadless steering tubes with clamps of differing lengths are available. It's a lot cheaper and easier than replacing the steering tube.

If you have a traditional rigid (non-suspension) fork, you probably can't just replace the steering tube without having it done by a frame builder. At this point, you might as well replace the fork. On most suspension forks, however, you can simply replace the steering tube and crown assembly and bolt your existing fork legs into it.

Steering tube too long: If the top of the steering tube is less than 3mm (1/8") below the top edge of the stem clamp (or if sticks up above the top of the stem clamp) you have a choice. If you want the option to raise the stem for a higher handlebar position, stack some headset spacers on top of the stem clamp until the spacers overlap the top edge of the steering tube by at least 3mm.

If, on the other hand, you want the stem to be as low as possible, go ahead and cut off the excess tube. First, mark the steering tube along the top edge of the stem clamp and remove the fork from the bike. Make another mark on the steering tube 3 mm below the first mark. Place the steering tube in a padded vise or bike stand clamp. Using the lower mark as a guide, cut the excess steering tube off with a hacksaw or tube cutter.

There is a star-shaped nut that is inserted inside the steering tube. The bolt through the stem-top cap screws into it to adjust the headset bearings. If the star nut is already inside of the steering tube, and you are certain that the saw is going to hit it, thread the adjusting bolt into the nut and tap on the bolt with a hammer. That should move it out of the way.

Make your cut straight. If you are not sure your cut will be straight, start it a little higher and file it down flat to the

mark. If you really want to be safe, use a tool specifically designed to help you make a straight cut. Park Tool's "threadless saw guide" is a good example. Remember that you can always shorten the steering tube a little more, but you cannot make it longer! So, apply the old adage of "measure twice, cut once." Use a round file on the inside of the tube and a flat file on the outside to file off any metal burrs left by the hacksaw or cutter.

When you have completed cutting and deburring, put the fork back in, replacing all headset parts the way they were originally installed. Return to Step 1 above.

❹ Check that the edges of the star-shaped nut are at least 12mm below the top edge of the steering tube. The nut must be far enough down that the bottom of the headset top cap does not hit it once the adjusting bolt is tightened. If the nut is not in deeply enough, you need to drive it deeper into the steering tube after removing the stem. This is best done with the star nut installation tool. The tool threads into the nut, and you hit it with a hammer until it stops; the star nut will now be set 15mm deep in the steering tube. If you do not have this tool, you can go to a bike shop to have the nut set for you. That's probably the best approach, but if you insist on doing it yourself follow the steps outlined below. Just remember that it is easy to mess up the installation this way.

a. Put the adjusting bolt through the

handlebars, stems and headsets

changing
steering tube
length

top cap, and thread it six turns into the star nut.

b. Set the star nut over the end of the steering tube, and tap the top of the bolt with a soft hammer. Use the top cap as guide to keep it going in straight.

c. Tap the bolt in until the star nut is 15mm below the top of the steering tube.
Note: Even pros sometimes mangle star nuts. When you do, replacements can be purchased separately. If the wall thickness of the steering tube is greater than standard, the star nut will not fit in, and it will just bend when you try to install it. If this happens, take a long punch or rod, set it on the star nut, and drive it all of the way out of the bottom of the steering tube. Dispose of the star nut, and get another.

If the internal diameter (I.D.) of the steering tube is undersized — (standard I.D. is 22.2mm (7/8″) on a 1″ steering tube, 25.4mm (1″) on a 1-1/8″ steering tube, and 28.6mm (1-1/8″) on a 1-1/4″ steering tube) — you will need to modify the star nut or it will be ruined. To do this, squeeze each pair of opposite leaves of the star nut with a pair of channel-lock pliers to bend the leaves in and reduce the nut's width. Now you can insert the nut.

5 Install the headset top cap on the top of the stem clamp (or spacers you set above it). Grease the threads of the top-cap adjusting bolt, and thread it into the star nut inside the steering tube.

6 Adjust the headset. The steps are outlined later in this chapter.

STEM MAINTENANCE AND REPLACEMENT SCHEDULE

A bike cannot be controlled if the stem breaks, so make sure yours doesn't break. Since aluminum has no fatigue limit, *all aluminum parts will eventually fail.* Steel and titanium parts repeatedly stressed more than about one-half of their tensile strength will eventually fail as well. Stems and handlebars are not permanent accessories on your bike. Replace them before they fail on you.

Clean your stem regularly. Whenever you clean it, look for corrosion, cracks, bends and stressed areas. If you find any, replace the stem immediately. If you crash hard on your bike, especially hard enough to bend the bars, replace your stem. It makes sense to err on the side of caution.

Italian stem maker 3T recommends replacing stems and bars every four years. As with a set of handlebars, if you rarely ride the bike, this is overkill. If you ride hard and ride often every four years may not be frequent enough. Do what is appropriate for you, and be aware of the risks.

SETTING STEM AND BAR POSITIONS

I recommend setting your handlebar twist so that the bends in the bars are pointed up and back toward you. I also recommend setting your bar ends so that they are horizontal or tipped up between 5 and 15 degrees from horizontal.

Setting handlebar height and reach is very personal. Much depends on your physique, your flexibility, your frame, your riding style, and a few other preferences. This subject is covered in depth in the appendix on page 266. Since I do not know anything about you personally, I will leave you with a few simple guidelines:

• If you climb a lot, you will want your bars lower and further forward to keep weight on the front wheel on steep uphills.

• If you descend technical trails a lot, you will want your bars higher and with less forward reach.

• If you ride a lot on pavement, a low, stretched-out position is better aerodynamically. A low position means that the handlebar grips are about 5-10cm lower than your saddle. A

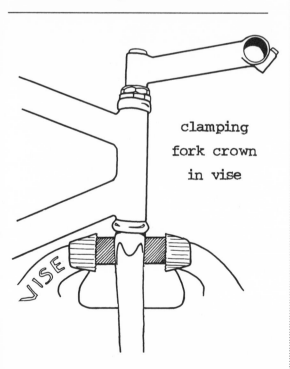

clamping
fork crown
in vise

stretched-out position would place your elbow at least two inches in front of your knee at the top of the pedal stroke.

REMOVING STUCK STEM

 If your stem is really stuck, be careful. You can ruin your fork as well as your stem and headset trying to get it out. In fact, you're better off having a shop work on it, unless you *really* know what you are doing and are willing to accept the risk of destroying a lot of expensive parts.

Removing a stuck stem from a threaded fork:

❶ Unscrew the stem bolt on top of the stem three turns or more. Smack the bolt (or the Allen wrench in the bolt) with a soft hammer to completely disengage the wedge.

❷ Grasping the front wheel between your knees, make one last attempt to free the stem by pushing and pulling back and forth on the bars. Don't use all of your strength, because you can ruin a fork this way.

❸ If your stem didn't budge, squirt penetrating oil around the stem where it enters the headset. Let the bike sit for several hours and add more penetrating oil every hour or so.

❹ Turn the bike over, and squirt penetrating oil into the bottom of the fork steering tube so that it runs down around the stem quill. Let the bike sit for several hours and add more penetrating oil every hour or so.

❺ Now that it is totally soaked in

xI

handlebars, stems
and headsets

removing a
stuck stem

183

penetrating oil, try Step 2 again. If the stem does not come this time, keep going. Now you have to go to your workbench and use that heavy-duty vise. It's solidly mounted, isn't it? Good, because you'll need it to be.

❻ Remove the front wheel and disconnect the front brake cable. Put pieces of wood on both sides of the vise. Clamp the fork crown into the vise. With some forks (and/or some vises), you may have to remove the brakes and perhaps the fork brace to do this.

❼ Grab both ends of the handlebar and twist. You still need to be careful not to use your full strength. Keep twisting back and forth. If this doesn't work, you may have to unscrew the headset parts and then saw off either the stem quill or the steering tube on the fork. Of course, you will have to replace both parts. I told you that you should have gone to a bike shop.

Removing a stuck stem from a threadless fork:

❶ Remove the bolts clamping the stem to the steering tube.

❷ Grasp the front wheel between your knees and give it one last try to free the stem by pushing and pulling back and forth on the bars. Again, don't use all of your strength, because you can ruin a fork this way. If the stem does not budge, go on to next step.

❸ Squirt penetrating oil around the stem clamp from both sides so that it runs between the steering tube and the

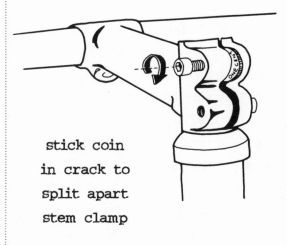

stick coin
in crack to
split apart
stem clamp

clamp. Let it sit for a few hours, adding more oil every hour or so.

❹ (If your stem is the type that comes with a single bolt in the side of the stem shaft *ahead* of the steering tube, skip to Step 6.)

You may be able to force the stem off by spreading the stem clamp slot. First, reverse the pinch bolt(s), and thread them into the threaded end of each binder lug until they just appear at the edge of the clamp slot.

❺ Insert a coin into the slot between each bolt end and the opposing unthreaded half of the binder lug. Tighten each bolt against the coin so that it spreads the clamp slot open wider.

❻ Repeat Step 2. It should come loose. I have never seen Step 5 not work. But, if it *still* does not budge, go on to the next step.

❼ Remove the front wheel and disconnect the front brake cable. Put a piece of wood against both sides of the vise jaws. Clamp the fork crown in the vise. With some forks (and/or some vises), you may have to remove the brakes and even the fork brace to do this. ❻ Grab either end of the handlebar and twist back and forth. If this does not free it, you may have to saw through the steering tube at the base of the stem clamp and replace both the stem and the fork (or the steering tube, if it is replaceable).

HEADSETS

There are two basic types of headsets, threaded and unthreaded. The different standard mountain bike headset sizes are 1", 1-1/8" and 1-1/4".

The top bearing cup on a threaded headset has wrench flats, a toothed washer stacked on top of it, and a locknut that covers the top of the steering tube. That locknut tightens against the washer and top cup. A brake cable hanger and extra spacers may be included under the locknut.

Prior to the 1990s, practically all headsets and steering tubes were threaded. Dia-Compe's AheadSet was the first widely available threadless headset. Threadless headsets are lighter because they eliminate the stem quill, bolt, and wedge. The connection between the handlebars and the stem is more rigid on bikes with threadless headsets. Of course fork manufacturers prefer them because they do not have to thread their forks and only have to offer three different size steering tubes.

On most unthreaded headsets, the top cup and a conical compression ring slide onto the steering tube. The stem clamps around the top of the steering tube and above the compression ring. A nut with two layers of spring-steel teeth sticking out from it (called a "Star Fangled Nut" by Dia-Compe) fits into the steering tube and grabs the inner walls. A top cap sits atop the stem clamp and pushes it down by means of a long bolt threaded into the star nut to adjust the headset. The stem clamped around the steering tube holds the headset in adjustment.

needle bearings

Threaded and threadless headsets use either loose or sealed cartridge bearings. Most headsets use loose ball bearings held in some type of steel or plastic retainer (or "cage") so that you are not chasing dozens of separate balls around when you work on the bike. A variation on this (Stronglight) has needle bearings held in conical plastic retainers riding on conical steel bearing surfaces.

Cartridge-sealed-bearing headsets usually employ "angular contact" bearings, since normal cartridge bearings cannot take the side forces

headsets

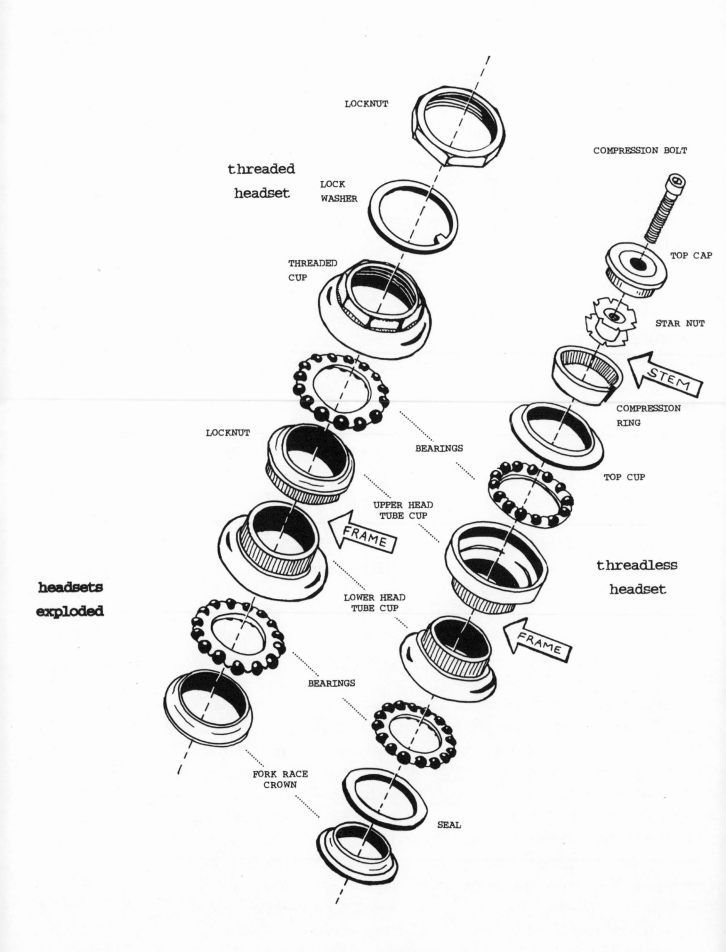

LOCKNUT

threaded
headset

LOCK
WASHER

THREADED
CUP

COMPRESSION BOLT

TOP CAP

STAR NUT

STEM

COMPRESSION
RING

BEARINGS

LOCKNUT

BEARINGS

TOP CUP

UPPER HEAD
TUBE CUP

FRAME

threadless
headset

headsets
exploded

LOWER HEAD
TUBE CUP

FRAME

BEARINGS

FORK RACE
CROWN

SEAL

encountered by a headset. Each bearing is a separate, sealed, internally-greased unit.

CHECK HEADSET ADJUSTMENT

If your headset is too loose, it will rattle or clunk while you ride. You might even notice some "play" in the fork as you apply the front brake. If your headset is too tight, the fork will be difficult to turn.

❶ **Check for headset looseness** by holding the front brake and rocking the bike forward and back. Try it with the front wheel pointed straight ahead and then with the wheel turned at 90° to the bike. Feel for back and forth movement (or "play") at the lower head cup with your other hand. If there is play, you need to adjust your headset because it is too loose.

If there is play, skip to **Adjusting a headset** instructions later in the chapter.

❷ **Check for headset tightness** by turning the stem with your hand. Feel for any binding or stiffness of movement. Also, check for the chunk-chunk-chunk movement to fixed positions characterizing a pitted headset (if you feel this, you need a new headset; skip to **Remove headset** below). Lean the bike to one side and then the other; the front wheel should turn as the bike is leaned (be aware that cable housings can resist the turning of the front wheel). Lift the bike by the saddle so it is tipped down at an angle with both wheels off of the ground. Turn the handlebar one way and let go of it. See if it returns to center

quickly and smoothly on its own. If the headset does not turn easily on any of the above steps, it is too tight. Skip to **Adjusting a headset** later in chapter.

❸ If yours is a threaded headset, try to unscrew or tighten either the top nut or the threaded cup with your hand. They should be so tight against each other that they can only be loosened with wrenches. If you can hand tighten or loosen either part, you need to adjust your headset.

ADJUSTING A THREADED HEADSET

 Note: Perform the adjustment with the stem installed. Not only does it give you something to hold on to that keeps the fork from turning during the installation, but there are slight differences in adjustment when the stem is in place as opposed when it is not. Tightening the stem bolt can sometimes bulge the walls of the steering tube very slightly, but just

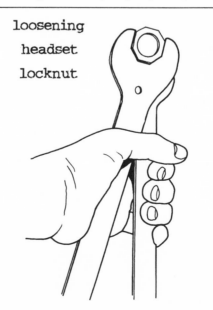

loosening
headset
locknut

adjusting
threaded
headset

enough for it to shorten the steering tube and throw your original headset adjustment off.

❶ Follow the steps outlined on the previous page and determine whether the headset is too loose or too tight.

❷ Put a pair of headset wrenches that fit your headset on the headset's top nut (which I will also call the "locknut") and top bearing cup (or "threaded cup"). Headset nuts come in a wide variety of sizes, so make sure you have purchased the proper wrenches. Place the wrenches so that the top one is slightly offset to left of the bottom wrench. That way you can squeeze them together to free the nut.

❸ Hold the lower wrench in place and turn the top wrench counterclockwise about 1/4 turn to loosen the locknut. It may take considerable force to break it loose, since it needs to be installed very tightly to keep the headset from loosening up.

❹ *If the headset was too loose.* Turn the lower (or threaded) cup clockwise about 1/16 of a turn while holding the stem with your other hand. Be very careful; if you over-tighten the cup, you can ruin the headset by pressing the bearings into the bearing surfaces. This makes little indentations in the bearing surfaces so that the headset stops at those spots rather than turns smoothly; this condition is known as a "pitted headset."

If the headset was too tight, loosen the threaded cup counterclockwise 1/16

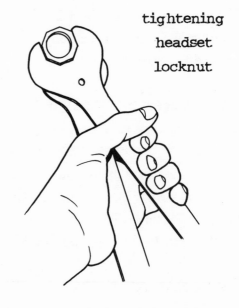

tightening headset locknut

turn while holding the stem with your other hand. Loosen it until the bearings turn freely, but be sure not to loosen to the point that you allow any play to develop.

❺ Hold the stem, and tighten the locknut clockwise with a single wrench. Make sure that the threaded cup does not turn while you tighten the locknut. If it does turn, you either are missing the toothed washer, or the washer you have is missing its tooth. In this case, remove the locknut and replace the toothed washer. Put it on the steering tube so that the tooth engages the longitudinal groove in the steering tube. Tighten the locknut on again.

❻ Check the headset adjustment again. Repeat Steps 4 and 5 until properly adjusted.

❼ Once properly adjusted, place one wrench on the locknut and the other on the threaded cup. Hold the threaded cup in place and turn the locknut

adjusting threaded headset

clockwise to tighten it. Tighten the locknut firmly against the washer(s) and threaded cup to hold the headset adjustment in place.

8 Check the headset adjustment again. If it is off, follow Steps 2-7 again. If it is adjusted properly, make sure the stem is aligned with the front wheel. Go ride your bike.

Notes: If you constantly get what you believe to be the proper adjustment, and then find it to be too loose after you tighten the locknut and threaded cup against each other, your steering tube may be too long. Remove the stem and examine the inside of the steering tube. If the top end of the tube is resting against the lip on the top of the locknut, the steering tube is too long. Remove the locknut and add another spacer.

If you don't want to add another spacer, file off one or two millimeters of the steering tube. Be sure to deburr it inside and out afterwards. Replace the locknut and return to Step 5.

• Wheels Manufacturing makes a headset locknut called the "Growler." It replaces your locknut and will not come loose, even on bumpy terrain. It slides on just like a normal locknut and is adjusted the same way. The only difference between a Growler and a standard locknut is that the Growler is split down one side and has a pinch bolt bridging the split. Once your headset is adjusted, tighten the pinch bolt to keep it in adjustment.

ADJUSTING A THREADLESS HEADSET

Adjusting a threadless headset is much easier than adjusting a threaded one. It's a Level 1 procedure and usually only takes a 5mm Allen wrench.

1 Check the headset adjustment. Determine whether the headset is too tight or too loose.

2 Loosen the bolt(s) that clamp the stem to the steering tube.

3 *If the headset is too tight*, loosen the 5mm Allen bolt on the top of the top cap about 1/16 of a turn.

If the headset is too loose, tighten the 5mm Allen bolt on the top of the headset top cap about 1/16 turn. Be careful not to over-tighten it and pit the headset. If you're using a torque wrench, Dia-Compe recommends a tightening torque on this bolt of 22 inch-pounds.

If the cap does not move down and push the stem down, make sure the stem is not stuck to the steering tube. If it is, go to **Remove stuck stem from threadless steering tube** earlier in this chapter. If the stem is not stuck, and the cap does not

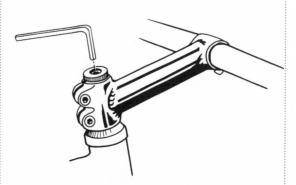

loosening and tightening bolt on threadless-style headset

adjusting threadless headset

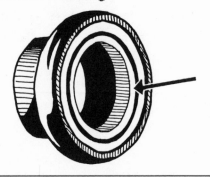

Chris King—style pressed sealed bearings

push the stem down, remove the cap. Check to see if the steering tube is too long and is hitting the lip of the top cap. The steering tube's top should be about 3mm below the top edge of the stem. Check the star nut. Be certain that it is far enough into the steering tube to be effective. The highest point of the star nut should be 12-15mm below the top of the steering tube. If the steering tube is too long, add a spacer or you can cut or file off the excess tubing. If the star nut is too high, move it down to 15mm below the top of the steering tube. Use a star-nut-installation tool, or put the bolt through the top cap, thread it five turns into the star nut, and gently tap it in with a soft hammer, using the top cap to keep it going in straight. Replace the top cap and bolt, and go back to the beginning of this step (Step 3).

❹ Tighten the stem clamp bolts. If using a torque wrench, Dia-Compe recommends a tightening torque of 130 inch-pounds.

❺ Re-check the headset adjustment. Repeat Steps 2-4 if necessary. If it is adjusted properly, make sure the stem is

aligned straight with the front wheel. Once the headset is adjusted properly, go find something else to do because you are done.

OVERHAUL THREADED HEADSET

Like any other bike part with bearings, headsets need periodic overhauls. If you use your bike regularly, you should probably overhaul your loose-bearing headset once a year. Headsets with sealed cartridge bearings usually never need to be overhauled; if a bearing fails, you either replace the bearing (Shimano) or, if it has press-in bearings (like Chris King and Dia-Compe's "S" series), you replace the entire cup. If you have a Shimano cartridge-bearing headset, continue with these instructions, if you are replacing a Chris King or Dia-Compe "S" headset cup, move on to the instructions for headset removal.

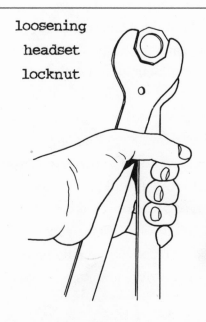

loosening headset locknut

(margin) **overhauling threaded headset**

A bike stand is highly recommended when overhauling a headset.

❶ Disconnect the front brake (Chapter 7), and remove the stem by loosening the stem bolt three turns, tapping the bolt down with a hammer to free the wedge, and pulling it out.

❷ Either turn your bike upside down or be prepared to catch your fork as you remove the upper portion of the headset. To remove the top headset cup, unscrew the locknut and threaded cup with headset wrenches. Place one on the locknut and one on the threaded cup. Loosen the locknut by turning it counterclockwise. Unscrew the locknut and the cup from the steering tube. The headset washer or washers will slide off of the steering tube as you unscrew the threaded cup.

❸ Pull the fork out of the frame.

❹ Remove any seals that surround the edges of the cups. Make a point of remembering the position and orientation of each.

❺ Remove the bearings from the cups. Be careful not to lose any. Separate top and bottom sets if they are of different sizes.

❻ Clean or replace the bearings.

With standard ball-bearing or needle-bearing headsets, put the bearings in a jar or old water bottle along with some citrus-based solvent. Shake. If the bearings from the top and bottom are of different sizes, keep them in separate containers to avoid confusion.

With sealed cartridge bearings, check to see if they turn smoothly. If they do not, buy new ones. Skip to Step 8.

❼ Blot the bearings dry with a clean rag. Plug the sink, and wash the bearings in soap and water in your hands, just as if you were washing your palms by rubbing them together. This helps keep your hands clean for the assembly steps as well. Rinse bearings thoroughly and blot them dry. Let them air dry completely.

❽ Wipe all of the bearing surfaces with clean rags. Wipe the steering tube clean, especially the threads, and wipe the inside of the head tube clean with a rag stuck to the end of a screwdriver.

❾ Inspect all bearing surfaces for wear and pitting. If you see pits (separate indentations made by bearings in the bearing surfaces), you need to replace the headset. If that's the case, skip to **Remove headset** later in this chapter.

❿ Liberally apply grease to all bearing surfaces. A thin film will do if you are using sealed cartridge bearings.

⓫ Turn the bike upside down in the bike stand. Place a set of bearings in the top cup and a set in the cup on the lower end of the head tube. Make sure you have the bearing retainer right side up so that only the bearings contact the bearing surfaces. If you have installed the retainer upside down it will come in contact with one of the bearing surfaces, and the headset does not turn well. This is a bad thing, since assembling and riding it that way will turn the retainer

handlebars, stems and headsets

overhauling headset

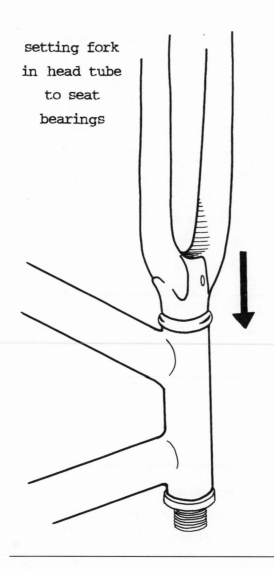

setting fork
in head tube
to seat
bearings

**setting fork
in frame**

of separate conical steel rings. These are the bearing surfaces that sit on both sides of the needle bearings. On each set of conical rings, you will find that one is smaller than the other. Place the smaller one on the lower surface of each pair: the fork crown race and the cup on top of the head tube.

• If you have loose ball bearings with *no bearing retainer*, stick the balls into the grease in the cups one at a time, making sure that you replace the same number you started with in each cup.

⓬ Re-install any seals that you removed from the headset parts.

⓭ Drop the fork-steering tube into the head tube so that the lower headset bearing set seats properly.

⓮ Screw on the top cup, with the bearings in it, onto the steering tube. Keeping the bike upside down at this point not only keeps the fork in place, it also prevents grit from falling into the bearings as you thread the cup on.

⓯ Slide on the toothed washer. Align the tooth in the groove going down the length of the steering tube threads. If you have one, install the brake cable hanger the same way. Screw on the locknut with your hand.

⓰ Turn the bike over. Grease the stem quill and insert it into the steering tube. Make certain that it is in deeper than the imprinted limit line. Line the stem up with the front wheel, and tighten the stem bolt.

⓱ Adjust the headset. As outlined in **Adjusting a threaded headset** earlier in this chapter.

into jagged chunks of broken metal. To be safe, double and triple check the retainer placement with each cup pair before proceeding. Most headsets have the bearings set up symmetrically top and bottom. This way the top piece of each pair is a cup, and the bottom piece is a cone and the bearing retainer rides the same way in both sets. Some headsets, however, place both cups facing outward from the head tube (See exploded headset diagram on page 188). **Notes:** Stronglight or similar needle-bearing headsets come with two pairs

OVERHAUL THREADLESS HEADSET

1 Either place the bike upside down in the work stand or be ready to catch the fork when you remove the stem. Disconnect the front brake (Chapter 7), and unscrew the top cap bolt and the stem clamp bolts. Remove the top cap and the stem.

2 Remove the top headset cup by sliding the top cup, conical washer, and any other spacers above it, off of the steering tube.

3 Pull the fork out of the frame.

4 Remove any seals that surround the edges of the cups. Remember the position and orientation of each.

5 Remove the bearings from the cups. Be careful not to lose any. Separate top and bottom sets if they are of different sizes.

6 Clean or replace the bearings:

With standard ball-bearing or needle-bearing headsets, put the bearings in a jar or old water bottle along with some citrus-based solvent. Shake. If the bearings from the top and bottom are of different sizes, keep them in separate containers to avoid confusion.

With sealed cartridge bearings, check to see if they turn smoothly. If they do not, buy new ones. Skip to Step 8.

7 Blot the bearings dry with a clean rag. Plug the sink, and wash the bearings in soap and water in your hands, just as if you were washing your palms by rubbing them together. Your hands will get clean for the assembly steps as well. Rinse bearings thoroughly and blot them dry. Air dry completely.

8 Wipe all of the bearing surfaces with clean rags. Wipe the steering tube clean, especially the threads, and wipe the inside of the head tube clean with a rag on the end of a screwdriver.

9 Inspect all bearing surfaces for wear and pitting. If you see pits (separate indentations made by bearings in the bearing surfaces), you need to replace the headset. If so, skip to **Remove headset** later in this chapter.

10 Liberally apply grease to all bearing surfaces. If you are using sealed-cartridge bearings, apply grease conservatively.

11 Turn the bike upside down in the bike stand. Place a set of bearings into the top cup and a set into the cup on the lower end of the head tube. Make sure you have the bearing retainer right side up so that only the bearings contact the bearing surfaces. If you have installed the retainer upside down, it will come in contact with one of the bearing surfaces, and the headset does not turn well. This is a bad thing since assembling and riding it that way will turn the retainer into jagged chunks of broken metal. To be safe, double and triple check the retainer placement with each cup pair before proceeding. Most headsets have the bearings set up symmetrically top and bottom. This way the top piece of

overhauling
threadless
headset

193

each pair is a cup and the bottom piece is a cone, and the bearing retainer rides the same way in both sets. Some headsets, however, place both cups facing outward from the head tube. (See exploded headset diagram on page 188).

Note: If you have loose ball bearings with *no bearing retainer*, stick the balls into the grease in the cups one at a time, making sure that you replace the same number you started with in each cup.

12 Re-install any seals that you removed from the headset parts.

13 Drop the fork-steering tube into the head tube so that the lower headset bearing set seats properly (see illustration on page 194).

14 Slide the top cup, with the bearings in it, onto the steering tube. Keep the bike upside down at this point; it not only keeps the fork in place, it also prevents grit from falling into the bearings as you put the cup on.

15 Slide on the compression ring so the narrower end slides into the conical space in the top of the top cup. Slide on any spacers you had under the stem. Slide the stem on, and tighten one stem clamp bolt to hold it in place.

16 Turn the bike over. Check that the stem clamp extends 3-6mm above the top of the steering tube. If it does, install the top cap on the top of the stem clamp and steering tube, and screw the bolt into the star nut set inside the steering tube.

If the steering tube is too long, remove

the stem. Add a spacer or file the steering shorter until the stem clamp overlaps it by 3mm. If the steering tube is too short, remove spacers from below the stem, if there are any. If there are no spacers to remove, try a new stem with a shorter clamp.

17 Adjust the headset. Go ride your bike.

REMOVE HEADSET

1 Remove the fork and bearings by following Steps 1-5 under **Overhaul threaded headset** or **Overhaul threadless headset** outlined earlier in this chapter.

2 Slide the solid end of the headset-cup remover through one end of the head tube. As you pull the headset-cup remover through the head tube, the splayed-out tangs on the opposite end of the tool pull through the cup and spread out.

3 Strike the solid end of the cup remover with a hammer, and drive the cup out.

4 Remove the other cup by placing the cup remover into the opposite end of the head tube and repeating Steps 2 and 3 on the opposite end of the end tube.

5 If you have a suspension fork (or a rigid fork with a clamp-together crown), you will find a groove under the fork crown race on the front and back of the fork crown. Turn the fork upside down so that the top of the steering tube is sitting on the workbench. Place the blade of a large screwdriver into the groove on one side of the crown so it butts against the

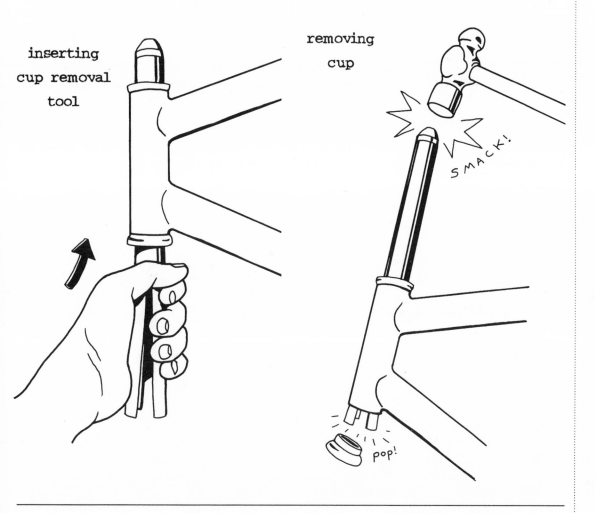

inserting
cup removal
tool

removing
cup

SMACK!

POP!

bottom of the headset fork crown race. Tap the handle of the screwdriver with a hammer to drive the crown race up the steering tube a bit. Move the screwdriver to the groove on the other side, and tap it again to move that side of the crown race up a bit. Continue in this way, alternately tapping either side of the crown race up the steering tube, bit by bit, until it gets over the enlarge section of the steering tube and slides off.

If you have a rigid fork, you can use a screwdriver to tap the crown race off as outlined above. You can also do it more elegantly with a crown race remover or an appropriately sized bench vise. Stand

the fork upside down on the top of the steering tube. Place the U-shaped crown race remover so it straddles the underside of the fork crown and its ledges engage the front and back edges of the crown race. Smack the top of the crown race remover with a hammer to knock the race off.

To do it with a bench vise, flip the brakes out of the way and slide the fork in, straddling the center shaft of the vise. Tighten the vise so its faces lightly contact the front and back of the fork crown with the lower side of the crown race sitting on top of them. Put a block of wood on the top of the steering tube to pad it. Strike

**removing
headset**

195

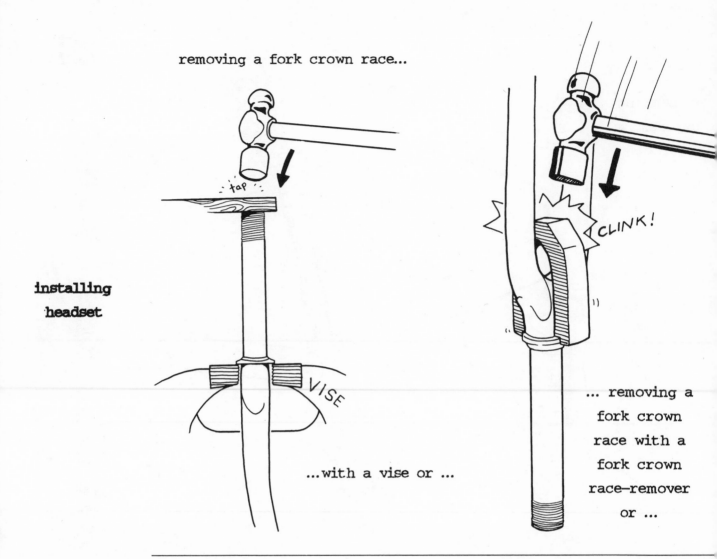

removing a fork crown race...

installing headset

...with a vise or ...

CLINK!

... removing a fork crown race with a fork crown race—remover or ...

the block with a hammer to drive the fork down and knock the crown race off of it.

INSTALL HEADSET

level 3 When you get a new headset, you can install it yourself if you have the necessary tools. Otherwise, get a shop to do it.

❶ *Frame and fork preparation:* If this is a new frame (or one that has "eaten" headsets in the past), make sure that the head tube has been reamed and faced. If not, you will need a bike shop equipped with the proper tools to do it for you. Reaming makes the head tube ends round inside and of the correct diameter

for the headset cups to press in. Facing makes both ends of the head tube parallel so the bearings can turn smoothly and uniformly.

The base of the steering tube also needs to be turned down to the correct diameter for the crown race. The crown race seat on top of the fork crown must be faced in a way that places the crown race parallel to the head tube cups. This is generally only a concern with rigid forks. Suspension forks are usually shipped with the tube properly machined to accept the fork crown race.

The fork (threaded or threadless) must also be cut to the proper length. You can

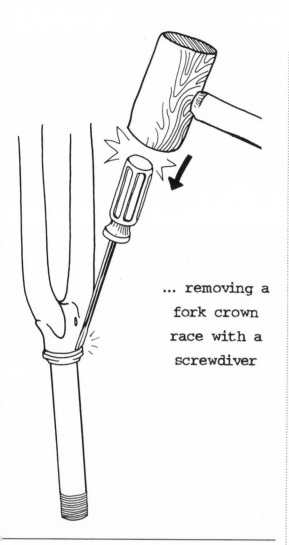

... removing a
fork crown
race with a
screwdiver

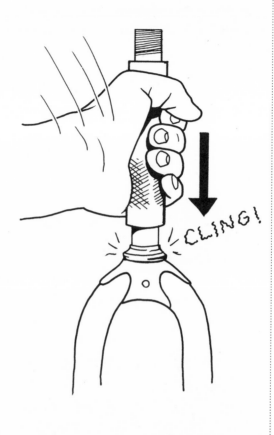

setting fork crown race

CLING!

handlebars, stems
and headsets

installing
headset

wait until the headset (and stem, in the case of a threadless headset) are installed, or you can figure out the length you need and cut it now. Remember, you can always go back and cut more off. You can't go back and add any, so be careful! (see illustration on page 200)

If you are using a threaded headset, and you know its stack height (the stack height is often listed in the headset owner's manual, or a bike shop can look it up in their *Sutherland's Manual*), measure the length of the head tube and add the headset-stack height to this length. If you are adding extra spacers or a brake cable hanger between the

headset nuts, add their thickness in as well. This figure represents the length that the fork-steering tube must be. If the steering tube is already more than 3-5mm shorter than this, you need to find another headset with a shorter stack height (or if include spacers, remove a few). If the steering tube is longer than this sum, saw it down to length and then file off the burrs the hacksaw left on the inside and outside edges of the steering tube end.

You can pretty much follow the same steps if you are using a threadless headset. Add the headset-stack height to the length of the steering tube and the

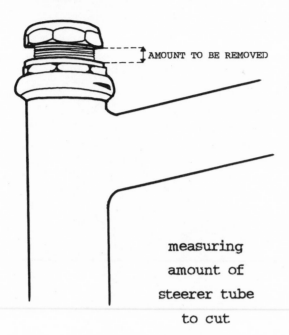

LOCKNUT SCREWED DOWN

AMOUNT TO BE REMOVED

measuring
amount of
steerer tube
to cut

stem clamp. Then, subtract 3mm from the total. This is the length from the fork crown race seat to the top of the steering tube. I recommend waiting until it is assembled and the stem is installed, however, so you can see if you want some spacers under the stem to raise your bars higher.

If you do not know the headset-stack height, you're afraid you'll cut the steering tube too short, or you want to see how it goes together before you cut it down, continue with the installation and assembly. When you are ready, cut it down using the method explained in Step 6 below.

2 Put a thin layer of grease on the surfaces of the head-tube cups that will be pressed into the head tube, inside the hole in the fork crown race, inside the ends of the head tube itself, and on the

base of the steering tube.

3 Slide the fork crown race down on the fork steering tube until it hits the enlarged section at the bottom. Slide the crown race slide punch up and down the steering tube, pounding the crown race down until it sits flat on top of its seat on the fork crown. Some crown race punches are longer and closed on the top and are meant to be hit with a hammer rather than be slid up and down by hand. Hold the fork up against the light to see if there are any gaps between the crown race and the crown. **Note:** Extra-thin crown races can be easily bent or broken by the crown race punch. Chris King and Shimano both make support tools that sit over the race and distribute the impact from the punch.

4 Place the headset cups into the ends of the head tube. Slide the headset cup press shaft through the head tube. Press the button on the detachable end of the tool and slide it onto the shaft until it bumps into one of the cups. Find the nearest notch on the shaft and release the button. Some headset presses use a system of spacers and cones on both ends of the cups. Follow the instructions to set yours up properly. Whatever you do, be certain that the parts that contact the cups are not touching the bearing races.

Note: Dia-Compe "S" and Chris King headsets have bearings that are pressed into the cups and cannot be removed. If you use a headset press that pushes on

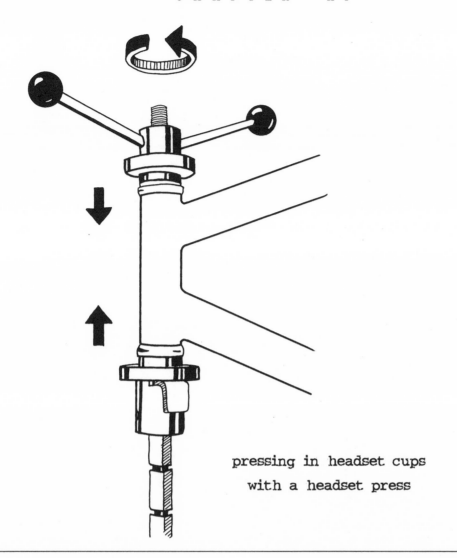

pressing in headset cups
with a headset press

the center of the cups, you will ruin the bearings. You need a press that pushes the outer portion of the cup and does not touch the bearings. Chris King makes tool inserts for this that fit most headset presses, and Park has a headset press with large flat ends that also works.

❺ Hold the lower end of the cup press shaft with a wrench. That will keep the tool from turning as you press in the cups. Tighten the press by turning the handle on the top clockwise. Keep tightening down on the tool until the cups are fully pressed into the ends of the head tube. Examine them carefully to make sure there are no gaps between the cups and the ends of the head tube.

❻ Liberally apply grease to all bearing surfaces. If you are using sealed cartridge bearings, a thin film will do.

❼ See the procedures outlined earlier in this chapter for details on how to adjust and install your style of headset and stem.

TROUBLESHOOTING STEM, BAR, AND HEADSET PROBLEMS

❶ Bars slip.

Tighten the pinch bolt on the stem that holds the bars.

❷ Bars make creaking noise while riding.

Loosen stem clamp, grease area of bar

TROUBLE-
SHOOTING

that fits in stem, slide bar back in place, and tighten stem bolt.

❸ Bar end slips.

Tighten bar-end clamp bolt.

❹ Stem is not pointed straight ahead.

Loosen bolt (or bolts) securing stem to fork steering tube, align stem with front wheel, and tighten stem bolt (or bolts) again. (With a threaded headset, the bolt you are interested in is a single vertical bolt on top of the stem; loosen it about two turns, and tap the top of the bolt with a soft hammer to disengage the wedge on the other end from the bottom of the stem. With a threadless headset, there are one, two, or three horizontal bolts pinching the stem around the steering tube. *Do not* loosen the bolt on the top of the stem cap; you'll have to readjust your headset if you do.)

❺ Fork and headset rattle or clunk when riding.

The headset is too loose. Tighten headset, as in **Adjust headset**.

❻ Stem/bar/fork assembly does not turn smoothly but instead stops in certain fixed positions.

Headset is pitted and needs to be replaced. See **Remove headset** and **Install headset**.

❼ Stem/bar/fork assembly does not turn freely.

Headset is too tight. The front wheel should swing easily from side to side when leaning the bike or lifting the front end. Loosen headset, as under

Adjusting a headset.

❽ Stem is stuck in fork steering tube.

See **Removing stuck stem**.

wheel building

"**A** child of five could understand this. Fetch me a child of five."

— Groucho Marx

tools

spoke wrench
truing stand
wheel dishing tool
13mm, 14mm, 15mm
   cone wrenches
17mm open end
   wrench (or
   an adjustable
   wrench)
spoke prep
   (follow
   application
   instructions
   on container)

OPTIONAL
linseed oil

Congratulations. You have arrived at the task most often used to gauge the talents of a bike mechanic. Next to building a frame or fork, building a good set of wheels is the most critical and most creative of a bike mechanic's tasks. Despite the air of mystery surrounding the art of wheel building, the construction of a good set of bicycle wheels is really a pretty straightforward task.

Clearly, wheels are the central component of a bike. For any bike to perform well, its wheels must be well-made and properly tensioned. Once you learn how, it is quite rewarding to turn a pile of small parts into a set of strong and light wheels upon which you can bash around with confidence. You will be amazed at what they can withstand, and you will no longer go through life thinking that building wheels is just something the "experts" do. With practice, you can build wheels at your house that are just as good as any custom-made set, and far superior to those built by machine.

This is not meant to be an exhaustive description of how to build all types of wheel spoking patterns; there are entire books written on that. (If you are interested in a more comprehensive treatment of the subject of wheel building, I recommend reading *The Barnett's Manual* by John Barnett or *The Bicycle Wheel* by Jobst Brandt.) You can build great wheels in the classic "three-cross" spoking pattern following this method. So, let's get started.

the whole thing

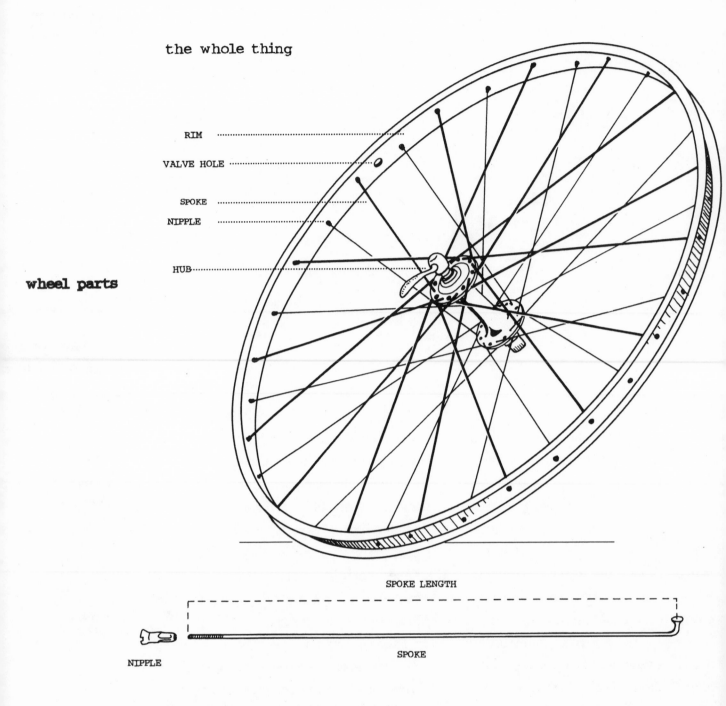

RIM

VALVE HOLE

SPOKE

NIPPLE

HUB

wheel parts

SPOKE LENGTH

NIPPLE   SPOKE

PARTS:

❶ Get together the parts you need: a rim, a hub (make sure that the hub you are using has the same number of holes as the rim does), properly-sized spokes and nipples to match. I suggest getting the spokes from your local bike shop. This

way, a mechanic can help make sure you are getting the right spoke lengths and can counsel you on what gauges (thickness) of spoke to buy, as well as what rim makes sense for your weight and kind of riding you plan on doing. Remember: you must specify that you

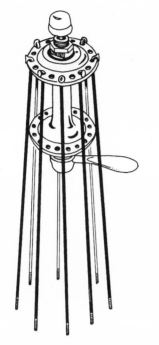

first half
of
right—side
spokes
placed
in hub

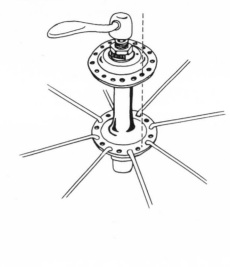

spoke—hole
offset

will be using a "three cross" spoking pattern.

Note: If you are just replacing a rim on an old wheel, do **not** use the old spokes. You won't save all that much money re-using the old spokes, and the rounded-out nipples and weakened spokes will soon make you wish you had gone ahead and spent the extra money on a new set.

LACING THE WHEEL

❶ Divide your spokes into four separate groups, two sets for each side of each hub flange. Remember: if you are building a rear wheel, you should be working with two different spoke lengths, since spokes on the right-hand side, or drive side, are almost always shorter.

❷ Hold the rim on your lap with the valve hole away from you. Notice that the holes alternate being offset upward

or downward from the rim centerline.

❸ Hold the hub in the center of the rim, with the right side of the hub pointing up. On a rear hub, the right side is the drive side. Front hubs are symmetrical; pick a side to be the right side. You may find it helpful to put a rubber band around the "right side" of a front hub, so you don't get the sides confused. In the illusratiions, the right sides has the nut end of the quick release.

First set of spokes

❹ Drop a spoke down into every other hole in the top (right side) hub flange, so that the spoke heads are facing you. Make sure if it's a rear wheel that you put the shorter spokes on the right side. If half the holes you are looking at are coumtersunk deeper into the hub flange, use those holes.

❺ Put a spoke into the first hole to the left of the valve hole and screw the

first spoke —
right side up

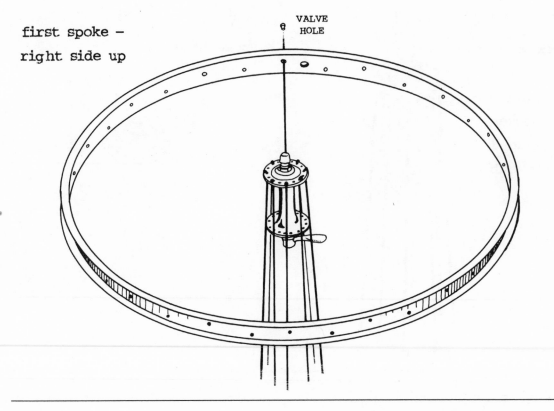

VALVE HOLE

**lacing the
wheel**

—

**second set
of spokes**

first set
of spokes
laced up

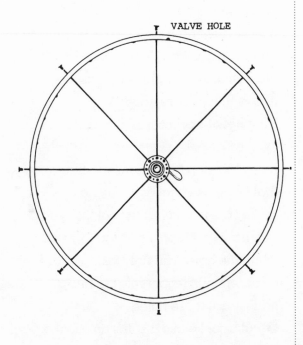

VALVE HOLE

nipple on three turns. Notice that this hole is offset upward. (If it isn't, you have a weird rim, and you must offset all instructions one hole.)

❻ Working counterclockwise, put the next spoke on the hub into the hole in the rim four holes away from the first spoke, and screw a nipple on three turns. There should be three open rim holes between these spokes, and the hole you put the second spoke into should also be offset upward.

❼ Continue counterclockwise around the wheel in the same manner. You should now have used half of the rim holes that are offset upward, and there should be three open holes between each spoke.

❽ Flip the wheel over.

Second set of spokes

❾ Sight down the length of the hub from

204

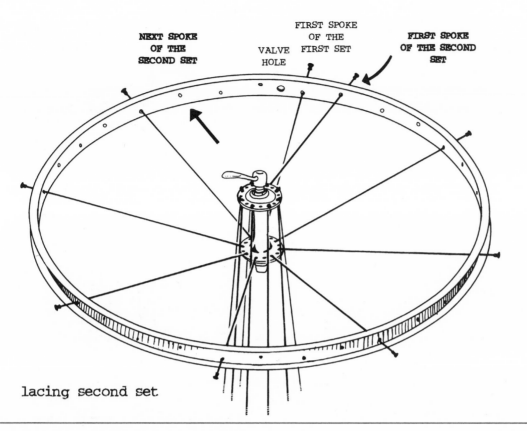

NEXT SPOKE
OF THE
SECOND SET

FIRST SPOKE
OF THE
FIRST SET

VALVE
HOLE

FIRST SPOKE
OF THE SECOND
SET

lacing second set

wheel building

one flange across to the other. Notice that the holes in one flange do not line up with the holes in the other; each hole lines up in between two holes on the opposite flange.

❿ Drop a spoke down through the hole in the top flange that is immediately to the right of the first spoke you installed (the spoke that is just to the right of the valve hole).

⓫ Put this new spoke into the second hole to the right of the valve hole, next to the first spoke you installed. This hole will be offset upward from the rim centerline.

⓬ Thread the nipple on three turns.

⓭ Double check to make sure that the spoke you just installed starts at a hole in the hub's top (left side) flange that is one-half-a-hole space to the right of the hole in the lower flange where the first spoke you installed started. These two spokes

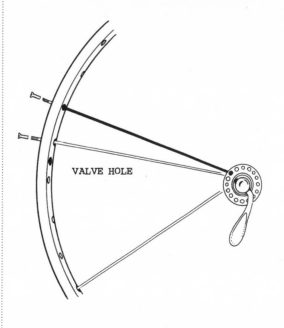

**diverging
parallel spokes**

VALVE HOLE

lacing the
wheel
————
second set
of spokes

second set of spokes laced up

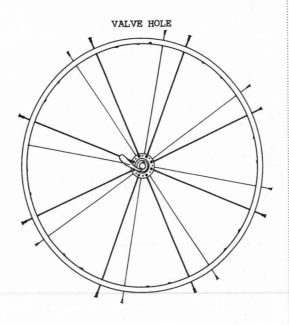

VALVE HOLE

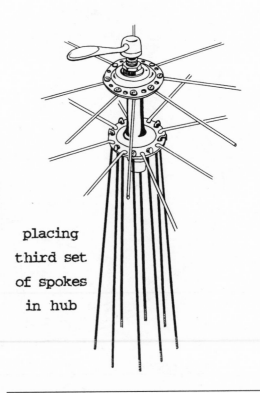

placing
third set
of spokes
in hub

should be diverging but still nearly parallel.

14 Drop a spoke down through the hole in the top (left side) flange two holes away in either direction, and continue around until every other hole has a spoke hanging down through it.

15 Working counterclockwise, take the next spoke and put it in the rim hole that is three holes to the left of the valve hole. This hole should be offset upward and four holes to the left of the spoke you just installed. Thread the nipple on three turns.

16 Follow this pattern counter-clockwise around the wheel. You should have now used half of the rim holes that are offset upwards, as well as half of the total rim holes. The second set of spokes should all be in upwardly offset holes, one hole to the right of each

spoke of the first set.

Third set of spokes

17 Drop spokes through the remaining holes on the right side of the hub, from the inside out. Remember: if it's a rear wheel, these spokes should be shorter than the spokes used on the left side.

18 Flip the wheel over, grabbing the spokes you've just dropped through to keep them from falling out.

19 Fan the spokes out, so they cannot fall back down through the hub holes.

20 Grab the hub and rotate it counterclockwise as far as you can.

21 Pick any spoke on the top (right hand) flange that is already laced to the rim. Now find the spoke five hub holes away in a clockwise direction.

22 Take this new spoke, cross it under the spoke you counted from (the one five holes away), and stick it into the rim hole

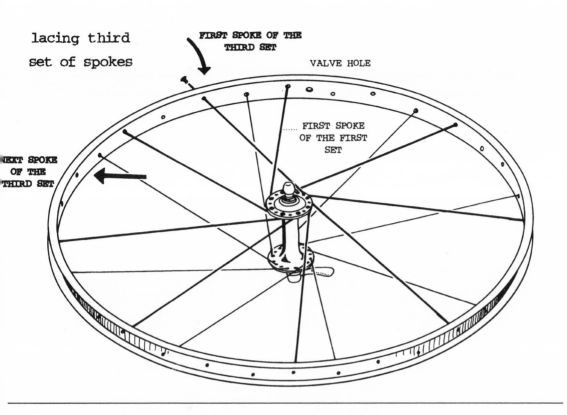

lacing third
set of spokes

FIRST SPOKE OF THE
THIRD SET

VALVE HOLE

FIRST SPOKE
OF THE FIRST
SET

NEXT SPOKE
OF THE
THIRD SET

two holes counterclockwise from that
spoke. Thread a nipple on three turns.

23 Continue around the wheel, doing the
same thing. You may find that some of
the spokes don't quite reach far enough.
If that's the case, push down on each one
about an inch from the spoke elbow to

help them reach.

24 Make sure that every spoke coming
out of the upper side of the top flange
(the spokes that come out towards you
with their spoke heads hidden from view)
crosses over two spokes and under a
third. All three of these "crossing" spokes

rotating hub counterclockwise

third set laced

valve hole

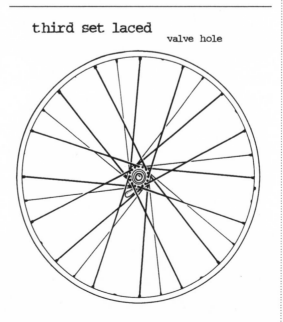

lacing the
wheel

———

third set
of spokes

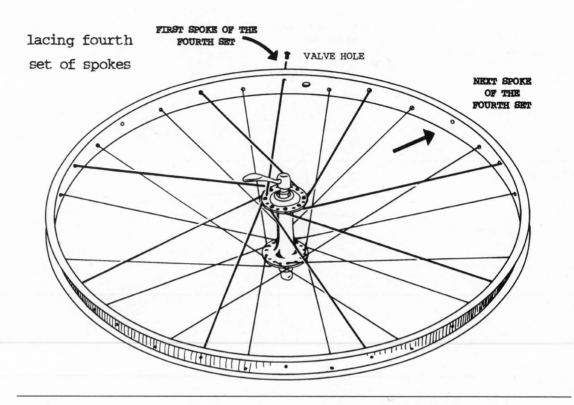

lacing fourth
set of spokes

FIRST SPOKE OF THE
FOURTH SET

VALVE HOLE

NEXT SPOKE
OF THE
FOURTH SET

come from the underside of the same flange, and have their spoke heads facing towards you. These "crossing" spokes begin 1, 3 and 5 hub holes counterclockwise from the spoke that you just inserted into the rim. This is called a "three cross" pattern because every spoke crosses three others on its way to the rim (over, over, under). Every upwardly offset hole should now be occupied on the rim.

Fourth (and final) set of spokes

25 Drop spokes down through the remaining hub holes in the bottom flange from the inside out.

26 Flip the wheel over, grabbing the spokes to keep them from falling back down through the holes.

27 Fan the spokes out.

28 Count in a counterclockwise direction to the spoke that is five hub holes from

any spoke on the top (left) flange that is already laced to the rim.

29 Take that spoke then cross it over two spokes, under the spoke you counted from, and stick it into the rim hole two holes clockwise from the spoke it crosses under. Thread a nipple on three turns.

30 Continue around the wheel, doing the same thing. You may find that some of the spokes don't quite reach far enough. If that's the case, push down on each one about an inch from the spoke elbow to help them reach.

31 Make sure that every spoke coming out from the upper side of the top flange (the spokes that come out towards you with their spoke heads hidden from view) crosses over two spokes and under a third. All three of these "crossing" spokes come from the underside of the same flange, and have their spoke heads

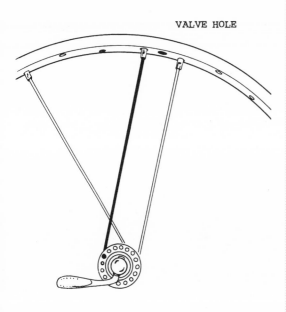

VALVE HOLE

converging parallel spokes

facing towards you. The "crossing" spokes begin 1, 3 and 5 hub holes clockwise from each spoke yemerging from the top of upper (left) hub flange. This is called a "three cross" pattern because every spoke crosses three others on its way to the rim (over, over, under). Every hole should now be occupied on the rim. The valve hole should be between "converging parallel" spokes to make room for the pump head.

TENSIONING THE WHEEL

❶ Put the wheel in the truing stand.

❷ Tighten each nipple with a spoke wrench until only three threads are visible beyond the bottom of the nipple. (This assumes that you are using standard length nipples and not the long ones that are rarely seen any more on high-quality wheels. With these, tighten

them until the spoke end is four threads from popping out of the top of the nipple toward the tube.)

❸ Press the spokes coming outward from the outer side of the hub flanges down with your thumb at the elbow to straighten out their line to the rim. Spokes coming out of the inner side of the flange do not need this.

❹ Go around the wheel, tightening each nipple 1/2 turn. Do this uniformly, so that the wheel is not thrown out of true.

❺ Check to see if the spokes are tight enough to give a tone when plucked.

❻ Repeat Steps 4 and 5 until the spokes all make a tone.

TRUING THE WHEEL
Lateral true

❶ Make sure the hub axle has no end play. If it does, adjust the hub (see **Chapter 6**) to eliminate the end play.

❷ (Optional) Put a drop of linseed oil on each nipple as it comes up out of the rim to lubricate the contact area between it and the inside of the rim hole.

❸ Set the truing stand feelers so that one of them scrapes the side of the rim at the worst lateral wobble.

❹ Where the rim scrapes, tighten the spokes coming from the opposite side of the hub and loosen the spokes coming from the same side of the hub. Start with 1/4 turn, and decrease it as you move away from the center of the scraping area. This pulls the rim away from the feeler.If it does the opposite, you are turning the spokes the wrong direction.

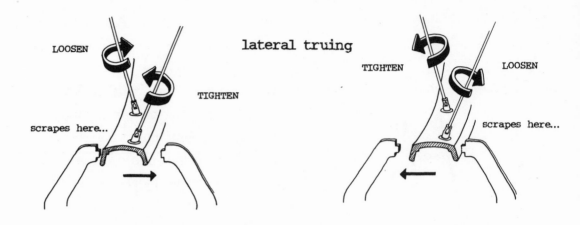

lateral truing

LOOSEN
TIGHTEN
scrapes here...
TIGHTEN
LOOSEN
scrapes here...

Remember: you normally turn something to the right to tighten and to the left to loosen, but tightening and loosening spoke nipples at the bottom of the wheel is the opposite of what you would normally do. This is because the nipple head is underneath your spoke wrench. Try opening a jar that is upside down and you will immediately understand the principles involved.

❺ Work around the wheel in this way, bringing in the feelers as the wheel gets truer.

Radial true

❻ Set the truing stand feelers so that they now contact the circumferemce of the rim, rather than the sides.

❼ Bring the feelers in until they scrape against the highest spot on the rim.

❽ Tighten the spokes where the rim scrapes by a 1/4 turn. This will pull the rim inward. Decrease the amount of each turn (to 1/8 turn and less) as you move away from the center of the scraping area.

❾ Work around the wheel this way, bringing the feelers in as the wheel becomes rounder. Loosen the spokes at a dip in the rim. (If the spokes are too tight at this point, they will be hard to turn and

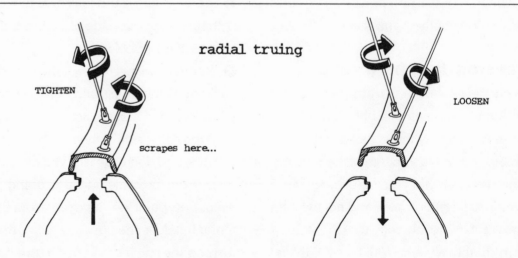

radial truing

TIGHTEN
scrapes here...
LOOSEN

creak and groan as you turn them. When
the spokes become hard to turn, loosen
all of the spokes in the wheel 1/4 turn
before continuing.)

DISHING THE WHEEL

❶ Place the dishing tool across the right
side of the wheel, bisecting the center.

❷ Tighten or loosen the dishing gauge
screw until the gauge contacts the outer
face of the axle end nut.

❸ Flip the wheel over.

❹ Place the dishing tool across the other
side of the wheel.

❺ Check the gap of the dishing gauge
with this axle end-nut face. Any gap
between the dishing gauge and the axle
end-nut face indicates the amount the
rim is offset from the centerline of the
wheel. If there is no gap but an overlap
instead, reset the dishing gauge on *this*
side (the previously overlapped side).
Then flip it over and check the other side
(i.e., repeat Steps 3, 4, and 5).

❻ Put the wheel back in the truing stand.

❼ Pull the rim toward the center
(reducing the gap between the dishing
tool and the axle end face) by tightening
the spokes on the opposite side of the
wheel from the axle end that had the gap
between it and the dishing gauge.
Tighten 1/2 turn each. If the spokes start
getting really tight (they creak a lot when
tightening, and they feel much tighter
than the spokes in a comparable wheel),
then loosen the spokes on the opposite
side of the wheel.

❽ Recheck the wheel with the dishing

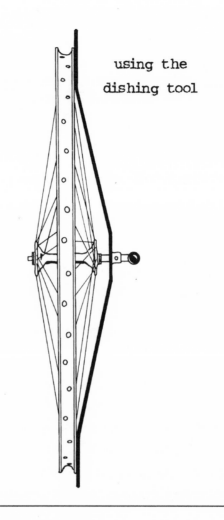

using the
dishing tool

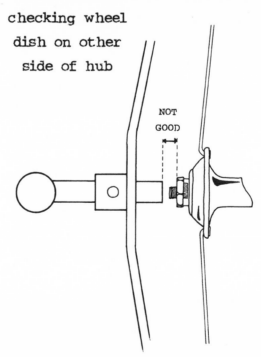

checking wheel
dish on other
side of hub

NOT
GOOD

dishing the
wheel

gauge by repeating Steps 1-5.

❾ If the wheel is still off dish (there is still a gap between the dishing gauge and the end nut when you flip it over), repeat Steps 6-8 until the dish is correct (the gap is zero).

❿ Pre-stress the spokes by squeezing each pair of spokes together with your hands. They will make a "ping" noise as they unwind. If pre-stressing throws the wheel way out of true, the spokes are probably too tight. Loosen them all 1/8 turn. Some loss of wheel "trueness" is normal. If the loss is minor, you may overlook it

⓫ Repeat "Truing the wheel" steps, followed by the "Dishing the wheel" steps. Keep bringing in the accuracy this way until the wheel is as you want it.

⓬ If the rim is oily, wipe it down with a citrus-based biodegradable solvent.

⓭ Congratulate yourself on building your wheel, and show it off to your friends.

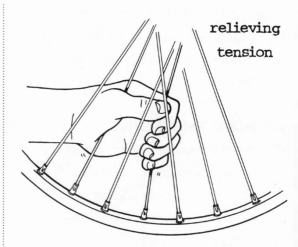

relieving tension

COMMENTS

Your wheel has some features that you won't find on machine-built wheels. Most significantly, on your rear wheel, the "pulling spokes are to the outside." In plain speak, this means that you have a spoking pattern that resists the twisting force on the hub produced by pedaling forces on the chain. Half of the spokes are called "pulling" or "dynamic" spokes, and the other half are called "static" spokes. The pulling spokes are the ones directed in such a way that a clockwise

twist on the hub increases the tension in them. If you look at the wheel from the drive side, you will see what I am talking about. On the other hand, the static spokes do not oppose a clockwise twist on the hub. In fact, their tension *decreases* when you stomp on the pedals. By placing all of the pulling spokes so that they come from the inside of the hub flanges out (i.e., the spoke heads are on the inward side of the flanges), we have attached the spokes doing the most work the farthest outward on the hub, increasing their angle to the rim, and hence their ability to oppose forces acting on the rim.

If you choose the appropriate parts for your weight and riding style, and have the proper spoke tension, then you should have a strong wheel that will last you a long time. Congratulations!

XIII

forks

"If you come to a fork in the road, take it."

— YOGI BERRA

The fork serves a number of purposes. Most obviously, it connects the front wheel to the handlebars. Of course, the fork allows the bike to be steered, and supports the front brake. Forks also offset the front hub some distance forward of the steering axis. This offset distance (called the "fork rake"), combined with the steering axis (the "head angle") and the wheel size, determine how your bike is going to handle; how it will respond in an emergency and how it steers through corners.

All forks — suspended or rigid — provide at least a minimum amount of suspension by allowing the front wheel to move up and down. The simple fact that a fork is angled forward from purely vertical makes it possible for the fork to flex along its length and absorb vertical shocks. Suspension forks add a much greater range of travel.

Virtually any mountain bike fork is made up of a simple combination of components: the steering tube, the fork crown, the fork legs (sometimes called "blades"), the brake bosses (usually cantilever posts, but there are also disc brake, roller-cam and U-brake mounts), and the fork ends (also called

tools

metric Allen wrenches
metric open-end wrenches
adjustable wrench
needle-nose pliers
safety glasses
soft hammer
long screwdriver
non-lithium grease
citrus degreaser

OPTIONAL
torque wrench
ruler or calipers
a pair of dropout alignment tools
solid bench vise
snap-ring pliers
air pump for fork
metric socket wrenches
bike stand
medium thread lock compound (like Loctite 242)
titanium bolt anti-seize compound

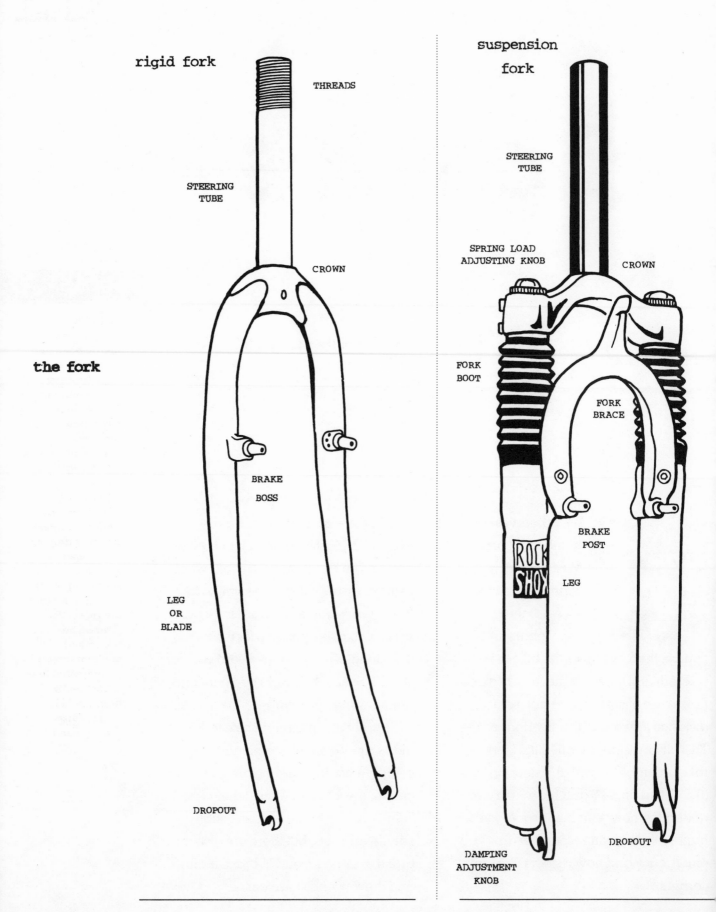

rigid fork

THREADS

STEERING
TUBE

CROWN

the fork

BRAKE

BOSS

LEG
OR
BLADE

DROPOUT

**suspension
fork**

STEERING
TUBE

SPRING LOAD
ADJUSTING KNOB

CROWN

FORK
BOOT

FORK
BRACE

ROCK
SHOX

BRAKE
POST

LEG

DROPOUT

DAMPING
ADJUSTMENT
KNOB

"dropouts" or "fork tips"). Mountain bike forks are manufactured from steel, aluminum, titanium, carbon fiber and countless mixes of these materials.

These days, a large percentage of mountain bikes come equipped with suspension forks. Their most distinguishing feature is, of course, the spring. That spring can be made up of elastic polymer bumpers (elastomers), compressed air, or steel coils. A lot of suspension forks also include a damping system to control how fast the spring compresses and to slow the rebound of the spring. It acts much like a shock absorber on a car.

Hydraulic damping systems are the most common, relying on the controlled movement of hydraulic fluid from one chamber to another. That flow is usually regulated by a system of holes that act to slow the rate of flow. Some dampers operate on a similar principle, but use compressed air to control compression and rebound.

The most commonly used suspension design uses "telescoping" fork legs that consist of two sections. The inner portion is attached to the fork, while the outer leg grips the front hub and slides up and down over the inner leg. There are a number of variations that vie for the rest of the fork market, but the vast majority of forks on the market fall into the first group: There have been a number of "upside down" telescoping forks introduced in recent years. On these models, the smaller lower leg fits inside

how it works

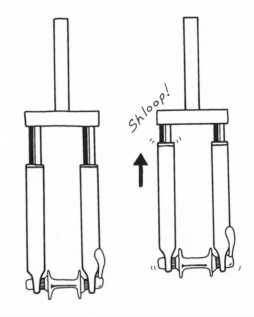

Shloop!

the larger-diameter upper leg. Cannondale's "Head Shock" design incorporates rigid fork legs and places a single shock unit into the head tube. There are also lots of "linkage" suspension forks on the market that use a system of pivots and movable arms attached to a spring.

FORK INSPECTION

For the most part, forks are pretty durable, but they *do break* sometimes. A fork failure could really ruin your day, since the means of control of the bike is eliminated. Such loss of control usually involves the rapid transfer of your body directly onto the ground. This often results in substantial pain.

Ever since I first opened a frame shop, people have regularly brought me an amazing collection of broken forks. Some of those fork failures involved steering tubes broken either at the top of

fork
inspection

215

the threaded section or at the base above the fork crown. I've seen fork crowns that broke or separated (releasing a fork leg or two), fork crown bolts that broke or fell out, fork legs that folded, cantilever posts that snapped, and front dropouts that broke off. Failures like that often involve some very serious and catastrophic consequences. I have also heard about pivot pins or pivot mounts on linkage forks breaking or falling out. There have been cases when the air in an air-sprung shock suddenly rushed out, causing the fork to bottom out. Fork braces, which hold the brake cable on, can break off, causing all sorts of problems. You can go a long way toward preventing these problems simply by regularly inspecting your fork.

With that in mind, get into the habit of checking your fork regularly for any warning signs of impending failure — bends, cracks and stressed paint. If you have crashed your bike, give your fork a complete and very thorough inspection. If you find any indication that your fork has been damaged, get a new fork. Saving money on a fork doesn't make a lot of sense when you weigh the risks.

When you inspect a fork, remove the front wheel, clean the mud off, and look under the crown and between the fork legs. Carefully examine all of the outside areas. Look for any areas where the paint or finish looks cracked or stretched. Look for bent parts, from little

ripples in fork legs to skewed cantilever posts and bent dropouts.

Put your wheel back in, and watch to see if the fork legs twist when you tighten the hub into the dropouts. Check to make sure that a true wheel centers under the fork crown. If it doesn't, turn the wheel around and put it back in the fork. That way you can confirm whether the misalignment is in your fork or a result of an out-of-dish wheel. If the wheel lines up off to one side when it is in one way and off the same amount to the other side when it is in the other way, the wheel is off, and the fork is straight. If the wheel skews off to the same side in the fork no matter which direction you place the wheel, the fork is misaligned.

I recommend overhauling your headset annually (Chapter 11), and, when you do, carefully examine the steering tube for any signs of stress or damage. Check for bent, cracked or stretched areas, and for bulging where the stem expands inside. Hold the stem up next to the steering tube to make sure that when your stem is inserted the way you have been using it, that the bottom of the stem is always over an inch below the bottom of the steering tube threads. If you expand your stem in the threaded region, you are asking for trouble. The threads cut the steering tube wall thickness down by about 50 percent, and each thread offers a sharp breakage plane along which the tube can cleave.

fork inspection

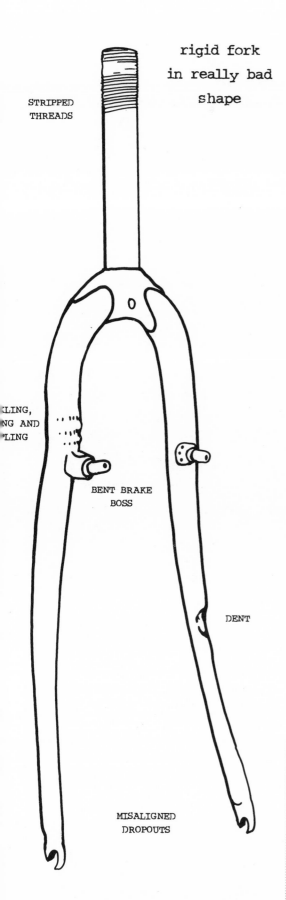

rigid fork
in really bad
shape

STRIPPED
THREADS

KLING,
NG AND
*LING

BENT BRAKE
BOSS

DENT

MISALIGNED
DROPOUTS

On telescoping suspension forks:
Check that any clamp bolts are tight (ideally, you would do this with a torque wrench to check that they are tightened to the torque recommended by the fork manufacturer). If you have titanium clamp bolts on your fork crown and you do lots of fast and rough downhill riding, consider replacing them annually; the heads of titanium fork crown bolts have been known to snap off. Check for oil leaks, either from around the top of the outer leg or around the bolt at the bottom of the outer leg. Check for torn, cracked or missing seals around the top of the outer leg.

On linkage forks, there are a lot of bolts, pins and pivots, and they all need to be checked regularly. Check to see that the bolts or pins at the pivot points are all secure. This means making sure that any bolts are tight and any pins have their circlips or other retaining devices in place so they do not fall out. Check for cracks and bends around the pivot points.

If you have any doubts about anything on your fork or think that something looks suspicious, take it to the expert at your bike shop. When it comes to forks, err on the side of caution. Replace them before they need it.

FORK DAMAGE

If your inspection has uncovered some damage that does not automatically require fork replacement, here are some guidelines to go by and means of repair.

forks

fork damage

Dents

Not all fork dents threaten the integrity of the fork. On a rigid fork, a small dent usually poses little risk. A large dent, of course, does. On a suspension fork, almost any dent can adversely affect the fork's operation, even if it does not pose a breakage threat. Most suspension fork parts are replaceable. If, for example, an inner leg gets dented, you can get a new one and install it without replacing — or even removing — the fork.

Fork misalignment

Within limits, a rigid steel fork can be realigned if it is slightly off-center. (See **Align dropouts on steel rigid fork** later in this chapter.) Suspension forks and rigid aluminum, carbon-fiber, and titanium forks *cannot* be re-aligned. Don't try it!

Stripped steering tube threads

If the threads on the steering tube are damaged so that the headset slips when you try to tighten it, you need to replace it. The steering tube and fork crown assembly can usually be replaced on a suspension fork. You don't usually have that option when it comes to rigid forks, so you have to replace the whole thing.

Obvious bend, ripple or crease in fork legs

Replace the fork. The poor handling and potential breakage pose too great a threat to your safety to be worth saving a few bucks.

Bent or stripped cantilever bosses

On most suspension forks (and even on some rigid forks), the cantilever bosses can be unscrewed with an open end wrench (usually 8mm) and replaced. It is a good idea to use a thread-locking compound like Loctite 242 on the threads of the new mount. With few exceptions, bent or stripped cantilever bosses on a rigid fork usually mean that you have to buy a new fork. If you have a framebuilder in your area, he or she may be able to weld or braze a new one on a steel fork. You will also need to repaint the fork.

MAINTAINING RIGID FORKS

Beyond touching up the paint on steel forks and performing regular inspections, there really isn't much maintenance you can do with a rigid fork. You can check the alignment, if your bike is handling badly. You can even perform some minor realignment on a steel fork if you find that it is off center. Note that it is risky enough to qualify as a Level 3 job. *Do not* try to realign titanium, carbon-fiber or aluminum forks. (You've probably noticed that I am repeating myself here.)

CHECK FORK ALIGNMENT

 You will need a ruler or caliper, a true front wheel and dropout alignment tools. If you have an aluminum, titanium, carbon-fiber fork, or a suspension fork, this procedure is useful only as a way to find out if there is something wrong with your fork. Because you should *not* try to realign titanium, carbon-fiber or

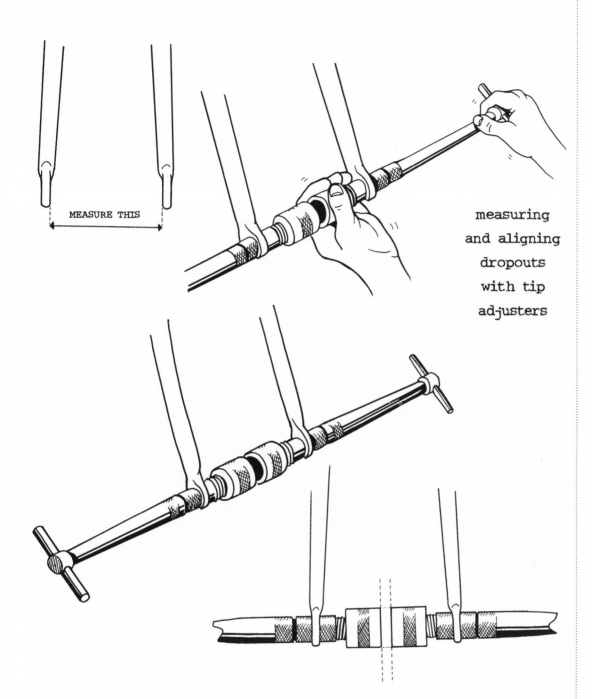

MEASURE THIS

measuring
and aligning
dropouts
with tip
adjusters

checking fork
alignment

aluminum forks. (You've probably noticed that I am repeating myself again.) Checking the alignment may help explain bike-handling problems you may be having. If you find the alignment to be off more than a couple of millimeters in any direction with one of these forks, you need a new fork. If your fork is new, it should be a warranty item. Otherwise, you need to buy a new one.

If your steel fork is more than 8mm off in any direction, you ought to get a new fork. If the dropouts of a steel fork are slightly bent, you can realign them. You can also take a moderately bent (between 2mm and 8mm off) steel fork to a framebuilder or a bike shop for realignment. Make sure that whomever you take it to is properly equipped with a fork jig or alignment table and is well versed in the art of "cold setting" (a fancy term for bending) steel forks.

❶ Remove the fork from the bike. (Chapter 11)

❷ With the front wheel out, measure the spacing between the faces of the dropouts. Adult and higher-quality childrens' bikes should have a spacing of 100mm between the inner surfaces of the dropouts. (Some low-end kids' bikes have narrower spacing — about 90mm or so. If that's the type of bike you are working with, don't bother with this step. It really isn't worth the trouble.) Remember that you are measuring the distance between the surfaces that the hub faces contact, not between wheel-retaining bumps. Dropout spacing up to 102mm and down to 99mm is acceptable. Beyond that in either direction means a trip to the bike shop for a new fork. If you have a steel fork, you can go to a bike shop or framebuilder for realignment.

❸ Clamp the steering tube of the fork in a bike stand or a padded vise. Install the dropout-alignment tools. The tools are made so that they can be used on both the fork and the rear triangle of the bike, so they have spacers for use in the wider rear dropouts. Unscrew the alignment cups enough to create a space large enough so that you can slide the tool into the dropouts. Move all of the spacers to the outside of the dropouts so that only the cups of the tools are placed inside of the dropouts. Install the tool so that the shaft is seated up against the top of the dropout slot. Tighten the handles down.

❹ Ideally, the ends of the cups on the dropout aligning tools should be parallel, lined up with each other, and about 0.1-0.5mm apart (the cups of the dropout alignment tools are nominally 50mm in length). The cups on some dropout aligning tools are adjustable in length, so that you can bring them up close to each other to see their alignment more clearly. If they are lined up with each other, and the dropouts are spaced between 99mm and 102mm apart, go to the next step. If they are not lined up straight across with each other and the dropouts are within the 99-102mm spacing range, skip to **Align dropouts on steel rigid fork** later in this chapter.

Note: It is very important that the fork dropout faces are parallel before continuing with step 5, or the rest of the alignment procedures will be a waste of time. Clamping the hub into misaligned dropouts will force the fork legs to twist. If your dropouts are misaligned, any measurement of the side-to-side and fore-aft alignment of the fork legs will not be accurate.

❺ Remove the tire from a front wheel Make sure the wheel is true and properly dished (Chapter 12).

❻ Install the wheel in the fork. Make

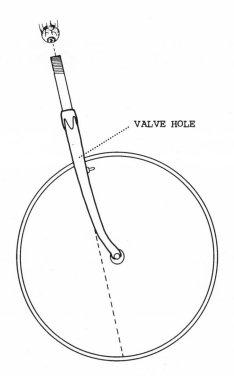

VALVE HOLE

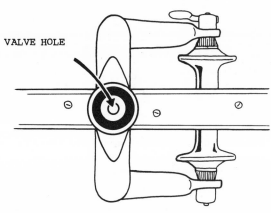

VALVE HOLE

checking fork alignment
by sighting through
the steering tube

checking fork
alignment

sure the axle is seated against the top of the dropout slot on both sides, and make sure the quick-release skewer is tight. Lightly push the rim from side to side to make certain that there is no play in the front hub. If there is play, you first must adjust the hub (Chapter 6).

❼ Look down the steering tube and through the valve hole to the bottom side of the rim. The steering tube should be lined up with this line of sight through the wheel. When you are sighting through the steering tube and the valve hole, you should see the same amount of space between either side of the rim and the sides of the steering tube. Turn the wheel around and install it again so that what was the right end of the hub is now the left, and vice versa. Sight through the steering tube and the wheel valve hole

again. Placing the wheel in the fork both ways corrects for deformation in the axle or any wobble in the wheel. If the wheel is true, properly dished and the axle is in good shape, the wheel should line up exactly as it did before. If it does not, but the wheel is off by the same amount to one side as it is to the other when the wheel is turned around, the wheel is off and the fork is fine side to side.

If this test indicates the fork is up to 2-3mm off to the side, that is close enough; continue on, please. If it is off by more than 3mm, get a new fork or have it aligned by a framebuilder (if it is steel ... because, by now you know that you should *not* try to realign titanium, carbon-fiber or aluminum forks).

Note: If you are sighting through the wheel in this way, and you cannot see

checking fork alignment with a ruler

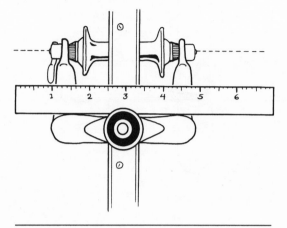

the bottom side of the rim through the valve hole because the hub is in the way, your fork has big problems. In order for the bike to handle properly, the fork must have some forward offset from the front hub from the steering axis. This offset, or "rake," is usually around 4cm on a mountain bike. If you sight through the steering tube and see the front hub, the fork is bent backward so much that it has little or no offset. If this is the case, you need a new fork.

❽ With the wheel in the fork, place a ruler on edge across the fork legs just below the fork crown. Make sure the ruler is exactly perpendicular to the steering tube.

❾ Holding the ruler in place, lift the fork toward a light source so that you are sighting across the ruler and the front hub toward the light. The ruler's edge should line up parallel with the axle ends sticking out of either end of the hub. This will tell you if one fork leg is bent back relative to the other one. If the two line up parallel or very close to that, your

aligning dropouts on rigid steel forks

fork alignment has checked out completely, and you can put it back in the bike. If one fork leg is considerably behind the other, you need to get a new fork or have this one aligned.

ALIGN DROPOUTS ON RIGID STEEL FORK

You can only do this with a steel, non-suspension fork!

You can knock your dropouts out of alignment by simply pulling the bike off of a roof rack and failing to lift it high enough to clear the rack skewer. Of course, your forks can come with misaligned dropouts to start with. If the dropout is bent more than 7 degrees or so, or if the paint is cracked at the dropout where it is bent, it is too dangerous to bend it back. Replace the fork.

❶ Install dropout-alignment tools as described in Step 3 under **Check fork alignment** earlier in this chapter. Check the alignment as in Step 4.

❷ If they are not lined up with each other, and the fork spacing is between 99mm and 102mm, you can align the dropouts. If the fork spacing is wider than 102mm or less than 99mm, there is no point in aligning the dropout faces, because you must bend the fork legs as well to correct the spacing. Without an alignment table or fork jig, you cannot do this accurately. You should get a new fork, or have a qualified mechanic or framebuilder align it.

If your fork spacing is between 99mm

and 102mm apart, clamp the crown or unicrown of the fork very tightly between two wood blocks in a well-anchored vise.

❸ Grab the end of the dropout-alignment tool handle with one hand and the cup of the tool with the other. Bend each dropout until the open faces of the dropout-alignment tools are parallel, and the edges line straight up with each other.

❹ Remove the tools, go back to Step 5 under **Check fork alignment** earlier in this chapter. Repeat the alignment steps if necessary.

MAINTAINING SUSPENSION FORKS

Suspension forks are rapidly becoming the standard on mountain bikes. They offer a significant performance advantage and increase the versatility of the bike. Rapid improvements in the science of bicycle suspension have resulted in a proliferation of numerous types of forks. Of course, with this rush of technology, older models quickly become obsolete. Because of that, you should remember that the details outlined here are applicable to forks commonly used in 1996. As of this writing, the market is dominated by telescoping forks with elastomer springs inside. Some also come equipped with hydraulic damping systems.

This chapter also outlines maintenance and adjustment pro-cedures for air-sprung forks. You will be

on your own if you have linkage-style forks or aftermarket upgrades retrofitted to forks. Most come with a set of maintenance instructions and an owners manual. Read them carefully. Linkage-style forks rely on several pivot points, so there are more places for more things to go wrong. Be especially vigilant about inspecting these forks regularly. Since a lot of forks require snap-ring pliers for service, they are included on the tool list, even though most elastomer forks do not require them.

Elastomer and air-oil telescoping forks

Since these two types of forks operate on the same basic principle, many of the basic service steps apply to both.

Remove fork legs from fork crown

If you want to add or replace dust boots on your fork, you first need to remove the legs. You can leave the fork brace and brakes on when you do that. You can also leave the headset/crown/steering tube assembly in the bike. It is not necessary to remove the fork legs from the crown to change the elastomer stack in an elastomer fork or to pump an air/oil fork.

Note: Some fork legs are pressed into the fork crown, rather than clamped in. These fork legs cannot be removed from the crown. Instead, installation and removal of dust boots on these forks requires the removal of the outer legs and fork brace structure. For example,

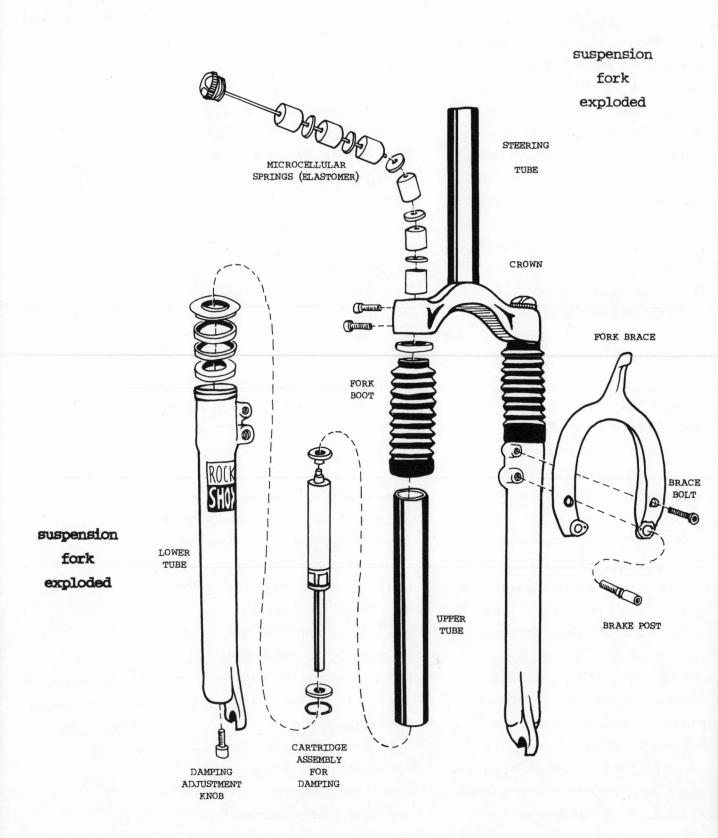

suspension
fork
exploded

MICROCELLULAR
SPRINGS (ELASTOMER)

STEERING
TUBE

CROWN

FORK BRACE

FORK
BOOT

BRACE
BOLT

suspension
fork
exploded

LOWER
TUBE

UPPER
TUBE

BRAKE POST

DAMPING
ADJUSTMENT
KNOB

CARTRIDGE
ASSEMBLY
FOR
DAMPING

ROCK SHOX

XIII

forks

1996 Rock Shox Judy forks use pressed-in crowns. (For instructions on how to remove the outer legs see **Overhaul fork legs on Judy and Mach 5** later in this chapter.)

❶ Disconnect the brake cable by removing the cable end from the brake lever (Chapter 7).

❷ Loosen the crown bolts on both sides of the crown. If there are two on each side of your fork crown, do not completely undo one bolt while leaving the other fully tightened. Doing that places a great deal of clamping force on the remaining tight bolt and you can strip the head trying to get it loose. Instead, turn one bolt about 1/4 of a turn and then do the same to the other. Then back to the first bolt and loosen by another 1/4 turn. Repeat until the crown is loose enough to free the leg.

❸ Pull the inner legs out of the crown using a very slight rocking motion.

Remove and install fork boots

With all telescoping forks, I recommend keeping fork boots on the inner legs (between the outer legs and the crown) to keep them clean and reduce maintenance and wear. You will need to remove the boots when you are checking your fork's travel.

❶ Remove the fork legs from the crown (see above).

❷ Pull the fork boots off.

❸ To install boots, slide them on to the inner legs, with the large end down toward the outer legs. Make sure that you are using boots designed for your fork.

❹ Pull the lip of each fork boot into the groove in the top of the outer leg. You may need to stretch the boot with a pair of needle-nose pliers to get it to slide over the outer leg behind the fork brace.

❺ Replace the inner legs (fork tubes) in the fork crown (see below).

Install fork legs in fork crown

❶ Wipe the inner legs clean, and make sure the fork crown bolts are loose.

❷ Insert the inner legs into the fork crown. Some Manitou forks have a lip against which the inner leg is supposed to rest. Slide the inner leg up into the crown until it hits the lip. Other Manitous and all Rock Shox forks slide all the way through the crown. Push the inner leg through the crown until the top of the leg sticks up no more than 3mm above the top of the crown.

❸ Tighten the crown bolts, again alternating between the two bolts on each side. Manitou's single 6mm crown bolts are to be tightened to a torque of 110-130 inch-pounds, and Rock Shox's smaller paired crown bolts are to be tightened to 60 inch-pounds. Use anti-seize compound on titanium bolts and medium thread-lock compound on steel bolts.

Measuring fork travel

MEASURE SAG

"Sag" is the amount of fork compression that occurs when the rider sits on the bike without moving. You'll need a friend to help you measure the distance from the top of the outer leg to the bottom of the fork crown when you are both on and off of the bike. The difference between the two measurements is the sag.

The sag can also be measured using the trusty zip-ie method:

❶ Tighten a plastic zip tie around one inner leg, and slide it down against the top of the outer leg.

❷ Get on your bike.

❸ Get off your bike. When you are off your bike, measure the distance from the top of the outer leg to the zip tie.

Notes: a. If you want to measure the amount of travel you normally use while riding, go ride with the zip tie on. Hit bumps and check the travel.

b. If you have protective fork boots installed over the inner legs, you will need to remove at least one of the boots when checking the travel. To remove the boots, you must remove the fork legs from the crown. Ssee **Remove and install fork bolts.**)

MEASURE MAXIMUM POSSIBLE TRAVEL

The fork's full travel can be measured by eliminating the spring from the fork. You can also go by the manufacturer's advertised travel for your fork, though I have often found that figure to be overstated.

❶ Remove the spring from both fork legs. **With an elastomer fork,** remove the elastomer stack cap from both sides of the fork crown. Some forks have hand-turned nuts; some need to be removed with a wrench (usually 22mm). On some forks, loosening the crown bolts makes it

elastomer forks

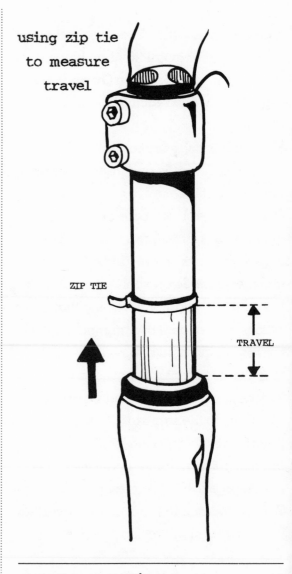

using zip tie to measure travel

ZIP TIE

TRAVEL

easier to unscrew the cap.

With an air-oil fork, release the air from both legs. On Rock Shox air-oil forks, remove either the Phillips screw or the plastic snap-on cap covering the air hole, turn the compression damping adjustment to the highest setting, moisten the needle of a ball-pumping adapter, and stick it down into the hole to release the air. On forks with Schrader valves, simply remove the valve cap and push down on the valve pin to let the air out.

❷ Measure the distance from the bottom of the crown to the top of the outer leg forks

when the fork is fully extended and when it is fully compressed. The difference between these numbers is the total available travel you have.

When riding with zip-ties on the inner legs, check if you are using up the total travel when you hit big bumps. This helps you determine the proper amount of spring tension to use.

Minor maintenance

If you do this procedure frequently and keep the inner legs covered with fork boots, you can greatly increase the life of the seals as well as the time between fork overhauls. Stickiness in suspension forks is usually caused by a dry or dirty dust seal rubbing on a dry or dirty inner leg.

❶ Wipe off the outside of the seal on top of each outer leg and the length of the inner leg between the outer leg and crown.

❷ Use a **non-lithium** grease and put a thin coat of grease on the outside of the seals and inner legs. Cover them back up with the fork boots. You may need to stretch the bottom of each fork boot with needle-nose pliers to get it in the groove around the top of the outer leg and behind the fork brace.

ELASTOMER FORKS

Telescoping elastomer suspension forks are beautiful in their simplicity. They have relatively few parts, are easy to tune to a rider's weight and riding style and are really easy to maintain. They have very few things that can go wrong with them.

Tuning elastomer forks
SETTING SPRING PRELOAD.

Spring preload can be adjusted on most mid- to high-end elastomer forks. Preload determines the way a spring responds to the forces applied to it. On an elastomer fork, you can simply adjust the preload by turning the adjuster knobs on the top of the fork crown. With most forks, you can adjust the preload while riding as you encounter terrain variations.

Rotating the adjuster knobs clockwise gives a firmer ride by tightening down on (and thus shortening) the elastomer spring stack. Rotating the adjuster knobs counterclockwise softens the ride. Make sure the top cap surrounding the

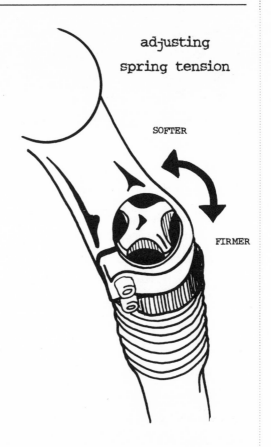

adjusting
spring tension

SOFTER

FIRMER

replacing
elastomers

knob does not unscrew from the fork crown; you may need to hold it tight with one hand (or a wrench) while you loosen the adjuster knob.

Preloading the springs does not limit the full travel for large bumps. It alters the force required to initially move the springs when you encounter smaller bumps. Varying the preload also changes the fork's sag.

REPLACING ELASTOMERS

To make major changes in the fork's spring rate, you must change the elastomer springs inside of the fork. Manufacturers usually color-code the elastomers for stiffness, though it's pretty easy to tell the difference between stiff and soft elastomer bumpers by simply squeezing them between your fingers. Extra elastomers usually come with the fork, or you can buy them from a dealer (some manufacturers refer to the elastomers as "MCUs" for "Micro-Cellular Units," referring to the small air chambers trapped inside the elastomers).

The fork needs stiffer elastomers (or more spring pre-load) if it sags excessively when you sit on it. Long-travel forks (those with more than 2 1/2-inches of travel) should sag around one-half inch. Short-travel forks should sag no more than a quarter of an inch or so. The fork needs softer elastomers if hard impacts with large bumps do not use the fork's full travel.

❶ Locate the top caps. Rock Shox

adjusting damping on Rock Shox Judy fork

2MM ALLEN WRENCH

recommends that you first loosen the crown bolts to relieve inward pressure on the fork legs before unscrewing the caps. Turn the top cap counterclockwise to loosen it. On many high-end forks, like Rock Shox Judy and Manitou Mach 5 and EFC, this can be done with your fingers. Many other forks use a wrench (22mm on Rock Shox Quadra) to unscrew the top cap.

❷ Pull the top caps straight up out of the fork. On many forks, the top cap is connected to a rod that runs through each of the elastomer bumpers. By pulling straight up on the top cap, you will remove all of the bumpers as well. Elastomer Rock Shox forks produced after mid-1995 use plastic spacers with nubs on both sides to hold the elastomer bumpers together. These are called "Judy Jax." Some forks have no system to hold the elastomers to the caps, so you need to turn the bike upside down to get them to fall out.

❸ Clean any old grease off of the skewers, elastomers, Judy Jax or whatever else you removed from the fork. Chose the combination of elastomers that you prefer and apply a new coating of grease to everything you just cleaned.

❹ Replace the elastomer stack in the fork legs, and screw the cap down. Be sure to re-tighten the crown bolts, if you loosened them. (Rock Shox recommends 60 inch-pounds).

FINE TUNING DAMPING

Some high-end elastomer forks have a hydraulic damping cartridge or cylinder inside one or both lower legs. Most elastomer forks do not have these (if there is no bolt at the bottom of the fork legs, it does not have one). Of those with damping cartridges, not all are adjustable. Manitou Mach 5 and EFC and all 1996 and later Rock Shox Judy forks do have adjustable damping.

Rebound damping controls the speed at which the fork returns to its original position after it has been compressed and released.

Compression damping controls the speed at which the spring compresses during the fork's downstroke.

On a Manitou Mach 5 or EFC, the compression damping is permanently set at the factory. Only the rebound damping is adjustable. Both forks have a damping adjustment finger knob at the bottom of the left outer leg. The Mach 5 knob is tall and made of black plastic; the EFC knob is flat and aluminum. Turning the knob clockwise increases rebound damping (and slows the return stroke), and counterclockwise decreases rebound damping. It is not recommended to ride with full damping, as it will almost prevent the fork from returning after compression.

On all three Rock Shox Judy models (DH, SL and XC), the compression damping is adjusted by inserting a 2mm hex key through the center of the bolt at the bottom of the left leg. Clockwise rotation increases compression damping.

Only Judy DH forks (the red ones) include an additional adjustable cartridge in the right leg to control rebound damping. It can also be adjusted with a 2mm hex key through the center of the bolt on the bottom of the fork leg. Clockwise rotation increases rebound damping (slows the return stroke). It is very important that you do *not* turn this adjuster any more than two full turns counterclockwise!

OVERHAULING FORK LEGS ON JUDY AND MACH 5

 This section only applies to Rock Shox Judy and Manitou Mach 5 forks. There are many other systems on the market. Each disassembles in a different way. I could not include all of them so I opted to include those that are most likely to be regularly overhauled. I am assuming that someone with a high-end fork like the Judy or the Mach 5 will be the most likely to regularly perform this task.

❶ Disconnect the front brake (Chapter 7) and remove the front wheel.

❷ Locate the bolts on the bottoms of the fork legs. But before you unscrew them, tighten the preload adjuster all of the way down. (See **Setting spring preload** earlier in this chapter.) This way, when you undo the bolts on the bottom of the fork leg you won't turn the dampers and the shafts along with them. That done, unscrew the bolts at the bottom of both fork legs until there are only a few threads still engaged.

Note: A 5mm Allen wrench is required to turn these bolts on a Judy. On a Mach 5, the right bolt takes a 5mm hex key, but the large aluminum bolt on the left leg requires an 8mm hex key. That 8mm hex is located beneath the plastic damper-adjustment knob. The knob is actually connected to the 5mm hex located in the center of the 8mm hex (this all makes sense when you see it). To get at the 8mm hex, simply pull the knob straight out. It should come out easily.

WARNING: Do not unscrew the 5mm bolt in the center of the Mach 5's 8mm aluminum bolt. This is the damping adjuster. If you remove it, you will break it. That means that you will have an oil spill all over your work area and you will have to buy a new damping unit.

❸ Before unscrewing the bolts completely, tap them with a soft hammer to free the inner legs from their bushings. Remove the bolts. Pull the entire assembly that includes both lower legs and the fork brace off of the inner legs.

❹ With a clean, lint-free rag, clean the inner legs. Clean the seals and bushings inside of the lower tubes. There are two bushings in each outer leg: one at the top and one more way down at the bottom. You need to reach the bottom one with the rag wrapped around a long rod.

Note: On the Mach 5, there is an elastomer around the damper shaft that extends from the right inner leg. It is a good idea to clean and grease it, but, if you remove it, be ready to catch the steel ball that will fall out. This is the "detent" ball for the damper that puts the clicks in the damper adjustment!

❺ Apply a thin layer of **non-lithium** grease (like "Judy Butter") to the bushings and seals in the outer legs. To grease the lower bushings, use a long rod (make sure it is clean), slather grease on the end of it, and reach down to the lower bushings with it. With your (clean) hand, smear a thin layer of the same grease on the inner legs.

❻ Slide the outer legs gently over the inner legs. Take care not to damage the upper dust seals or the lower bushings. Push the outer legs on completely. It may help if you spread the outer tube and fork brace assembly slightly while you rock it side to side to engage the bushings on the inner legs.

ovehauling fork legs

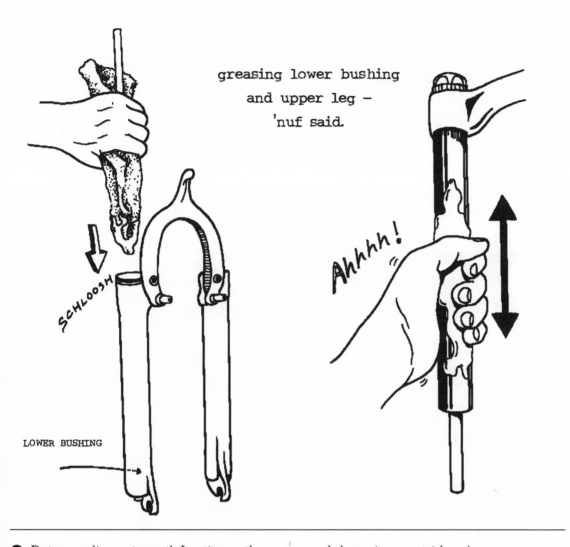

greasing lower bushing
and upper leg –
'nuf said.

SCHLOOSH

Ahhhh!

LOWER BUSHING

❼ Put a medium-strength Loctite on the bolts. Put them back in the bottom of the outer legs, engaging the threads in the damper and neutral shaft. Repeat Step 6 if the threads do not engage.

❽ Tighten the bolts down. Rock Shox recommends 60 in-lbs of torque; Manitou recommends 110-130 in-lbs.

CHANGING TRAVEL

 The travel can be changed with many elastomer forks. Consult the owner's manual for instructions and to see which parts are required (like neutral shafts and damping cartridges).

OVERHAUL HYDRAULIC DAMPING UNIT AND REPLACE BUSHINGS

The damping unit is overhaulable on Rock Shox Judy and Manitou Mach 5 and EFC forks. The bushings are also replaceable. Bushing replacement and cartridge overhaul is beyond the scope of this book, mainly because of the special manufacturer-specific tools and steps required. The Judy cartridge requires special Rock Shox seal installation tools. It is also quite a complex overhaul. The Manitou Mach 5 cartridge is easier to overhaul, and it takes standard tools, but it helps if they are set up in a certain way (like a 15/16-inch socket welded to a piece of angle iron, and tipped back at an angle to allow bleeding air from the damper as you replace the cap).

ADJUSTING AIR/OIL FORKS

Because of the complex system of precise seals and the oil damping system, air/oil forks are much more difficult to work on than elastomer forks. Despite the complexity, air springs do offer a distinct weight advantage over other springs. It would, after all, be hard to come up with a spring lighter than one made of air!

Tuning air/oil fork

❶ Adjust air pressure

Compressed air acts as the spring in this type of fork. Greater air pressure means a stiffer fork, and vice versa. It is a good idea to pump your fork every couple of weeks, since all forks lose pressure over time.

Use the pump designed for your fork. Pump it up to the pressure recommended for your weight by your fork manufacturer. You might want to experiment with different pressures to find what you like best.

Do not use a tire pump on the fork; the large size of the chamber puts way too much air into the fork much too quickly. As a result, the gauge won't read

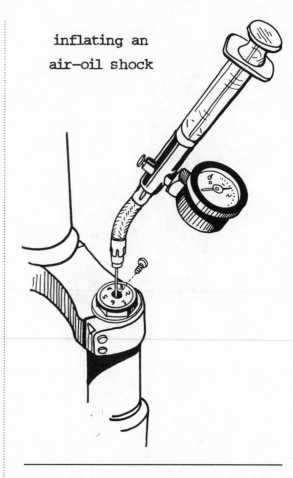

inflating an air–oil shock

accurately. Most non-Rock Shox air/oil forks use Schrader valves. Rock Shox Mag 10, 20, 21, and 21 SLTi all take a ball pump needle.

Rock Shox: Rock Shox's pump looks like a large syringe with a gauge on it. The ball valve on each leg is located beneath either a Phillips screw or a plastic pry-off cap on top of the compression-damping adjusting knob. Tighten down the compression-damping adjustment before inserting the pump needle. This will help you avoid pinching the rubber valve on the top of the adjuster rod inside, causing it to leak. This is especially important on Mag 20 forks. Moisten the needle, and insert it into the valve hole. Pump it up to the desired pressure. Forty pounds is a good starting point for a medium-weight rider.

❷ Compression-damping adjustment
The compression damping determines how large an impact is required to initiate the movement of the fork.

Compression damping with most air/oil forks can be adjusted by turning the knobs on top of the fork crown. Doing so varies the size of orifices separating the oil-filled chambers. Turning the knob clockwise increases the compression damping, meaning that a larger bump (or pedaling force) is required to start the fork moving. When riding on a paved road, tighten it all of the way down to minimize the fork movement due to pedaling.

❸ Other adjustments You can make several other adjustments to air/oil forks, including oil height, oil viscosity, valve-spring preload, rebound bleed hole size, compression bleed hole size and travel.

The following briefly describes how to determine if you wish to change your settings. I do not, however, go into the details of how to perform these adjustments with various forks. You will have to refer to your owner's manual for details.

Generally, heavier riders and heavier use (i.e., downhilling) will benefit from lower oil height (which increases the volume of air), higher oil viscosity (to slow the compression and rebound of the fork), higher valve-spring preload, smaller rebound and compression bleed holes, and longer travel. The reverse is true for smaller riders and lighter use. The factory settings are usually for an average rider and average use, and, as such, probably work better for most people than if they monkeyed with them.

MAINTENANCE
Other than the minor maintenance mentioned above under both kinds of forks, any maintenance of an air/oil fork involves considerable complexity and differs widely from brand to brand. If you ride your bike a lot, especially in dirty and rough conditions, it is a good idea to change the oil, replace the seals, and check wear on things like valve springs periodically. You will need to have a shop do it, or consult your owner's manual for the details.

OTHER SUSPENSION SYSTEMS AND UPGRADES
There are a number of variations on suspension forks. If you have something other than those described in this chapter, you should consult the owner's manual for service requirements and procedures.

There are also a number of retrofit units designed to improve the performance of the forks covered above. So, you need not feel that you are stuck with a certain low level of performance from your fork. You can significantly upgrade a fork's performance without replacing it. Modern upgrades involve a

XIII

forks

maintenance
———
other
suspension
systems

lot more than just a few lightweight titanium fork bolts. Englund, for example, offers hydraulic damping units that install inside standard elastomer forks. These improve performance by controlling compression and rebound speed. Englund also offers entire compressed-air units to replace the elastomer spring *and* the hydraulic damper in a high-end elastomer-sprung fluid-damped fork. The air spring works the same as in an air/oil fork, but the damping is controlled by air flow through orifices rather than by oil. The advantage is that air is lighter than elastomers or oil, and the fork does not change performance with temperature the way both air/oil and elastomer forks do.

frames

"**C**ome to kindly terms with your Ass for it bears you."

— as quoted by JOHN MUIR in *HOW TO KEEP YOUR VOLKSWAGEN ALIVE*

Your Volkswagen is not a donkey ... and your mountain bike is not a Volkswagen. Still, you'd be well served to follow the sage advice given above and stay on good terms with your bike. In doing so, pay close attention to the frame, because it is the most important part of your bike. It is the one part of your bike that is nearly impossible to fix on the trail, and when it fails, the consequences can be serious. So, get to know your bike. Come to kindly terms with it ... for it bears your ass ... or something like that.

FRAME DESIGN

The traditional "diamond," or "double-diamond," mountain-bike frame design evolved directly from the cruiser-style of road frame. The rigid design of a road bike relies on a "front triangle", and a "rear triangle." Never mind that the front triangle is not actually a triangle — or much of a diamond, for that matter. While the basic concept is similar, there are some notable differences between road and mountain bike geometries. Mountain-bike frames feature a higher bottom bracket for more ground clearance, a longer and wider rear triangle for more tire clearance, a shorter seat tube for more standover clearance, and brake bosses. Mountain frames also use larger-diameter tubing and are often welded rather than brazed. Another rigid frame variation is the "elevated

tools

ruler or caliper
string
bike stand
metric wrenches
and hex keys

OPTIONAL
dropout-alignment
tools
derailleur hanger-
alignment tool
metric taps
English-thread
bottom-bracket
tap set
thread-cutting oil
drill and drill bits
16mm cone wrench

rigid frame

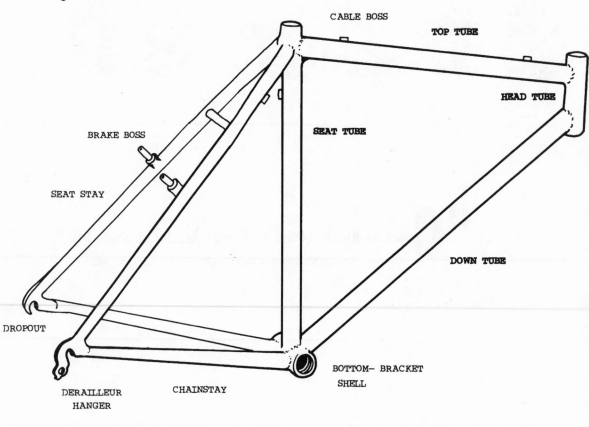

CABLE BOSS

TOP TUBE

HEAD TUBE

SEAT TUBE

BRAKE BOSS

SEAT STAY

DOWN TUBE

DROPOUT

BOTTOM— BRACKET SHELL

DERAILLEUR HANGER

CHAINSTAY

chainstay" design, in which the chainstays attach to the seat tube rather than to the bottom-bracket shell. This design enjoyed great popularity for a few years. Its primary benefit is the elimination of "chain suck," the jamming of the chain between the chainring and the chainstay, and its primary drawback is added weight. When the chainstay-mounted U-brake and roller-cam brake went out of fashion, many chain suck problems evaporated, and so did sales of elevated chainstay rigid frames.

These and other modifications — sloping top tubes, large-diameter head tubes and the use of materials other than steel — are generally aimed at

bringing a bike closer to the Holy Grail of bicycle design: low frame weight, and price, coupled with high frame stiffness and strength.

As a result of this pursuit, mountain-bike frame design has changed radically in the short time since the inception of the sport. Take a look at a modern mountain bike and compare it to the Marin County Repack-style bikes of the late '70s or the Crested Butte off-road "cruisers" that popped onto the scene around the same time. The difference is amazing, even if you are just comparing one of the older bikes to a simple rigid design with no moving suspension. Start looking at full-suspension models, and you have a

rear suspension frame

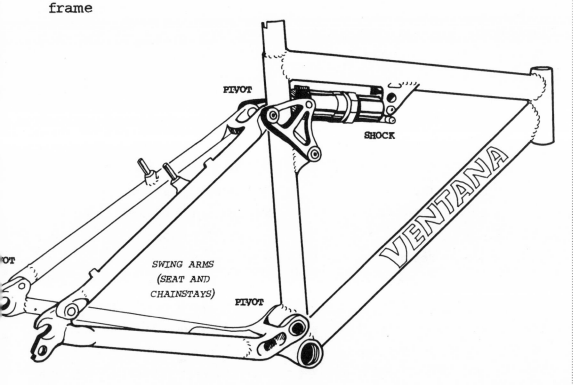

PIVOT

SHOCK

VENTANA

SWING ARMS
(SEAT AND
CHAINSTAYS)

PIVOT

suspension
frame
design

whole new breed of animal. As of this writing, most mountain bikes still use a rigid frame, but rear-suspension designs are rapidly working their way into lower and lower price-point bikes.

SUSPENSION FRAME DESIGN

Rear suspension (also called "full suspension," because it is usually combined with a suspension fork) usually involves a design totally different than the traditional double diamond. Most suspension frames have a front triangle and a "rear swingarm."

There are almost as many rear suspension designs (and names for them) as there are suspension frame designers. Over the past few years, the changes have come fast and furious, and I'd wager that eventually there will be a whole new crop of popular designs and whole new crop of high-zoot names. It would be pointless to go on at length about specifics of current designs and their maintenance. This chapter will divide suspension frames into some very broad categories and give only general maintenance guidelines for them.

FRAME MATERIALS

The bicycle-frame-material revolution has been going on since the birth of the bicycle. Wood was the material of choice for the first bicycles, but that was soon replaced by steel, aluminum, and even bamboo. Steel is still the material most commonly used to build mountain-bike frames, but aluminum, titanium, carbon composites, and metal matrix composites account for an ever-increasing share. Since the materials used in mountain-bike frames come in a variety of grades with varying costs and physical properties, assume that I am talking about the highest grades used in bicycles. For example, the aluminum used in window frames is a lot different than the 7000-series aluminum used in high-end bicycle frames.

Steel has the highest modulus of elasticity (a principal determiner of stiffness) as well as the highest density and tensile strength of any of the metals commonly used in frames. Aluminum has a much lower modulus, density or tensile strength than steel; and titanium has a modulus, density and tensile strength in between the two. With intelligent use of materials, long-lasting frames with stiffness-to-weight and/or strength-to-weight ratios comparable to each other can be built out of any of these metals.

Carbon-fiber and similar composite frame materials consist of fibers embedded in a resin (plastic) matrix. These materials can be very light, very strong and very stiff. Bikes can be built by gluing carbon-fiber tubes into lugs (usually made of carbon fiber or aluminum), or they can be molded in a single piece ("monocoque"

construction). The big advantage of composites is that they can be molded to be thicker where extra strength is needed. The real tricky part is holding them together in a frame that does not come apart.

Metal-matrix composite frame materials contain hard materials included into the metal to increase its mechanical properties (usually its tensile strength). These added materials are not alloying materials (i.e., they are not melted together with the metal), since that would usually contaminate the metal. Rather, pieces of sand-like materials (aluminum oxide, silicon oxide, etc.) are worked into the metal without melting them. The trick with these materials is making them weldable without weakening the frame at the joints.

Framebuilders have and will continue to experiment with all sorts of exotic materials that offer their own mechanical advantages. Beryllium, for example, was commonly used in the defense industry. Its light weight and low density coupled with high strength and stiffness made it an ideal material to use on the nose cones of nuclear missiles. Well, they're not making too many of those any more, so a few folks have tried building bikes out of the stuff. It works great but has the drawback of being poisonous if ingested or inhaled ... so, I strongly recommend against trying to taste or snort a Beryllium frame.

FRAME INSPECTION

You can avoid potentially dangerous, or at least ride-shortening frame failures by inspecting your frame frequently. If you find damage, and you are not sure how dangerous the bike is to ride, take it to a bike shop for advice.

❶ Clean your frame every few rides, so that you can see any problems if they do occur.

❷ Inspect all tubes for cracks, bends, buckles, dents, and paint stretching or cracking, especially near the joints where stress is at its highest. If in doubt, take it to an expert for advice.

❸ Inspect the rear dropouts for cracks. Inspect the welds around the brake bosses for cracks. Check to be sure the brake bosses and cable hangers are not bent or broken. Some dropouts and brake bosses are the bolt-on replaceable type. Otherwise, badly bent or broken dropouts, brake bosses, and cable hangers need to be replaced; a framebuilder in your area may be able to do it.

❹ Look for deeply rusted areas on steel frames. Remove the seatpost every few months and invert the bike to see if water pours out of the seat tube. Look and feel for deep rusted areas inside, or for rust falling out. J. P. Weigle offers a rust protective spray for bicycles available at most bike shops. I recommend you spray that or something like it inside your tubes periodically. Remember to grease both the seatpost and inside of the seat tube when you reinsert the seatpost. After sanding off the rust, touch up any external areas where the paint has come off with touch-up paint or nail polish (hey, it's available in lots of cool colors).

❺ On suspension frames, disconnect the shock. Move the swingarm up and down, and flex it laterally, feeling for play or binding in the pivots. Check the shock for leaking oil, cracks, a bent shaft or other damage.

❻ Check that a true and properly dished wheel sits straight in the frame, centered between the chainstays and seatstays and lined up in the same plane as the front triangle. Tightening the hub skewer should not result in chainstay, or seatstay, bowing or twisting.

CHECK FRAME ALIGNMENT AND ADJUST DROPOUT ALIGNMENT

 These are inexact methods for determining frame alignment. If your alignment is way off, these methods will tell you. If you find alignment problems, other than perhaps moderately bent dropouts or derailleur hanger, do not attempt to correct them. Adjusting frame alignment, if it can be done at all, should only be performed with an accurate frame jig by someone who is practiced at its use.

❶ With the frame clamped in a bike stand, tie the end of a string to one rear dropout. Stretch it tightly around the head tube, and tie it symmetrically to the other dropout.

❷ Measure from the string to the seat

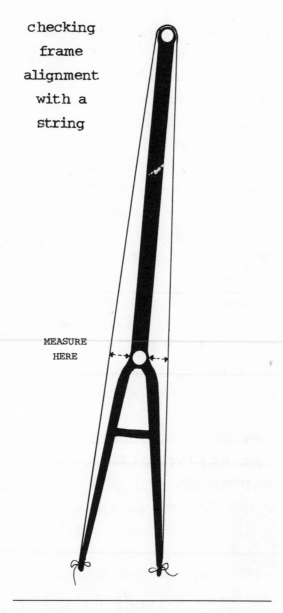

checking frame alignment with a string

MEASURE HERE

frame alignment

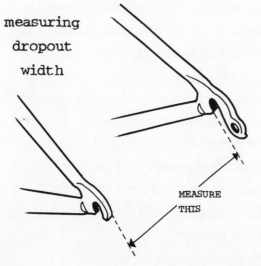

measuring dropout width

MEASURE THIS

tube on either side. The measurement should be at least within a millimeter of being the same on both sides.

❸ Put a true and properly dished rear wheel in the frame and check that it lines up in the same plane as the front triangle. Make certain that the wheel is centered between the seatstays and chainstays (or swingarms). The hub should easily slide into the dropouts without causing you to pull or push on the frame. Tightening the hub quick release should not result in chainstays or seatstays bowing or twisting.

❹ Remove the wheel and measure the spacing between the dropouts. On most mountain bikes made since 1990, this spacing should be 135mm. Mountain bikes made between 1984 and 1990 or so should have a rear spacing of 130mm. Mountain bikes made prior to 1984 are likely to have a rear spacing of 125mm. Some high-end mountain bikes (some Manitou, for instance) have custom rear hubs with wider spacing (like 150mm) to decrease wheel dish. Measure the width of the rear hub with a caliper to see what the rear-end spacing of the frame should be. No matter what the nominal measurement for your frame should be, if it is 1mm less or 1.5mm more than the nominal, it is acceptable. For instance, if you have a frame whose rear spacing should be 135mm, acceptable spacing is 134mm to 136.5mm.

❺ If you have dropout alignment tools, put them in the dropouts so their shafts are fully seated into the dropouts.

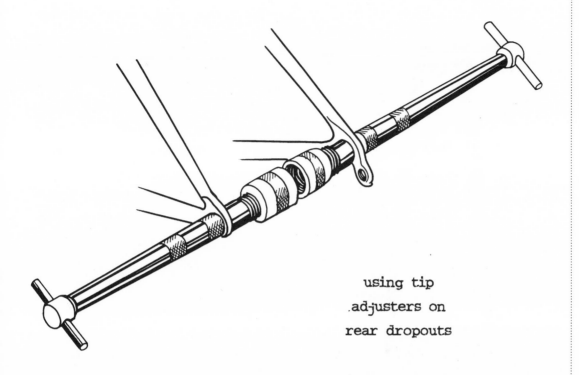

using tip
adjusters on
rear dropouts

Arrange the tool's spacers (and the cups, if they are adjustable) so that the faces of the cups are within a millimeter of each other. Tighten the handles on the tools. The tool's cups should line up straight across with each other, with their faces parallel.

If the tools do not line up with each other, one or both dropouts are bent. If you have replaceable bolt-on dropouts, go ahead and replace them. If you have a composite or bonded rear triangle of any kind, there is nothing you can do about it if your bike is not equipped with replaceable dropouts. If you have a steel rear triangle, you can align the dropouts by bending them carefully with the dropout alignment tools. Hold the cup of the tool with one hand and push or pull on the handle with the other. Aluminum or titanium rear dropouts can sometimes

be aligned, but it is something you should have a shop do. Titanium is hard to bend since it keeps springing back into place and you run a great risk of breaking aluminum if you apply too much pressure to it.

❻ If you have a derailleur-hanger-alignment tool, thread it into the derailleur hanger on the right dropout. Install a true rear wheel without a tire on it. Swing the tool around, measuring the spacing between its arm and the rim all of the way around. The arm of the tool should be the same distance from the rim at all points. Some tools have a set screw extending from the arm that you can adjust to check the spacing; others require you to measure it with a ruler or caliper. If your tool has play in it, keep it pushed inward lightly as you perform all of the measure-

**dropout
alignment**

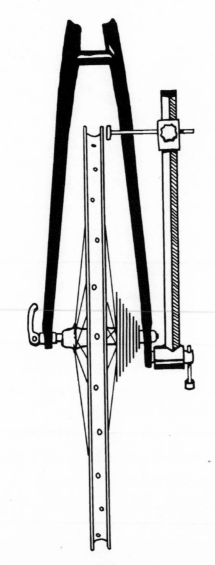

checking derailleur—hanger
alignment

ments, or you will get inconsistent data.

If the spacing between the tool arm and the rim is not consistent (within a millimeter or two all of the way around), carefully bend the hanger by pulling outward on the arm of the tool lightly where it is closest to the rim. If the derailleur hanger is really bent, you may not be able to align it without breaking it (you may even have trouble threading the tool in, because the threaded hole will be ovalized). If you have a replaceable bolt-on dropout, replace it. If you do not have a replaceable dropout, see **Fixing damaged threads** for other derailleur hanger options.

❼ Suspension frames have one other alignment feature not shared with rigid frames. To ensure proper swingarm movement, every separate link in the swingarm puzzle must be in perfect alignment with the next link, so that there are no side forces applied to the pivots. If, for example, the rear shock has to be really forced into position between the two pivot points it connects, then there is unnecessary strain on the frame. These stresses will accelerate the rate of wear of the parts and compromise the linkage's ability to move smoothly.

CORRECTING FRAME DAMAGE

Other than alignment items covered above, the only frame problems you can correct are damaged threads, chipped paint, and small dents. Broken braze-ons and bent, broken or deeply dented tubes require a framebuilder to replace them, or a new frame is called for.

FIXING DAMAGED THREADS

 A mountain-bike frame has threads in the bottom bracket shell, the cantilever (or U-brake) bosses, the waterbottle bosses, the rear derailleur hanger. Some bikes also have threads in the seat binder. Some also have a small hole in the

242

frames

bottom of the bottom-bracket shell to which a plastic derailleur cable guide is bolted. Bikes equipped with new XTR front derailleurs have a threaded front derailleur mount.

❶ If any threads on the frame are stripped or cross-threaded, try chasing through the threads with the appropriate-sized thread tap. Then replace the bolt or bottom bracket cup with a new one.

The following tap sizes are commonly found on most mountain bikes:

WATERBOTTLE BOSSES AND THE HOLE
    FOR A PLASTIC CABLE GUIDE: **5mm X 0.8**
SEAT BINDERS AND CANTILEVER
    OR U-BRAKE BOSSES: **6mm X 1**
DERAILLEUR HANGER: **10mm X 1**
BOTTOM-BRACKET SHELLS: **1.37 inches X 24**
(remember the chain side bottom-bracket threads are left-hand threaded; the other side is right-hand threaded)

Whenever you re-tap any threads, use oil on the tap (canola vegetable oil with titanium threads). Specific thread-cutting oil is not really necessary on old threads since they are already so worn.

❷ Turn the tap forward a bit, then turn it back, then forward (two steps forward and one back), etc. to prevent the tap from binding and possibly breaking. Be aware that taps are made of very hard, and brittle, steel. If you put any side or twisting forces on them they can easily break off. So, be careful. If it breaks you'll have a real mess, since the broken tap in the hole is harder than the frame, so it's impossible to drill the broken tap out. If you break off a tap in your frame, do not try to get it out yourself. Take it to a bike

shop, a machine shop, or a framebuilder before you break off what little is left sticking out. Unless you put the tap in crooked, breaking one should not be a problem when re-tapping damaged frame threads since these threads will be so worn; getting them to find any metal to bite into will probably be your biggest problem.

Important note: *Tapping a bottom-bracket shell takes a good amount of expertise. You really need expert supervision, if you have never done it before and still want to do it yourself. In addition to making sure that you place the correct tap in the correct end of the shell, you must also be certain that the taps go in straight. Most bottom-bracket taps have a shaft between the two taps to keep them parallel to each other. They must both be started at the same time from both ends.*

If you mess it up, you can ruin your frame. So, if in doubt, ask an expert.

If tapping the threads and using a new bolt does not work, here are some specific remedies:

Brake bosses

Some brake posts are replaceable. They have wrench flats (usually 8mm) at the base of the boss, and threads below that screw into a threaded boss which is welded to the frame. If yours are not like this, you must take it to a frame-builder to get a new post welded on.

Waterbottle bosses and threaded front derailleur braze-ons Some bike shops have a tool that rivets bottle bosses into

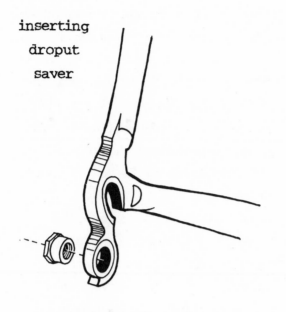

inserting
dropout
saver

the frame. Check for this first, since you can avoid a new paint job that way. Otherwise, take it to a framebuilder to get a new boss welded or brazed in.

Rear derailleur hanger threads

Some bikes have replaceable rear dropouts that bolt onto the frame. Another option is to use a "dropout saver" derailleur hanger backing nut made by Wheels Manufacturing (available at bike shops). The dropout saver is simply a sleeve threaded the same as your dropout was with a hex flange with wrench flats for a 16mm cone wrench. You drill out the hole in your damaged derailleur hanger with a 15/32" drill bit, push the dropout saver in from the back side, and screw in your derailleur. The dropout saver comes in two lengths, depending on the thickness of the dropout. Another option is to saw off the derailleur hanger with a hacksaw and use a separate derailleur hanger

from a really cheap bike that fits flat against the outside of the dropout and is held in by the hub axle bolts or quick release. The final options are to have the dropout replaced by a framebuilder ... or you could always get a new frame.

Seat binders

These can be drilled out and used with a quick release or a bolt and nut. Seat-binder threads rarely get stripped, however; it is usually the bolt that is the problem.

Bottom-bracket-shell threads

You can use a Mavic bottom bracket, since it does not depend on the threads in the shell to anchor it. You must have a shop bevel the ends of your bottom-bracket shell with a special Mavic tool, and they will have the tools to install the bottom bracket as well.

Bottom-bracket cable-guide threads

The hole in the bottom of the bottom bracket can be tapped out with larger threads for a larger screw, and the hole in the plastic derailleur cable guide can be drilled larger for the larger screw as well. Make sure the screw is short enough that it does not protrude into the inside of the bottom-bracket shell.

REPAIR CHIPPED PAINT AND SMALL DENTS

Fixing paint chips is simply a matter of cleaning the area and touching it up. Sand any chipped paint or rust completely away before touching up the spot. Use touch up paint that came with your bike, model paint, or

frames

fingernail polish.

Small dents can be filled with body putty, but there is little point to filling them if you are only doing a touch up, since the area probably doesn't look that great anyway.

There are plenty of frame painters around the country who can fill dents, repaint frames, and can even match original decals. Many of them advertise in bike magazines.

SUSPENSION FRAME SETUP AND MAINTENANCE

There are so many types of suspension frames, I will simply divide them into two primary categories: those with pivots, and those without.

REAR SUSPENSION TUNING

 There are three variables to take into account when setting up the rear suspension system: sag, compression damping, and rebound damping. **Note:** *These instructions do not apply to beam bikes, such as Softride.*

The four main types of shocks are air/oil, air/air, coil spring (or "coil over"), and elastomer (or "elastomer over"). In both air/oil and air/air shocks, compressed air acts as the spring. Air/oil shocks rely on the flow of oil through a small opening separating two chambers to dampen the shock movement. Air/air shocks operate on the same basic principle but rely on the movement of air to damp the shock

movement. "Coil over" and "elastomer over" shocks use either a coil spring or an elastomer spring surrounding an oil chamber or gas/oil chamber. The oil provides the damping, and the pressurized gas provides an additional spring. The most commonly used gas is nitrogen, since it is less likely to emulsify with the oil. This type of shock is not to be pumped by the consumer.

Air/oil and air/air shocks are tuned for spring rate by varying the air pressure. You must have a shock pump to pump these or to check the air pressure, since the air volume is so small and the air pressure is so high. Start with the pressure recommended by the bike manufacturer for your weight, and experiment from there. Since the location of the shock and pressure requirements vary from bike to bike, the recommendations will come from the bike manufacturer and not the shock manufacturer.

You can change the spring rate of most "coil over" and "elastomer over" shocks by turning a threaded collar around the shock body.

On rear shocks with hydraulic damping systems, damping is adjusted by varying the size of the orifices through which the oil (or compressed air) flows or by changing the viscosity of the oil. On many models, the damping orifices are adjusted with a knob, but the technique varies from shock to shock, so be sure to read the owner's manual that came with yours.

tuning rear
suspension

Setting sag

On a rear-suspension bike, "sag" represents the amount of shock compression that takes place when a rider gets on the saddle. As a general rule of thumb, sag should equal about one quarter of the total amount of travel available.

On some shocks, you can put a zip tie around the piston or piston shaft, slide it against the cylinder, and measure how much it moves with the suspension.

To measure the total travel available, deflate or disconnect the shock. Measure the height of the saddle above the ground with the swingarm fully compressed and fully extended. The difference between these two measurements is the total available travel. On some shocks, you can put a zip tie around the piston or piston shaft, slide it against the deflated cylinder, and measure how much it moves with the suspension (or bottom the shock out on a big bump when the spring is installed or inflated).

Adjust the sag by adjusting the air pressure in an air/oil shock and by adjusting the spring preload, and/or by changing the spring on either a "coil over" shock or an elastomer shock. The preload is usually set with both of these systems by turning a threaded collar surrounding the shock body that compresses the coil spring or the elastomers.

Compression damping

If adjustable, set the compression damping as light as possible without bottoming out the shock on the biggest bump you hit. Many shocks have a knob with which to adjust damping.

Rebound damping

If adjustable, set the rebound damping as light as you can get without causing the bike to "pogo" (bouncing repeatedly after a bump). Many shocks have a knob with which to set the rebound damping.

PIVOTLESS FRAME MAINTENANCE

Suspension frames without moving pivots fall into two categories: beam bikes, and bikes with a shock that depend on the flex of the chainstay, rather than on pivots.

The principal beam suspension used on mountain bikes is the Softride beam, and Softride, Breeze, Otis Guy, and Ritchey are some of the frame brands that have used it. Installation and replacement of the beam is covered in Chapter 10. Inspect the beam-mounting points on the frame periodically for fatigue indications (stretched, bulged, or cracking metal or paint). There is not much else to say about Softride beams; they are fairly maintenance-free.

One of the simplest and lightest rear-suspension designs out there relies on a small shock behind the seat tube and flexing chainstays. The design was originally used in Moots frames and later adopted by Ritchey. Beyond checking the chainstays for indications of fatigue (stretched, bulged, or cracking metal or paint) all you really need to do with these is to keep the shock lubricated and tuned to your weight and riding style.

MAINTENANCE OF FRAMES WITH PIVOTS

 The complexity of suspension frames varies, hence the ambiguity in the maintenance level. The maintenance to be performed, besides the regular inspections described early in this chapter, is on the shock and the pivots. Some systems, like the "unified rear triangle" — in which the bottom bracket and rear hub are both fixed to the swingarm — have a single pivot and a shock. Others utilize numerous pivots.

Shock maintenance

Generally, other than shock tuning described above, any maintenance of internal parts and oil changing must be done by a shop with the proper tools.

Pivot maintenance

The pivots on any suspension frame require periodic attention. Pivots usually rely on cartridge bearings or bushings (usually steel on brass, but some are made of ceramic or plastic). They are held together by clamps with pinch bolts surrounding the pivot shaft or by bolts, pins, cotters or snaprings.

The shock also pivots on brass bushings on both ends of the shock body.

Pivot bushings must be cleaned and greased after about 40 hours of riding. You should inspect them for signs of wear whenever you perform regular service. With the shock deflated or removed, check for wear by feeling for lateral play and binding. Look at the bushings for scoring and ovalization, and listen for squeaks that indicate a need for lubrication. If the bushings are worn, replace them.

Pivot bearings must be replaced when they wear out. Check them for lateral play and for binding.

appendices

This index is intended to assist you in finding and fixing problems. If you already know wherein the problem lies, consult the Table of Contents for the chapter covering that part of the bike. If you are not sure which part of the bike is affected, this index can be of assistance. It is organized alphabetically, but, since people's descriptions of the same problem vary, you may need to look through the entire list to find your symptom.

This index can assist you with a diagnosis and can recommend a course of action. Following each recommended action are listed chapter numbers to which you can refer for the repair procedure to fix the problem.

SYMPTOM	LIKELY CAUSES	ACTION	CHAPTER
bent wheel	1. maladjusted spokes	true wheel	6
	2. broken spoke	replace spoke	6
	3. bent rim	replace rim	12
bike pulls to one side	1. wheels not true	true wheels	6
	2. tight headset	adjust headset	11
	3. pitted headset	replace headset	11
	4. bent frame	replace or straighten	14
	5. bent fork	replace or straighten	13
	6. loose hub bearings	adjust hubs	6
	7. tire pressure really low	inflate tires	2, 6
bike shimmies at high speed	1. frame cracked	replace frame	14
	2. frame bent	replace or straighten	14
	3. wheels way out of true	true wheels	6
	4. loose hub bearings	adjust hubs	6
	5. headset too loose	tighten headset	11
	6. flexible frame/heavy rider	replace frame	14
bike vibrates when braking	see chattering and vibration when braking under "strange noises" below		
brake doesn't stop bike	1. maladjusted brake	adjust brake	7
	2. worn brake pads	replace pads	7
	3. greasy rims	clean rims	7
	4. sticky brake cable	lube or replace cable	7
	5. steel rims in wet weather	use aluminum rims	12
	6. brake damaged	replace brake	7
	7. sticky or bent brake lever	lube or replace lever	7
	8. air in hydraulic brake lines	bleed brake lines	7
	9. disc brake pads set wide	adjust disc brake	7

SYMPTOM	LIKELY CAUSES	ACTION	CHAPTER
chain falls off in front	1. maladjusted front derailleur	adjust front derailleur	5
	2. chain line off	adjust chain line	8
	3. chain ring bent or loose	replace or tighten	8
chain jams in front between chain ring and chainstay-called *chain suck*	1. dirty chain	clean chain	4
	2. bent chain ring teeth	replace chain ring	8
	3. chain too narrow	replace chain	4
	4. chain line off	adjust chain line	8
	5. stiff links in chain	free links, lube chain	4
chain jams in rear	1. maladjusted rear derailleur	adjust derailleur	5
	2. chain too wide	replace chain	4
	3. small cog not on spline	re-seat cogs	6
	4. poor frame clearance	return to dealer	14
chain skips	1. stretched chain	replace chain	4
	2. maladjusted derailleur	adjust derailleur	5
	3. worn rear cogs	replace cogs & chain	6, 4
	4. dirty or rusted chain	clean or replace chain	4
	5. tight chain link	loosen tight link	4
	6. bent rear derailleur	replace derailleur	5
	7. bent derailleur hanger	straighten hanger	14
	8. loose der. jockey wheels	tighten jockey wheels	5
	9. bent chain link	replace chain	4
	10. sticky rear shift cable	replace shift cable	5
chain slaps chainstay	1. chain too long	shorten chain	4
	2. weak rear derailleur spring	replace spring or der.	5
	3. terrain very bumpy	ignore noise	n/a
derailleur hits spokes	1. maladjusted rear derailleur	adjust derailleur	5
	2. broken spoke	replace spoke	6
	3. bent rear derailleur	replace derailleur	5
	4. bent derailleur hanger	straighten or replace	14
knee pain	1. poor shoe cleat position	reposition cleat	9
	2. saddle too low or high	adjust saddle	10
	3. foot rolled in or out	replace shoes or get orthotics	n/a
pain or fatigue when riding, particularly in the back, neck and arms	1. incorrect seat position	adjust seat position	10
	2. too much riding	build up miles gradually	
	3. incorrect stem length	replace stem	11
	4. poor frame fit	replace frame	14

troubleshooting index

SYMPTOM	LIKELY CAUSES	ACTION	CHAPTER
pedal(s) move laterally, clunk or twist while pedalling	1. loose crank arm	tighten crank bolt	8
	2. pedal loose in crank arm	tighten pedal to crank	9
	3. bent pedal axle	replace pedal or axle	9
	4. loose bottom bracket	adjust bottom bracket	8
	5. bent bottom bracket axle	replace bottom bracket or axle	8
	6. bent crank arm	replace crank arm	8
	7. loose pedal bearings	adjust pedal bearings	9
pedal entry difficult (with clipless pedals)	1. release tension set high	reduce release tension	9
	2. shoe sole knobs too tall	trim knobs	9
	3. cleat guide loose or gone	tighten or replace	9
pedal release difficult (with clipless pedals)	1. release tension set high	reduce release tension	9
	2. loose cleat on shoe	tighten cleat	9
	3. dry pedal spring pivots	oil spring pivots	9
	4. dirty pedals	clean and lube pedals	9
	5. bent pedal clips	replace pedals or clips	9
	6. dirty cleats	clean, lube cleats	9
pedal release too easy (with clipless pedals)	1. release tension set too low	increase release tension	9
	2. cleats worn out	replace cleats	9
rear shifting working poorly	1. maladjusted derailleur	adjust derailleur	5
	2. sticky or damaged cable	replace cable	5
	3. loose rear cogs	seat and tighten cogs	6
	4. worn rear cogs	replace cogs	6
	5. stretched/damaged chain	replace chain	4
	6. see also *chain jams in rear* and *chain skips* above		
resistance *while coasting or pedaling*	1. tire rubs frame or fork	make axle adjustments or true wheel	2, 6
	2. brake drags on rim	adjust brake	7
	3. tire pressure really low	inflate tire	2, 6
	4. hub bearings too tight	adjust hubs	6
	5. hub bearings dirty/worn	overhaul hubs	6
	6. mud packed around tires	clean bike	2
resistance *while pedaling only*	1. bottom bracket too tight	adjust bottom bracket	8
	2. bottom bracket dirty/worn	overhaul bottom bracket	8
	3. chain dry/dirty/rusted	clean/lube or replace	4
	4. pedal bearings too tight	adjust pedal bearings	9
	5. pedal bearings dirty/worn	overhaul pedals	9
	6. bent chain ring rubs frame	straighten or replace	8
	7. chain ring rubs frame	adjust chain line	8

STRANGE NOISES

Weird noises can be hard to locate; use this to assist in locating them.

SYMPTOM	LIKELY CAUSES	ACTION	CHAPTER
creaking noise	1. dry handlebar/stem joint	put grease inside stem clamp	11
	2. loose seatpost	tighten seatpost	10
	3. loose shoe cleats	tighten cleats	9
	4. loose crank arm	tighten crank arm bolt	8
	5. cracked frame	replace frame	14
	6. dry, rusty seatpost	grease seatpost	10
	7. see *squeaking* below	see *squeaking* below	
clicking noise	1. cracked shoe cleats	replace cleats	9
	2. cracked shoe sole	replace shoes	9
	3. loose bottom bracket	tighten BB	8
	4. loose crank arm	tighten crank arm	8
	5. loose pedal	tighten pedal	9
chattering and vibration when braking	1. bent or dented rim	replace rim	12
	2. loose headset	adjust headset	11
	3. brake pads toed out	adjust brake pads	7
	4. wheel way out of round	true wheel	6
	5. greasy sections of rim	clean rim	6
	6. loose brake pivot bolts	tighten brake bolts	7
rubbing or scraping noise *when pedaling*	1. crossed chain	avoid extreme gears	5
	2. front derailleur rubbing	adjust front derailleur	5
	3. chain ring rubs frame	longer bottom bracket	8
		or, move bottom bracket over	8
rubbing or scraping noise *when coasting or pedaling*	1. tire dragging on frame	straighten wheel	2, 6
	2. tire dragging on fork	straighten wheel	2, 6
	3. brake dragging on rim	adjust brake	7
squeaking noise	1. dry hub or BB bearings	overhaul hubs or BB	6, 8
	2. dry pedal bushings	overhaul pedals	9
	3. squeaky saddle	replace saddle	10
	4. dry suspension pivots	overhaul suspension	13, 14
	5. rusted or dry chain	lube or replace chain	4
	6. dry suspension fork	overhaul fork	13
	8. dry suspension seatpost	overhaul seatpost	10
squealing noise when braking	1. brake pads toed out	adjust brake pads	7
	2. greasy rims	clean rims and pads	7
	3. loose brake arms	tighten brake arms	7

strange noises

The gear table on the following page is based on a 26-inch (66cm) tire diameter. Your gear development numbers may be slightly different if the diameter of your rear tire, at inflation, with your weight on it, is not 26 inches. Unless your bike has 24-inch wheels or some other non-standard size, these numbers will be very close.

If you want to have totally accurate gear development numbers for the tire you happen to have on at the time, at a certain inflation pressure, then you can measure the tire diameter very precisely with the procedure below. You can come up with your own gear chart by plugging your tire diameter into the following gear development formula, or by multiplying each number in this chart by the ratio of your tire diameter divided by 26 inches (the tire diameter we used).

MEASURE DIAMETER OF YOUR TIRE

1. Sit on the bike with your tire pumped to your desired pressure.
2. Mark the spot on the rear rim that is at the bottom, and mark the floor adjacent to that spot.
3. Roll forward one wheel revolution, and mark the floor again where the mark on the rim is again at the bottom.
4. Measure the distance between the marks on the floor; this is the tire circumference at pressure with your weight on it.
5. Divide this number by π (*pi*) — 3.14159 — to get the diameter.

Note: This roll-out procedure is also the method to measure the wheel size with which to calibrate your bike computer, except you do it on the front wheel with most computers.

rear hub cogs	20	22	24	26	28	30	32	34	36	38	39	40
11	47	52	57	61	66	71	76	80	85	90	92	95
12	43	48	52	56	61	65	69	74	78	82	84	87
13	40	44	48	52	56	60	64	68	72	76	78	80
14	37	41	45	48	52	56	60	63	67	70	72	74
15	35	38	42	45	49	52	55	59	62	66	68	69
16	33	36	39	42	45	49	52	55	58	61	63	65
17	31	34	37	40	43	46	49	52	55	58	60	61
18	29	32	35	38	40	43	46	49	52	55	56	58
19	27	30	33	36	38	41	44	47	49	52	53	55
20	26	29	31	34	36	39	42	44	47	49	51	52
21	25	27	30	32	35	37	40	42	45	47	48	50
22	24	26	28	31	33	35	38	40	43	45	46	47
23	23	25	27	29	32	34	36	38	41	43	44	45
24	22	24	26	28	30	32	35	37	39	41	42	43
25	21	23	25	27	29	31	33	35	37	39	41	42
26	20	22	24	26	28	30	32	34	36	38	39	40
27	19	21	23	25	27	29	31	33	35	37	38	39
28	18	20	22	24	26	28	30	32	33	35	36	37
30	17	19	21	23	24	26	28	29	31	33	34	35
32	16	18	20	21	23	24	26	28	29	31	32	33
34	15	17	18	20	21	23	24	26	28	29	30	31
38	14	16	16	18	19	21	22	23	25	26	27	27
	20	22	24	26	28	30	32	34	36	38	39	40

chain ring gear teeth

THE FORMULA IS:

Gear development = (number of teeth on chainring) x (wheel diam

To find out how far you get with each pedal stroke in a given gear,
multiply the gear development by π (3.14159265).

B

chain ring gear teeth

43	44	45	46	47	48	49	50	51	52	53	
102	104	106	109	111	113	116	118	121	123	125	11
93	95	97	100	102	104	106	108	111	113	115	12
86	88	90	92	94	96	98	100	102	104	106	13
80	82	84	85	87	89	91	93	95	97	98	14
75	76	78	80	81	83	85	87	88	90	92	15
70	72	73	75	76	78	80	81	83	85	86	16
66	67	69	70	72	73	75	76	78	80	81	17
62	64	65	66	68	69	71	72	74	75	77	18
59	60	62	63	64	66	67	68	70	71	73	19
56	57	59	60	61	62	64	65	66	68	69	20
53	54	56	57	58	59	61	62	63	64	66	21
51	52	53	54	56	57	58	59	60	61	63	22
49	50	51	52	53	54	55	57	58	59	60	23
47	48	49	50	51	52	53	54	55	56	57	24
45	46	47	48	49	50	51	52	53	54	55	25
43	44	45	46	47	48	49	50	51	52	53	26
41	42	43	44	45	46	47	48	49	50	51	27
40	41	42	43	44	45	46	46	47	48	49	28
37	38	39	40	41	42	42	43	44	45	46	30
35	35	37	37	38	39	40	41	41	42	43	32
33	33	34	35	36	37	37	38	39	40	41	34
29	30	31	31	32	32	33	34	35	36	36	38
43	44	45	46	47	48	49	50	51	52	53	

chain ring gear teeth

ber of teeth on rear cog)

gear development

MOUNTAIN BIKE FITTING

If you are getting a new bike, you might as well get one that fits you properly. The simple need to protect your more sensitive parts should keep you away from a bike without sufficient standover clearance, but there are a lot of other factors to consider as well. You need to make certain that your bike has enough reach to ensure that you don't bang your knees on the handle bar; you also need to check that your weight is properly distributed over the wheels so that you don't end up going over the handlebars on downhills or unweighting the front end on steep climbs. An improperly-sized bike will cause you to ride with less efficiency and more discomfort. So, take some time and find out how you can pick the properly-sized bike.

I've outlined two methods for finding your frame size. The first is a simple method of checking your fit to fully assembled bikes at your local bike shop. The second is a bit more elaborate, since it involves taking body measurements. This more detailed approach will allow you to calculate the proper frame dimensions whether the bike is assembled or not.

SELECTING THE SIZE OF A BUILT-UP BIKE

❶ Standover height.

Stand over the bike's top tube and lift the bike straight up until the top tube hits your crotch. The wheels should be at least 2 inches off of the ground to ensure that you can jump off of the bike safely without hitting your crotch. There is no maximum dimension here. If you have 5 inches of standover height or more, that is fine, as long as

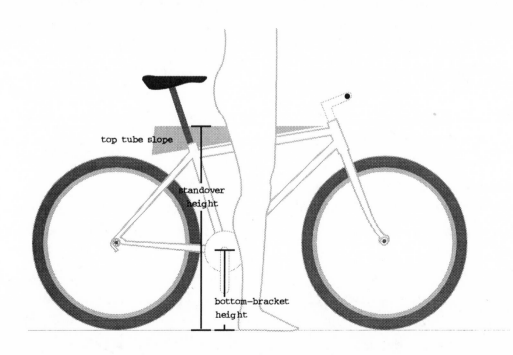

top tube slope

standover height

bottom-bracket height

the top tube is long enough for you, and the handlebar height can be set properly for you.

Note: If you have 2 inches of standover clearance over one bike, do not assume that another bike with the same listed frame size will also offer you the same standover clearance. Manufacturers measure frame size using a variety of methods. They also slope their top tubes differently, and use different bottom bracket heights, all of which affect the final standover height.

All manufacturers measure the frame size up the seat tube from the center of the bottom bracket, but the top of the measurement varies. Some manufacturers measure to the center of the top tube ("center-to-center" measurement), some measure to the top of the top tube ("center-to-top"), and others measure to the top of the seat tube (also called "center-to-top"), even though there is wide variation in the length of the seat post collar above the top tube. Obviously, each of these methods will give you a different "frame size" for the same frame.

No matter how the frame size is measured, the standover height of a bike depends on the slope of the top tube. Top tubes that slant up to the front are common, so standover clearance is obviously a function of where you are standing. With an up-angled top tube, stand over it a few inches forward of the nose of the saddle, and then lift the bike up into your crotch to measure

standover clearance.

A bike with a suspension fork will have a higher front end than a bike with a rigid fork would, since the suspension fork has to allow for travel. This makes it difficult even to compare listed frame sizes from the same manufacturer to determine standover height.

Standover height is also a function of bottom bracket height above the ground. There is substantial variation here, especially with bikes with rear suspension whose bottom brackets are often very high so that ground clearance is still sufficient when the suspension is fully compressed.

Unless the manufacturer lists the standover height in their brochure and you know your inseam length, you need to actually stand over the bike.

Another note: If you are short and cannot find a frame size small enough for you to get at least 2 inches of standover clearance, consider a bike with 24 -inch wheels instead of 26-inch.

❷ **Knee to handlebar clearance**
With one foot on the ground and one foot on the pedal, make sure your knee cannot hit the handlebar. Do this standing out of the saddle as well as seated and with the front wheel turned slightly, to make sure that the knee will not hit when you are in the most awkward pedaling position you might use.

3. Handlebar reach and drop Ride the bike. See if the reach feels comfortable to you when grabbing the bars or the bar ends. Make sure it is easy to grab

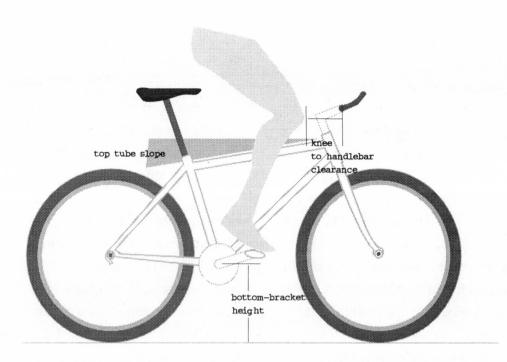

top tube slope

knee to handlebar clearance

bottom-bracket height

bike fit

the brake levers. Make sure your knees do not hit your elbows as you pedal. Make sure that the stem can be raised or lowered enough to achieve a comfortable handlebar height for you. **Note:** Check that your toe does not hit the front tire either.

CHOOSING A FRAME SIZE FROM YOUR BODY MEASUREMENTS

You will need a second person to assist you.

By taking three easy measurements, most people can get a very good frame fit. When designing a custom frame, I go through a more complex procedure than this, involving more measurements. For picking an off-the-shelf bike, this method works well.

❶ Measure your inseam
Spread your stocking feet about 2 inches apart, and measure up from the floor to a broomstick held level and lifted firmly up into your crotch. You can also use a large book and slide it up a wall to keep the top edge horizontal — as you pull it up as hard as you can — into your crotch. You can mark the top of the book on the wall and measure up from the floor to the mark.

❷ Measure your inseam plus torso length
Hold a pencil horizontally in your sternal notch, the U-shaped bone depression just below your Adam's Apple. Standing up straight in front of a wall, mark the wall with the horizontal pencil. Measure up from the floor to the mark.

❸ Measure your arm length
Hold your arm out from your side at a 45 degree angle with your elbow straight. Measure from the sharp bone point directly behind your shoulder

joint to the wrist bone on your little finger side.

❹ Find your frame seat tube length
Subtract 34 to 42cm (13.5 inches-16.5 inches) from your inseam length. This length is your frame size measured from the center of the bottom bracket to the top of a horizontal top tube. If the frame you are interested in has a sloping top tube, you need a bike with an even shorter seat tube length. With a sloping top tube bike, project a horizontal line back to the seat tube (or seat post) from the top of the top tube at the center of its length. Mark the seat tube or seat post at this line. Measure from the center of the bottom bracket to this mark; this length should be 34-42cm less than your inseam measurement.

Also, if the bike has a bottom bracket higher than 29cm (11-1/2 inches), subtract the additional bottom-bracket height from the seat tube length as well.

Generally, smaller riders will want to subtract close to 34cm from their inseam, while taller riders will subtract closer to 40cm. There is considerable range here. The top tube length is more important in a frame than any specific "frame size", and, if you have short torso and arms, you can use a small frame to get the right top tube length, as long as you can raise your bars as high as you need them.

You really want to make sure you have plenty of standover clearance, so do not subtract less than 34cm from your inseam for your seat-tube length; this should insure at least 2 inches (5cm) of standover clearance. If you are short and cannot find a bike small enough for you to get at least 2 inches of standover clearance, consider one with 24 inches wheels instead of 26 inches.

❺ Find your top tube length
To find your torso length, subtract your inseam measurement (found in Step 1) from your inseam-plus-torso measurement (found in Step 2). Add this torso length to your arm length measurement (found in Step 3). To find the top tube length, multiply this arm-plus-torso measurement by a factor in the range between 0.47 and 0.5. If you are a casual rider, use 0.47; if you are a very aggressive rider, use 0.5, and, if you are in between, use a factor in between. This top-tube length is measured horizontally from the center of the seat tube to the center of the head tube. Obviously, the horizontal top-tube length is less than the length measured along the top tube on a sloping top tube bike.

❻ Find your stem length
Multiply the arm-plus-torso length you found in step 5 by 0.10 up to 0.14 to find the stem length. Again, a casual rider will multiply by 0.10 or so, while an aggressive rider will multiply by closer to 0.14. This is a starting stem length. Finalize the stem length once you are sitting on the bike and see

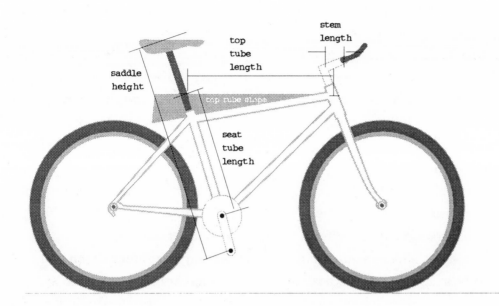

saddle height

top tube length

stem length

top tube slope

seat tube length

what feels best.

POSITIONING OF YOUR SADDLE AND HANDLEBARS

The frame fit is only part of the equation. Except for the standover clearance, a good frame fit is relatively meaningless if the seat setback, seat height, handlebar height, and handlebar reach are not set correctly for you.

❶ Saddle height

When your foot is at the bottom of the stroke, lock your knee without rocking your hips. Do this sitting on your bike on a trainer with someone else observing. Your foot should be level, or the heel should be slightly higher than the ball of the foot. Another way to determine seat height is to take your inseam measurement (found in step 1 under "Choosing frame size from your body measurements", above) and multiply it by 1.09; this is the length from the center of the pedal spindle (when the

pedal is down) to one of the points on the top of the saddle where your butt bones (ischial tuberosities) contact it. Adjust the seat height (Chapter 10) until you get it the proper height.

Note: These two methods yield similar results, although the measurement-multiplying method is dependent on shoe sole and pedal thicknesses. They yield a biomechanically efficient pedaling position, but if you do a lot of technical riding and descending, you may wish to have a lower saddle for better bike-handling control.

❷ Saddle setback

Sit on your bike on a stationary trainer with your cranks horizontal and your foot at the angle it is at that point when pedaling. Have a friend drop a plumb line from the front of your knee below your knee cap. You can use a heavy ring, washer, etc. tied to a string for the plumb line. The plumb line should bisect the pedal axle or pass up to two centimeters behind it (you will need to lean the knee out to get the string to hang clear). A saddle centered in this manner encourages smooth pedaling at high RPMs, while two centimeters behind the pedal spindle encourages powerful seated climbing.

Slide the saddle back and forth on the seatpost (Chapter 10), until you achieve the desired fore-aft saddle position. Set the saddle level or very close to it. Re-check the seat height in Step 1 above, since fore-aft saddle movements affect seat-to-pedal distance as well.

❸ Handlebar height

Measure the handlebar height relative to the saddle height by measuring the vertical distance of the saddle and bar up from the floor. How much higher the saddle is than your bar (or vice versa) depends on your flexibility, riding style, overall size, and type of riding you prefer.

Aggressive and tall cross-country riders will prefer to have their saddle 10 cm or more higher than the bars. Shorter riders will want proportionately less drop, as will less aggressive riders. Riders doing lots of downhills will want their bars higher; downhill racers often have 2-4 cm of drop from saddle to bar, and mountain bike slalom riders' bars are usually higher than their saddles. Generally, people beginning mountain bike riding will like their bars high and can lower them as they become more comfortable with the bike, with going

fast, and with riding more technical terrain.

If in doubt, start with 4 cm of drop and vary it from there. The higher the bar, the greater the tendency is for the front wheel to pull up off of the ground when climbing, and the more wind resistance you can expect. Change the bar height by raising or lowering the stem (Chapter 11), or by switching stems and/or bars.

❹ Setting handlebar reach

The reach from the saddle to the handlebar is also very dependent on personal preference. More aggressive riders will want a more stretched out position than will casual riders. This length is subjective, and I find that I need to look at the rider on the bike and get a feel for how they would be comfortable and efficient.

A useful starting place is to drop a plumb line from the back of your elbow with your arms bent in a comfortable riding position. This plane determined by your elbows and the plumb line should be 2-4 cm horizontally ahead of each knee at the point in the pedal stroke when the crank arm is horizontal forward. The idea is to select a position you find comfortable and efficient; listen to what your body wants.

Vary the saddle-bar distance by changing stem length (Chapter 11), not by changing the seat fore-aft position, which is based on pedaling efficiency (Step 2 above) and not on reach.

Note: There is no single formula for

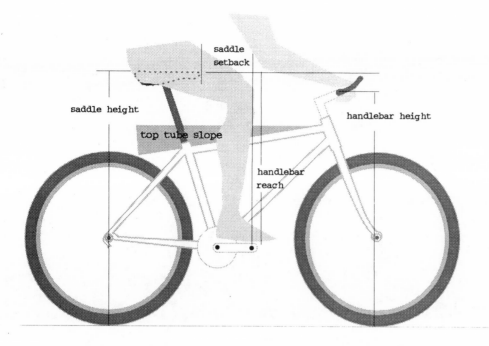

saddle setback

saddle height

top tube slope

handlebar height

handlebar reach

bike fit

determining handlebar reach and height. I can tell you that using a method of placing your elbow against the saddle and seeing if your fingertips reach the handlebar is close to useless. Similarly, the oft suggested method of seeing if the handlebar obscures your vision of the front hub is not worth the brief time it takes to look, being dependent on elbow bend and front end geometry. Another method involving dropping a plumb bob from the rider's nose is dependent on the handlebar height and elbow bend and thus does not lend itself to a proscribed relationship for all riders.

❺ Bar end position

The bar ends should be set up in the range between horizontal and pointed up 15 degrees. Find the position you find comfortable for pulling on when climbing standing or seated, and for when pedaling seated for long stretch-

es on paved roads.

Note: Do not use the bar ends to raise your hand position by pointing them vertically up. If you want a higher hand position, get a taller or more up-angled stem, and/or a higher-rise handlebar. Bar ends are not meant to be stood straight up and held on to for cruising along sitting up high; that is the mountain bike equivalent of flipping a road drop bar upside down to lift the hands. As with the road bar equivalent, you cannot reach the brakes when you need them.

15 degrees

bar end angle

adjustable cup: The non-drive side cup in the bottom bracket. This cup is removed for maintenance of the bottom bracket spindle and bearings, and it adjusts the bearings.

AheadSet: a style of headset that allows the use of a fork with a threadless steering tube.

Allen key (Allen wrench, hex key): a hexagonal wrench that fits inside the head of the bolt.

all-terrain bike (ATB): another term for mountain bike.

barrel adjuster: a threaded cable stop that allows for fine adjustment of cable tension. Barrel adjusters are commonly found on rear derailleurs, shifters and brake levers.

binder bolt: a bolt clamping a seat post in a frame, a handlebar inside a stem, or a threadless steering tube inside a stem clamp.

bottom bracket (BB): the assembly that allows the crank to rotate. Generally the bottom bracket assembly includes bearings, an axle, a fixed cup and adjustable cup, and a lockring.

bottom-bracket shell: the cylindrical housing at the bottomof a bicycle frame through which the bottom-bracket axle passes.

brake boss (brake post, cantilever post): a fork- or frame-mounted pivot for a brake arm.

brake pad (brake block): a block of rubber or similar material used to slow the bike by creating friction on the rim or other braking surface.

brake shoe: the metal pad holder that holds the brake pad to the brake arm.

braze-on: a generic term for most metal frame attachments, even those connected by means other than brazing.

brazing: a method commonly used to construct steel bicycle frames. Brazing involves the use of brass or silver solder to connect frame tubes and attach various "braze-on" items including brake bosses, cable guides and rack mounts to the frame.

bushing: a metal or plastic sleeve that acts as a simple bearing on pedals, suspension forks, suspension swing arms, and jockey wheels.

butted tubing: a common type of frame tubing with varying wall thicknesses. Butted tubing is designed to accommodate high stress points at the ends of the tube by being thicker there.

cable end: a cap on the end of a cable to keep it from fraying.

cable housing: an exterior sleeve for protecting shifter cables and brake cables from moisture and rust.

cable-fixing bolt: an anchor bolt that attaches cables to brakes or derailleurs.

cable stop: a fitting on the frame, fork, or stem at which a cable housing segment terminates.

cage: two guiding plates through which the chain travels. Both the front and rear derailleurs have cages. The cage on the rear also holds the jockey pulleys.

cantilever brake: a brake that relies on cable tension to move two opposing arms — which pivot on posts attached to the frame or fork, toward the braking surface of the rim. Cantilevers are the most common brake found on mountain bikes.

cantilever post: (see "brake boss.")

cassette hub: a rear hub that has a built-in freewheel mechanism.

chain: a series of metal links held together by pins and used to transmit energy from the crank to the rear wheel.

chain line: the imaginary line connecting the center of the middle chainring with the middle of the cogset. This line should in theory be straight and parallel with the vertical plane passing through the center of the bicycle. This is measured as the distance from the center of the seat tube to the center of the middle chainring (an easy way to measure this is to measure from the left side of the seat tube to the outside of the large chainring, measure the distance from the right side of the seat tube to the inside of the inner chainring, add these two measurements, and divide the sum by two).

chainring: a multiple tooth sprocket located on the cranks.

chainstays: the tubes leading from the bottom bracket shell to the rear hub axle.

chainring-nut spanner: a tool used to secure the chainring nuts while tightening the chainring bolts.

chain whip (chain wrench): a flat piece of steel, usually attached to two lengths of chain. This tool is used to remove the rear cogs on a freehub.

circlip (snapring, Jesus clip): a c-shaped snap ring that fits in a groove to hold parts together.

clipless pedals: a pedal that relies on spring-loaded clips to grip the rider's shoe, without the use of toe clips and straps.

cog: the sprockets located on the drive side of the rear hub.

cone: a threaded conical nut that serves to hold a set of bearings in place and also provides a smooth surface upon which those bearings can roll.

crankarm: the lever attached at the bottom bracket spindle used to transmit a rider's energy to the chain.

crankarm-fixing bolt: the bolt attaching the crank to the bottom bracket spindle on a cotterless drive train.

crankset: the assembly that includes two crank arms, chain rings and accompanying nuts and bolts.

cross three: a pattern used by wheel builders, that calls for each spoke to cross three others in its path from the hub to the rim.

cup: a cup-shaped bearing race that surrounds the bearings in a bottom bracket, headset or hub.

derailleur: a gear-changing device that allows a rider to move the chain from one cog or chainring to another while the bicycle is in motion.

derailleur hanger: a metal extension of the right rear drop-out to which the rear derailleur is mounted to the frame.

diamond frame: the traditional bicycle frame shape.

dish: a difference in spoke tension on the two sides of the rear wheel so that the wheel is centered.

disc brake: a brake that stops the bike by squeezing brake pads against a circular disc attached to the wheel.

down tube: the tube that connects to the head tube and bottom-bracket shell.

drivetrain: the crankset, bottom bracket, front derailleur, chain, rear derailleur, freewheel (or cassette).

drop: the perpendicular distance between a horizntal line passing through the wheel hub centers and the center of the bottom bracket.

dropouts: the slots in the forks and rear triangle where the wheel axles are placed.

dust cap: a protective cap keeping dirt away from a part.

elastomer: a urethane spring used in suspension forks and swing arms.

ferrule: a cap for the end of cable housing.

fixed cup: the non-adjustable cup of the bottom bracket located on the drive side of the bottom bracket.

flange: the largest diameter of the hub where the spoke heads are anchored.

fork: the part that attaches the front wheel to the frame.

fork crown: the cross piece connecting the fork legs to the steering tube.

fork rake (rake): the perpendicular offset distance of the front axle from an imaginary line through the steering tube that forms the steering axis.

fork tips (ends): the front dropouts of the fork where the front wheel axle attaches. Also called *dropouts*.

frame: the central structure of a bicycle to which all of the parts are attached.

freewheel: a removable cluster of cogs that allows a rider to stop pedaling as the bicycle is moving forward.

friction shifter: a traditional (non-indexed) shifter attached to the frame or handle bars. Cable tension is maintained by a combination of friction washers and bolts.

front triangle (main triangle): the head tube, top tube, down tube and seat tube of a bike frame.

Grip Shift: a shifter that is integrated with the handle bar grip of a mountain bike. The rider shifts gears by twisting the grip.

hex key: (see "Allen key.")

headset: the cup, lock ring, and bearings that hold the fork to the frame and allow the fork to spin in the frame.

head tube: the front tube of the frame. It is attached to the top tube and down tube and is where the steering tube of the fork and the headset are located.

hub: the central part of a wheel to which the spokes are anchored and within which the axle freely rotates.

hub brake: a disk, drum or coaster brake that stops the wheel with friction applied to a braking surface attached to the hub.

hydraulic brake: a type of brake that uses oil pressure to move the brake pads against the braking surface.

glossary

dish
—
hydraulic
brake

index shifter: a shifter that clicks into fixed positions as it moves the derailleur from gear to gear.

Jesus clip: (see "circlip.")

jockey wheel or jockey pulley: a circular cog-shaped-pulley used to direct the chain through the rear derailleur and onto the rear cogs.

knobby tire: an all terrain tire used on mountain bikes.

locknut: a nut that serves to hold the bearing adjustment in a headset, hub or pedal.

lock ring: the outer ring that tightens the adjustable cup of a bottom bracket against the face of the bottom-bracket shell.

lock washer: a notched washer that serves to hold surrounding nuts and washers in position.

master link: a detachable link that holds the chain together. The master link can be opened by hand and without a chain tool.

mounting bolt: (see "pivot bolt.")

nipple: a small nut specially designed to receive the end of a spoke and fit the holes of a rim.

pin spanner: a V-shaped wrench with two tip end pins that is used for tightening the adjustable cup of the bottom bracket.

pivot bolt: a fixing bolt that fastens the brake arm to the frame or fork.

Presta valve: thin, metal tire valve that uses a locking nut to stop air flow from the tire.

quick release: the tightening lever and part used to attach a wheel to the forks or rear dropout without using a wrench. Some bikes also come equip-ped with a quick- release lever at the seat post.

quill: the vertical tube of a stem. It has an expander plug and bolt inside and is used to secure the stem in the steering tube.

race: a ring-shaped surface on which the bearings roll freely.

Rapid-fire shifter: an indexing shifter manufactured by Shimano for use on mountain bikes with two separate levers operating each shift cable.

rear triangle: the rear portion of the bicycle frame, including the seat stays, the chain stays and the seat tube.

rim: the outer hoop of a wheel to which the tire is attached.

roller-cam brakes: a brake system using pulleys and a cam to force the brake pads against the rim surface.

saddle: a platform made of leather or plastic upon which the rider sits.

Schrader valve: a valve used by some bicycle tubes and most automobile tires for inflation and deflation of the tire.

sealed bearing: an enclosed bearing cartridge designed to keep contaminants out.

seat cluster: the intersection of the seat tube, top tube, and seat stays.

seat: (see "saddle.")

seat post: the post to which the saddle is secured.

skewer: a hub quick release or a shaft passing through a stack of elastomer bumpers in a suspension fork.

snapring: (see "circlip.")

spider: a star shaped piece of metal that connects the right crank arm to the chainrings.

spokes: metal rods that connect the hub to the rim of a wheel.

sprocket: a circular, multiple-toothed piece of metal that engages a chain. (See also: cog and chain ring.)

star nut: a tanged nut that is forced down into the steering tube and anchors the stem bolt of a threadless headset.

steering axis: the imaginary line about which the fork rotates.

steering tube: the vertical tube on a fork that is attached to the fork crown and fits inside the head tube.

straddle-cable holder: (see "yoke.")

swingarm: the movable rear end of a rear-suspension frame.

threadless headset: (see "AheadSet.")

three cross: (see "cross three.")

thumb shifter: a thumb-operated shift lever attached on top of the handle-bars.

top tube: the horizontal tube that is connected to the seat tube and head tube.

triple: a term used to describe the three chain ring combination attached to the right crankarm.

U-brake: a mountain-bike brake consisting of two arms shaped like invert-ed L's affixed to posts on the frame or fork.

wheel base: the horizontal distance between the two wheel axles.

yoke: the part attaching the brake cable to the straddle cable, or a cantilever or U-brake.

glossary

snapring
—
yoke

If you have a torque wrench, these are the standard tightnesses recommended by Shimano, Grip Shift, Rock Shox and Answer/Manitou for their products. Divide these numbers by 12 to convert them to foot-pounds.

brake assemblies

brake lever clamp bolt . . . . .52-69 inch-pounds
. . . .(22-26 inch-pounds for slotted screw type)
brake pivot bolt . . . . .43-61 inch-pounds
brake cable fixing bolt . . . . .52-69 inch-pounds
V-brake pad fixing bolt . . . . .52-69 inch-pounds
canti brake pad fixing bolt . . . . .70-78 inch-pounds
straddle cable yoke fixing nut . . . . .35-43 inch-pounds

derailleur and shifting assemblies

front derailleur cable fixing bolt . . . . .43-61 inch-pounds
front derailleur clamp bolt . . . . .43-61 inch-pounds
rear derailleur cable fixing bolt . . . . .35-52 inch-pounds
rear derailleur dropout mounting bolt . . . .70-86 inch-pounds
rear derailleur pulley center bolts . . . . .27-34 inch-pounds
thumb shifter clamp bolt . . . . .53-69 inch-pounds
. . . .(22-26 inch-pounds for slotted screw type)
shift lever parts fixing screw . . . . .22-24 inch-pounds
Gripshift lever mounting screw . . . . .17 inch-pounds

hubs, cassettes, quick releases

hub quick release lever closing . . . . .79-104 inch-pounds
quick release axle locknut . . . . .87-217 inch-pounds
freehub cassette body fixing bolt . . . . .305-434 inch-pounds
cassette cog lockring . . . . .260-434 inch-pounds.

crank, bottom bracket assemblies

crank arm fixing bolt . . . . .357-435 inch-pounds
chainchring fixing bolt . . . . .70-95 inch-pounds
cartridge bottom bracket cups . . . . .435-608 inch-pounds
standard bottom bracket fixed cup . . . . . . .609-695 inch-pounds
standard bottom bracket lockring . . . . .609-695 inch-pounds
pedal axle . . . . .307 inch-pounds or more

seats, stems

seat post clamp bolt . . . . .174-347 inch-pounds
stem handlebar clamping bolt . . . . .174-260 inch-pounds
stem expander bolt . . . . .174-260 inch-pounds
AheadSet stem clamp bolts . . . . .130 inch-pounds
Aheadset bearing preload . . . . .22 inch-pounds

suspension forks

Rock Shox fork crown clamp bolt . . . . .60 inch-pounds
Rock Shox brake post . . . . .60 inch-pounds
Rock Shox fork brace bolt . . . . .60 inch-pounds
Rock Shox Judy cartridge shaft bolt . . . . . .60 inch-pounds
Rock Shox Judy neutral shaft bolt . . . . .60 inch-pounds
Manitou fork crown clamp bolt . . . . .110-130 inch-pounds
Manitou brake post . . . . .90-110 inch-pounds
Manitou fork brace bolt . . . . .90-110 inch-pounds
Manitou EFC/Mach 5 cartridge bolt . . . . . .10-30 inch-pounds
Manitou neutral shaft bolt . . . . .10-30 inch-pounds
Manitou EFC/Mach 5 cartridge cap . . . . . .30-50 inch-pounds

shoes

shoe cleat fixing bolt . . . . .44-51 inch-pounds
shoe spike . . . . .34 inch-pounds

torque table

Barnett, John. *Barnett's Manual: Analysis and Procedures for Bicycle Mechanics.* Brattleboro, VT: Vitesse Press, 1989

Brandt, Jobst. *The Bicycle Wheel.* Menlo Park, CA: Avocet, 1988

Dushan, Allan. *Surviving the Trail*, Tumbleweed Films, 1993.

Editors of Bicycling and Mountain Bike magazines. *Bicycling Magazine's Complete Guide to Bicycle Maintenance and Repair.* Emmaus, PA: Rodale Press, 1994

Lindorf, W. *Mountain Bike Repair and Maintenance.* London: Ward Lock, 1995

Muir, John and Gregg, Tosh. *How to Keep Your Volkswagen Alive: a Manual of Step by Step Procedures for the Compleat Idiot.* Santa Fe, NM: John Muir Publications, 1969; 74, 75, 81, 85, 88, 90, 92, 94.

Pirsig, Robert. *Zen and the Art of Motorcycle Maintenance.* New York, NY: William Morrow & Co., 1974.

Stevenson, John, and Richards, Brant. *Mountain Bikes: Maintenance and Repair.* Mill Valley, CA: Bicycle Books, 1994

Taylor, Garrett, *Bicycle Wheelbuilding 101, a Video Lesson in the Art of Wheelbuilding.* Westwood, MA: Rexadog, 1994

Van der Plas, Robert. *The Bicycle Repair Book.* Mill Valley, CA: Bicycle Books, 1993

Van der Plas, Robert. *Mountain Bike Maintenance.* San Francisco: Bicycle Books, 1994

NOTES

NOTES

N O T E S

NOTES

NOTES

about the author

Lennard Zinn is a bike framebuilder, technical writer, and bike lover who has written about cycling for enthusiasts' magazines since 1986. He grew up in Los Alamos, New Mexico, cycling, skiing, running rivers, and tinkering with mechanical devices. He earned a degree in physics from Colorado College in 1980. From 1980 to 1982, he was a member of the U.S. Olympic Development Cycling Team (road racing, since mountain bike racing was virtually nonexistent then). He worked as a mountain bike framebuilder for Tom Ritchey at Ritchey Cycles in 1981, one of the principal pioneers of the mountain bike. He founded Zinn Cycles in 1982 and has been producing custom road and mountain frames and forks ever since. Starting in 1989, Zinn has written technical articles for *VeloNews*, the journal of record of bike racing, on a freelance basis. In 1993, he joined the staff and has served as the senior technical writer for both *VeloNews* and *Inside Triathlon* magazines ever since.

about the illustrator

A former mechanic and bike racer, Todd Telander devotes most of his time now to artistic endeavors. In addition to drawing mountain-bike parts, he paints and draws wildlife for publishers, museums, design companies and individuals. Birds are his favorite subject, so he has included a little house sparrow.